Association for Computing Machinery
11 West 42nd Street
New York, NY 10036

Compiled by the ACM Education Board

Price: ACM Members: $12.00
Non-members $16.00

Copies may be ordered, prepaid, from:
ACM Order Department
P.O.Box 64145
Baltimore, MD 21264

ACM order #201831

ISBN: 0-89791-117-2

CONTENTS

CURRICULUM 68

Recommendations for Academic Programs in Computer Science

A REPORT OF THE ACM CURRICULUM COMMITTEE ON COMPUTER SCIENCE

Dedicated to the Memory of Silvio O. Navarro

This report contains recommendations on academic programs in computer science which were developed by the ACM Curriculum Committee on Computer Science. A classification of the subject areas contained in computer science is presented and twenty-two courses in these areas are described. Prerequisites, catolog descriptions, detailed outlines, and annotated bibliographies for these courses are included. Specific recommendations which have evolved from the Committee's 1965 Preliminary Recommendations are given for undergraduate programs. Graduate programs in computer science are discussed, and some recommendations are presented for the development of master's degree programs. Ways of developing guidelines for doctoral programs are discussed, but no specific recommendations are made. The importance of service courses, minors, and continuing education in computer science is emphasized. Attention is given to the organization, staff requirements, computer resources, and other facilities needed to implement computer science educational programs.

KEY WORDS AND PHRASES: computer science courses, computer science curriculum, computer science education, computer science academic programs, computer science graduate programs, computer science undergraduate programs, computer science course bibliographies

CR CATEGORIES: 1.52

Preface

The Curriculum Committee on Computer Science (C^3S) was initially formed in 1962 as a subcommittee of the Education Committee of the Association for Computing Machinery. In the first few years of its existence this subcommittee functioned rather informally by sponsoring a number of panel discussions and other sessions at various national computer meetings. The Curriculum Committee became an independent committee of the ACM in 1964 and began an active effort to formulate detailed recommendations for curricula in computer science. Its first report, "An Undergraduate Program in Computer Science—Preliminary Recommendations" [1], was published in the September 1965 issue of *Communications of the ACM*.

The work of the Committee during the last two years has been devoted to revising these recommendations on undergraduate programs and developing recommendations for graduate programs as contained in this report. The primary support for this work has been from the National Science Foundation under Grant Number GY-305, received in July 1965.

The Committee membership during the preparation of this report was:

William F. Atchison, University of Maryland (Chairman)
Samuel D. Conte, Purdue University
John W. Hamblen, SREB and Georgia Institute of Technology
Thomas E. Hull, University of Toronto
Thomas A. Keenan, EDUCOM and the University of Rochester
William B. Kehl, University of California at Los Angeles
Edward J. McCluskey, Stanford University
Silvio O. Navarro,* University of Kentucky
Werner C. Rheinboldt, University of Maryland
Earl J. Schweppe, University of Maryland (Secretary)
William Viavant, University of Utah
David M. Young, Jr., University of Texas

* Dr. Navarro was killed in an airplane crash on April 3, 1967.

In addition to these members many others have made valuable contributions to the work of the Committee. Their names and affiliations are listed at the end of this report. Robert Ashenhurst and Peter Wegner have given especial assistance in the preparation of this report.

CONTENTS

1. Introduction

Following the appearance of its Preliminary Recommendations [1], the Curriculum Committee on Computer Science received many valuable comments, criticisms, and suggestions on computer science education. From these, the advice of numerous consultants, and the ideas of many other people, the Committee has prepared this report, "Curriculum 68," which is a substantial refinement and extension of the earlier recommendations. The Committee hopes that these new recommendations will stimulate further discussion in this area and evoke additional contributions to its future work from those in the computing profession. The Committee believes strongly that a continuing dialogue on the process and goals of education in computer science will be vital in the years to come.

In its Preliminary Recommendations the Committee devoted considerable attention to the justification and description of "computer science" as a discipline. Although debate on the existence of such a discipline still continues, there seems to be more discussion today on what this discipline should be called and what it should include. In a recent letter [2], Newell, Perlis, and Simon defend the name "computer science." Others, wishing perhaps to take in a broader scope and to emphasize the information being processed, advocate calling this discipline "information science" [3] or, as a compromise, "the computer and information sciences" [4]. The Committee has decided to use the term "computer science" throughout this report, although it fully realizes that other names may be used for essentially the same discipline.

In attempting to define the scope of this discipline, the Committee split computer science into three major subject divisions to which two groups of related areas were then added. Using this as a framework, the Committee developed a classification of the subject areas of computer science and some of its related fields, and this classification is presented in Section 2.

As was the case for its Preliminary Recommendations, the Committee has devoted considerable effort to the development of descriptions, detailed outlines, and bibliographies for courses in computer science. Of the sixteen courses proposed in the earlier recommendations, eleven have survived in spirit if not in detail. Two of the other five courses have been split into two courses each, and the remaining three have been omitted since they belong more properly to other disciplines closely related to computer science. In addition seven new courses have been proposed, of which Course B3 on "discrete structures" and Course I3 on "computer organization" are particularly notable. Thus this report contains detailed information—in the form of catalog descriptions and prerequisites in Section 3 and detailed outlines and annotated bibliographies in the Appendix—on a total of twenty-two courses.

Another important issue which concerned the Curriculum Committee is the extent to which undergraduate programs as opposed to graduate programs in computer science ought to be advocated. Certainly, both undergraduate and graduate programs in "computer science" do now exist, and more such programs operate under other names such as "information science" or "data processing" or as options in such fields as mathematics or electrical engineering. A recent survey [5], supported by the National Science Foundation and carried out by the Computer Sciences Project of the Southern Regional Education Board, contains estimates of the number of such degree programs operating in 1964–1965 and projections of the number planned to be operating by 1968–1969. These estimates and projections can be summarized as follows:

Program name	Bachelor's		Program level Master's		Doctoral	
	1964 1965	1968 1969	1964 1965	1968 1969	1964 1965	1968 1969
Computer Science	11	92	17	76	12	38
Data Processing	6	15	3	4	1	2
Information Science	2	4	12	17	4	13
Similar Programs	25	40	29	40	21	28

The information contained in these figures is interesting for two reasons. First, it shows that the number of computer science degree programs will continue to grow rapidly even if some of the programs now being planned do not come into being. Second, it shows a strong tendency to use the name "computer science," although the availability of academic work in computing is not limited to institutions having a department or a program operating under that title.

A major purpose of the Committee's recommendations on undergraduate programs and master's degree programs given in Sections 4 and 5 is to provide a sense of direction and a realizable set of goals for those colleges and universities which plan to provide computer science education for undergraduate and /or graduate students. The discussion in Section 6 of how guidelines for doctoral programs may be developed is very general, mainly because this is a difficult area in which to make detailed recommendations.

The importance of service courses, minors, and continued education in computer science has also been of concern to the Committee. Although detailed work still needs to be done, some preliminary discussion of the needs in these areas is given in Section 7. In Section 8 some of the problems of implementing an educational program in computer science are discussed.

In general the difficulties in establishing such programs are formidable; the practical problems of finding qualified faculty, of providing adequate laboratory facilities, and of beginning a program in a new area where there are few textbooks are severe. These problems are magnified for baccalaureate programs in comparison with graduate programs, where the admission can be more closely controlled.

The demand for substantially increased numbers of persons to work in all areas of computing has been noted in a report of the National Academy of Sciences-National Research Council [6] (commonly known as the "Rosser Report") and in a report of the President's Science Advisory Committee [7] (often called the "Pierce Report"). Although programs based on the recommendations of the Curriculum Committee can contribute substantially to satisfying this demand, such programs will not cover the full breadth of the need for personnel. For example, these recommendations are not directed to the training of computer operators, coders, and other service personnel. Training for such positions, as well as for many programming positions, can probably be supplied best by applied technology programs, vocational institutes, or junior colleges. It is also likely that the majority of applications programmers in such areas as business data processing, scientific research, and engineering analysis will continue to be specialists educated in the related subject matter areas, although such students can undoubtedly profit by taking a number of computer science courses.

In addition to this Committee, several other organizations have set forth guidelines to aid educational institutions in the establishment of programs pertinent to the needs of today's computer-oriented technology. Prominent among these are the reports of the Committee on the Undergraduate Program in Mathematics (CUPM) of the Mathematical Association of America [8], the COSINE Committee of the Commission on Engineering Education [9], and the Education Committee of the British Computer Society [10]. Also, the ACM Curriculum Committee on Computer Education for Management, chaired by Daniel Teichroew, is now beginning to consider educational matters related to the application of computers to "management information systems." The Curriculum Committee has benefited greatly from interchanging ideas with these other groups. In addition, the entire Committee was privileged to take part in "The Graduate Academic Conference in Computing Science" [11] held at Stony Brook in June 1967.

Computer science programs, in common with those of all disciplines, must attempt to provide a basis of knowledge and a mode of thinking which permit continuing growth on the part of their graduates. Thus, in addition to exposing the student to a depth of knowledge in computer science sufficient to lay the basis for professional competence, such programs must also provide the student with the intellectual maturity which will allow him to stay abreast of his own discipline and to interact with other disciplines.

2. Subject Classification

The scope of academic programs and curricula in computer science will necessarily vary from institution to institution as dictated by local needs, resources, and objectives. To provide a basis for discussion, however, it seems desirable to have a reasonably comprehensive system for classifying the subject areas within computer science and related fields. Although any such system is somewhat arbitrary, it is hoped that any substantial aspect of the computer field, unless specifically excluded for stated reasons, may be found within the system presented here. The subject areas within computer science will be classified first; those shared with or wholly within related fields will be discussed later in this section.

Computer Science. The subject areas of computer science are grouped into three major divisions: "information structures and processes," "information processing systems," and "methodologies." The subject areas contained in each of these divisions are given below together with lists of the topics within each subject area.

I. INFORMATION STRUCTURES AND PROCESSES

This subject division is concerned with representations and transformations of information structures and with theoretical models for such representations and transformations.

1. DATA STRUCTURES: includes the description, representation, and manipulation of numbers, arrays, lists, trees, files, etc.; storage organization, allocation, and access; enumeration, searching and sorting; generation, modification, transformation, and deletion techniques; the static and dynamic properties of structures; algorithms for the manipulation of sets, graphs, and other combinatoric structures.

2. PROGRAMMING LANGUAGES: includes the representation of algorithms; the syntactic and semantic specification of languages; the analysis of expressions, statements, declarations, control structures, and other features of programming languages; dynamic structures which arise during execution; the design, development and evaluation of languages; program efficiency and the simplification of programs; sequential transformations of program structures; special purpose languages; the relation between programming languages, formal languages, and linguistics.

3. MODELS OF COMPUTATION: includes the behavioral and structural analysis of switching circuits and sequential machines; the properties and classification of automata; algebraic automata theory and model theory; formal languages and formal grammars; the classification of languages by recognition devices; syntactic analysis; formal

specification of semantics; syntax directed processing; decidability problems for grammars; the treatment of programming languages as automata; other formal theories of programming languages and computation.

II. INFORMATION PROCESSING SYSTEMS

This subject division is concerned with systems having the ability to transform information. Such systems usually involve the interaction of hardware and software.

1. Computer Design and Organization: includes types of computer structure—von Neumann computers, array computers, and look-ahead computers; hierarchies of memory—flip-flop registers, cores, disks, drums, tapes—and their accessing techniques; microprogramming and implementation of control functions; arithmetic circuitry; instruction codes; input-output techniques; multiprocessing and multiprogramming structures.

2. Translators and Interpreters: includes the theory and techniques involved in building assemblers, compilers, interpreters, loaders, and editing or conversion routines (media, format, etc.).

3. Computer and Operating Systems: includes program monitoring and data management; accounting and utility routines; data and program libraries; modular organization of systems programs; interfaces and communication between modules; requirements of multi-access, multiprogram and multiprocess environments; large scale systems description and documentation; diagnostic and debugging techniques; measurement of performance.

4. Special Purpose Systems: includes analog and hybrid computers; special terminals for data transmission and display; peripheral and interface units for particular applications; special software to support these.

III. METHODOLOGIES

Methodologies are derived from broad areas of applications of computing which have common structures, processes, and techniques.

1. Numerical Mathematics: includes numerical algorithms and their theoretical and computational properties; computational error analysis (for rounding and truncation errors); automatic error estimates and convergence properties.

2. Data Processing and File Management: includes techniques applicable to library, biomedical, and management information systems; file processing languages.

3. Symbol Manipulation: includes formula operations such as simplification and formal differentiation; symbol manipulation languages.

4. Text Processing: includes text editing, correcting, and justification; the design of concordances; applied linguistic analysis; text processing languages.

5. Computer Graphics: includes digitizing and digital storage; display equipment and generation; picture compression and image enhancement; picture geometry and topology; perspective and rotation; picture analysis; graphics languages.

6. Simulation: includes natural and operational models; discrete simulation models; continuous change models; simulation languages.

7. Information Retrieval: includes indexing and classification; statistical techniques; automatic classification; matching and search strategies; secondary outputs such as abstracts and indexes; selective dissemination systems; automatic question answering systems.

8. Artificial Intelligence: includes heuristics; brain models; pattern recognition; theorem proving; problem solving; game playing; adaptive and cognitive systems; man-machine systems.

9. Process Control: includes machine tool control; experiment control; command and control systems.

10. Instructional Systems: includes computer aided instruction.

Related Areas. In addition to the areas of computer science listed under the three divisions above, there are many related areas of mathematics, statistics, electrical engineering, philosophy, linguistics, and industrial engineering or management which are essential to balanced computer science programs. Suitable courses in these areas should be developed cooperatively with the appropriate departments, although it may occasionally be desirable to develop some of these courses within the computer science program.

Since it is not feasible in this report to list all of the areas which might be related to a computer science program, let alone indicate where courses in these areas should be taught, the following listing is somewhat restricted. It is grouped into two major divisions: "mathematical sciences" and "physical and engineering sciences."

IV. MATHEMATICAL SCIENCES

1. Elementary Analysis
2. Linear Algebra
3. Differential Equations
4. Algebraic Structures
5. Theoretical Numerical Analysis
6. Methods of Applied Mathematics
7. Optimization Theory
8. Combinatorial Mathematics
9. Mathematical Logic
10. Number Theory
11. Probability and Statistics
12. Operations Analysis

V. PHYSICAL AND ENGINEERING SCIENCES

1. General Physics
2. Basic Electronics
3. Circuit Analysis and Design
4. Thermodynamics and Statistical Mechanics
5. Field Theory
6. Digital and Pulse Circuits
7. Coding and Information Theory
8. Communication and Control Theory
9. Quantum Mechanics

No attempt has been made to include within this classification system all the subject areas which make use of computer techniques, such as chemistry and economics; indeed, to list these would require inclusion of a major portion of the typical university catalog. Furthermore, the sociological, economic, and educational implications of developments in computer science are not discussed in this report. These issues are undoubtedly important, but they are not the exclusive nor even the major responsibility of computer science. Indeed, other departments such as philosophy and sociology should be urged to cooperate with computer scientists in the development of courses or seminars covering these topics, and computer science students should be encouraged to take these courses.

3. Description of Courses

The computer science courses specified in this report are divided into three categories: "basic," "intermediate," and "advanced." The basic courses are intended to be taught primarily at the freshman-sophomore level, whereas both the intermediate and the advanced courses may be taught at the junior-senior or the graduate level. In general, the intermediate courses are strongly recommended as part of undergraduate programs. The advanced courses are classified as such either because of their higher level of prerequisites and required maturity or because of their concern with special applications of computer science.

In addition to more elementary computer science courses, certain courses in mathematics are necessary, or at least highly desirable, as prerequisites for some of the proposed courses. More advanced mathematics courses may be included as supporting work in the programs of some students. Because of the considerable variation in the level and content of mathematics courses among (and even within) schools, the courses described by the Committee on the Undergraduate Program in Mathematics (CUPM) in the report, "A General Curriculum in Mathematics for Colleges" [12] have been used to specify the prerequisites for the proposed courses in computer science and requirements for degrees. Other pertinent mathematics courses are described in the CUPM reports, "Recommendations on the Undergraduate Mathematics Program for Engineers and Physicists" [13] and "A Curriculum in Applied Mathematics" [14].

The titles and numbers of all the courses proposed in this report and the pertinent courses recommended by CUPM are shown in Figure 1 along with the prerequisite structure linking these courses. The courses described below, which make up the core of the undergraduate program, are also singled out in Figure 1. The relatively strong prerequisite structure proposed for these core courses allows their content to be greatly expanded from what a weaker structure would permit. The Committee recognizes that other—perhaps weaker—prerequisite structures might also be effective and that the structure shown will change along with the course content as computer science education develops. Prerequisites proposed for the advanced courses are subject to modification based on many orientations which these courses may be given at individual institutions.

Most of the courses have been designed on the basis of three semester hours of credit. Laboratory sessions, in which the more practical aspects of the material can be presented more effectively than in formal lectures, have been included where appropriate. The proposed number of hours of lecture and laboratory each week and the number of semester hours of credit for the course are shown in parentheses in the catalog descriptions below. For example, (2-2-3) indicates two hours of lecture and two hours of laboratory per week for a total of three semester hours of credit.

Course Catalog Descriptions and Prerequisites

For each of the courses listed below, a brief statement on the approach which might be taken in teaching it is given in the Appendix along with the detailed outlines of its proposed contents and annotated bibliographies of pertinent source materials and textbooks.

□ The first course is designed to provide the student with the basic knowledge and experience necessary to use computers effectively in the solution of problems. It can be a service course for students in a number of other fields as well as an introductory course for majors in computer science. Although no prerequisites are listed, it is assumed that the student will have had a minimum of three years of high school mathematics. All of the computer science courses which follow will depend upon this introduction.

Course B1. Introduction to Computing (2-2-3)

Algorithms, programs, and computers. Basic programming and program structure. Programming and computing systems. Debugging and verification of programs. Data representation. Organization and characteristics of computers. Survey of computers, languages, systems, and applications. Computer solution of several numerical and nonnumerical problems using one or more programming languages.

□ The second course is intended to lay a foundation for more advanced study in computer science. By familiarizing the student with the basic structure and language of machines, the content of this course will give him a better understanding of the internal behavior of computers, some facility in the use of assembly languages, and an ability to use computers more effectively—even with procedure-oriented languages.

Course B2. Computers and Programming (2-2-3)

Prerequisite: Course B1.

Computer structure, machine language, instruction execution, addressing techniques, and digital representation of data. Computer

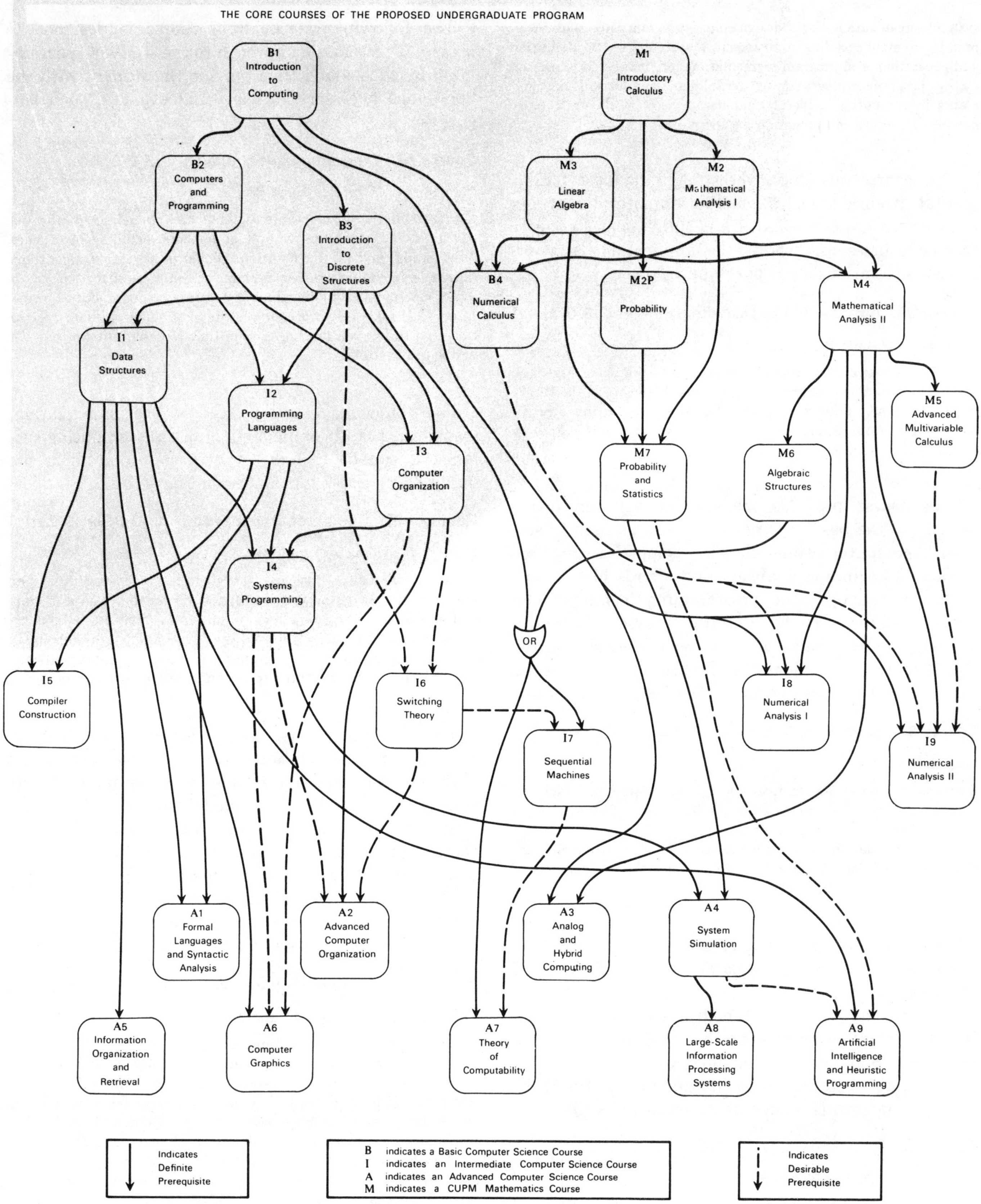

THE CORE COURSES OF THE PROPOSED UNDERGRADUATE PROGRAM

B1 Introduction to Computing

M1 Introductory Calculus

B2 Computers and Programming

B3 Introduction to Discrete Structures

M3 Linear Algebra

M2 Mathematical Analysis I

B4 Numerical Calculus

M2P Probability

M4 Mathematical Analysis II

I1 Data Structures

I2 Programming Languages

I3 Computer Organization

M5 Advanced Multivariable Calculus

M7 Probability and Statistics

M6 Algebraic Structures

I4 Systems Programming

OR

I5 Compiler Construction

I6 Switching Theory

I7 Sequential Machines

I8 Numerical Analysis I

I9 Numerical Analysis II

A1 Formal Languages and Syntactic Analysis

A2 Advanced Computer Organization

A3 Analog and Hybrid Computing

A4 System Simulation

A5 Information Organization and Retrieval

A6 Computer Graphics

A7 Theory of Computability

A8 Large-Scale Information Processing Systems

A9 Artificial Intelligence and Heuristic Programming

Indicates Definite Prerequisite

B indicates a Basic Computer Science Course
I indicates an Intermediate Computer Science Course
A indicates an Advanced Computer Science Course
M indicates a CUPM Mathematics Course

Indicates Desirable Prerequisite

FIG. 1. Prerequisite structure of courses

systems organization, logic design, micro-programming, and interpreters. Symbolic coding and assembly systems, macro definition and generation, and program segmentation and linkage. Systems and utility programs, programming techniques, and recent developments in computing. Several computer projects to illustrate basic machine structure and programming techniques.

☐This course introduces the student to those fundamental algebraic, logical, and combinatoric concepts from mathematics needed in the subsequent computer science courses and shows the applications of these concepts to various areas of computer science.

Course B3. Introduction to Discrete Structures (3-0-3)

Prerequisite: Course B1.

Review of set algebra including mappings and relations. Algebraic structures including semigroups and groups. Elements of the theory of directed and undirected graphs. Boolean algebra and propositional logic. Applications of these structures to various areas of computer science.

☐This course provides the student with an introduction to the basic numerical algorithms used in scientific computer work—thereby complementing his studies in beginning analysis—and affords him an opportunity to apply the programming techniques he has learned in Course B1. Because of these aims, many of the standard elementary numerical analysis courses now offered in mathematics departments cannot be considered as substitutes for this course.

Course B4. Numerical Calculus (2-2-3)

Prerequisites: Courses B1, M2, and M3.

An introduction to the numerical algorithms fundamental to scientific computer work. Includes elementary discussion of error, polynomial interpolation, quadrature, linear systems of equations, solution of nonlinear equations, and numerical solution of ordinary differential equations. The algorithmic approach and the efficient use of the computer are emphasized.

☐This course is concerned with one of the most fundamental—but often inadequately recognized—areas of computer science. Its purpose is to introduce the student to the relations which hold among the elements of data involved in problems, the structures of storage media and machines, the methods which are useful in representing structured data in storage, and the techniques for operating upon data structures.

Course I1. Data Structures (3-0-3)

Prerequisites: Courses B2 and B3.

Basic concepts of data. Linear lists, strings, arrays, and orthogonal lists. Representation of trees and graphs. Storage systems and structures, and storage allocation and collection. Multilinked structures. Symbol tables and searching techniques. Sorting (ordering) techniques. Formal specification of data structures, data structures in programming languages, and generalized data management systems.

☐The following intermediate course is designed to present a systematic approach to the study of programming languages and thus provide the student with the knowledge necessary to learn and evaluate such languages.

Course I2. Programming Languages (3-0-3)

Prerequisites: Courses B2 and B3.

Formal definition of programming languages including specification of syntax and semantics. Simple statements including precedence, infix, prefix, and postfix notation. Global properties of algorithmic languages including scope of declarations, storage allocation, grouping of statements, binding time of constituents, subroutines, coroutines, and tasks. List processing, string manipulation, data description, and simulation languages. Run-time representation of program and data structures.

☐The following course discusses the organization, logic design, and components of digital computing systems. It can be thought of as a continuation of the hardware concepts introduced in Course B2.

Course I3. Computer Organization (3-0-3) or (3-2-4)

Prerequisites: Courses B2 and B3.

Basic digital circuits, Boolean algebra and combinational logic, data representation and transfer, and digital arithmetic. Digital storage and accessing, control functions, input-output facilities, system organization, and reliability. Description and simulation techniques. Features needed for multiprogramming, multiprocessing, and real-time systems. Other advanced topics and alternate organizations.

☐The following course is concerned primarily with the software organization—and to a lesser extent the hardware—of computer systems which support a wide variety of users. It is intended to bring together the concepts and techniques developed in the previous courses on data structures, programming languages, and computer organization by considering their role in the design of general computer systems. The problems which arise in multiaccessing, multiprogramming, and multiprocessing are emphasized.

Course I4. Systems Programming (3-0-3)

Prerequisites: Courses I1, I2, and I3.

Review of batch process systems programs, their components, operating characteristics, user services and their limitations. Implementation techniques for parallel processing of input-output and interrupt handling. Overall structure of multiprogramming systems on multiprocessor hardware configurations. Details on addressing techniques, core management, file system design and management, system accounting, and other user-related services. Traffic control, interprocess communication, design of system modules, and interfaces. System updating, documentation, and operation.

☐The following course is intended to provide a detailed understanding of the techniques used in the design and implementation of compilers.

Course I5. Compiler Construction (3-0-3)

Prerequisites: Courses I1 and I2.

Review of program language structures, translation, loading, execution, and storage allocation. Compilation of simple expressions and statements. Organization of a compiler including compile-time and run-time symbol tables, lexical scan, syntax scan, object code generation, error diagnostics, object code optimization techniques, and overall design. Use of compiler writing languages and bootstrapping.

☐ This course introduces the theoretical principles and mathematical techniques involved in the design of digital system logic. A course compatible with the content and approach of this course is frequently taught in departments of electrical engineering.

Course I6. Switching Theory (3-0-3) or (2-2-3)

Prerequisites: Courses B3 (desirable) and I3 (desirable, as it would allow more meaningful examples to be used).

Switching algebra, gate network analysis and synthesis, Boolean algebra, combinational circuit minimization, sequential circuit analysis and synthesis, sequential circuit state minimization, hazards and races, and elementary number systems and codes.

☐ This theoretical course is especially recommended for undergraduate students planning to do graduate work in computer science. It is also an appropriate course for electrical engineers and may sometimes be available from or jointly developed with an electrical engineering department.

Course I7. Sequential Machines (3-0-3)

Prerequisites: Courses B3 or M6, and I6 (desirable).

Definition and representation of finite state automata and sequential machines. Equivalence of states and machines, congruence, reduced machines, and analysis and synthesis of machines. Decision problems of finite automata, partitions with the substitution property, generalized and incomplete machines, semigroups and machines, probabilistic automata, and other topics.

☐ The following two courses in numerical analysis are intended to be mathematically rigorous and at the same time computer-oriented.

Course I8. Numerical Analysis I (3-0-3)

Prerequisites: Courses B1, B4 (desirable), and M4.

A thorough treatment of solutions of equations, interpolation and approximations, numerical differentiation and integration, and numerical solution of initial value problems in ordinary differential equations. Selected algorithms will be programmed for solution on computers.

Course I9. Numerical Analysis II (3-0-3)

Prerequisites: Courses B1, B4 (desirable), M4, and M5 (desirable).

The solution of linear systems by direct and iterative methods, matrix inversion, the evaluation of determinants, and the calculation of eigenvalues and eigenvectors of matrices. Application to boundary value problems in ordinary differential equations. Introduction to the numerical solution of partial differential equations. Selected algorithms will be programmed for solution on computers.

☐ The following course serves as an introduction both to the theory of context-free grammars and formal languages, and to syntactic recognition techniques for recognizing languages specified by context-free grammars.

Course A1. Formal Languages and Syntactic Analysis (3-0-3)

Prerequisites: Courses I1 and I2.

Definition of formal grammars: arithmetic expressions and precedence grammars, context-free and finite-state grammars. Algorithms for syntactic analysis: recognizers, backtracking, operator precedence techniques. Semantics of grammatical constructs: reductive grammars, Floyd productions, simple syntactical compilation. Relationship between formal languages and automata.

☐ The following advanced course in computer organization is centered around the comparison of solutions to basic design problems which have been incorporated in a number of quite different computers.

Course A2. Advanced Computer Organization (3-0-3)

Prerequisites: Courses I3, I4 (desirable), and I6 (desirable).

Computer system design problems such as arithmetic and nonarithmetic processing, memory utilization, storage management, addressing, control, and input-output. Comparison of specific examples of various solutions to computer system design problems. Selected topics on novel computer organizations such as those of array or cellular computers and variable structure computers.

☐ This course is designed to give the computer science student some experience with analog, hybrid, and related techniques. It could also be very valuable as a service course.

Course A3. Analog and Hybrid Computing (2-2-3)

Prerequisites: Courses B1 and M4. (The CUPM mathematical analysis courses include some differential equations; more may be needed.)

Analog, hybrid and related digital techniques for the solution of differential equations. Analog simulation languages. Scaling methods. Operational characteristics of analog components. Digital differential analyzers. Analog-to-digital and digital-to-analog conversion. Stability problems. Modeling methods. Use of analog and hybrid equipment and of digital simulation of continuous systems.

☐ The following course is concerned with the simulation and modeling of discrete systems on a computer. Since simulation is one of the most common applications of computers and is used to a great extent in the design of computing machines and systems, students of computer science should become acquainted with simulation techniques and their use.

Course A4. System Simulation (3-0-3)

Prerequisites: Courses I4 and M7.

Introduction to simulation and comparison with other techniques. Discrete simulation models, and introduction to, or review of, queueing theory and stochastic processes. Comparison of discrete change simulation languages. Simulation methodology including generation of random numbers and variates, design of simulation experiments for optimization, analysis of data generated by simulation experiments, and validation of simulation models and results. Selected applications of simulation.

☐The purpose of the following course is to provide an introduction to natural language processing, particularly as it relates to the design and operation of automatic information systems. Included are techniques for organizing, storing, matching, and retrieving structured information on digital computers, as well as procedures useful for the optimization of search effectiveness.

Course A5. Information Organization and Retrieval (3-0-3)

Prerequisite: Course I1.

Structure of semiformal languages and models for the representation of structured information. Aspects of natural language processing on digital computers. The analysis of information content by statistical, syntactic, and logical methods. Search and matching techniques. Automatic retrieval systems, question-answering systems. Production of secondary outputs. Evaluation of retrieval effectiveness.

☐The objective of the following course is to study the problems of handling graphic information, such as line drawings, block diagrams, handwriting, and three-dimensional surfaces, in computers. Input-output and representation-storage of pictures will be introduced from the hardware and software points of view. The course is intended to serve both the student interested in specializing in computer graphics per se and the student who seeks to apply graphic techniques to his particular computing work.

Course A6. Computer Graphics (2-2-3)

Prerequisites: Courses I1, I3 (desirable), and I4 (desirable).

Display memory, generation of points, vectors, etc. Interactive versus passive graphics. Analog storage of images on microfilm, etc. Digitizing and digital storage. Pattern recognition by features, syntax tables, random nets, etc. Data structures and graphics software. The mathematics of three-dimensions, projections, and the hidden-line problem. "Graphical programs," computer-aided design and instruction, and animated movies.

☐The following course uses abstract machines as models in the study of computability and computational complexity. Emphasis is placed on the multi-tape Turing machine as a suitable model, but other models are also considered.

Course A7. Theory of Computability (3-0-3)

Prerequisites: Courses B3 or M6, and I7 (desirable).

Introduction to Turing machines, Wang machines, Shepherdson-Sturgis, and other machines. Gödel numbering and unsolvability results, the halting problem, Post's correspondence problem, and relative uncomputability. Machines with restricted memory access, limited memory, and limited computing time. Recursive function theory and complexity classification. Models of computation including relationships to algorithms and programming.

☐The following course is intended for students who are interested in the application of information technology in large-scale information processing systems. The term "information processing system" is used here to include the hardware, software, procedures, and techniques that are assembled and organized to achieve some desired objectives. Examples of such large-scale information processing systems are business data processing systems, information storage and retrieval systems, command and control systems, and computer centers.

Course A8. Large-scale Information Processing Systems (3-0-3)

Prerequisites: Course A4, and a course in operations research or optimization theory.

Organization of major types of information processing systems. Data organization and storage structure techniques. Designing "best" systems by organizing files and segmenting problems into computer programs to make efficient use of hardware devices. Documentation methods and techniques for modifying systems. Use of optimization and simulation as design techniques. Communication problems among individuals involved in system development.

☐The following course introduces the student to those nonarithmetical applications of computing machines that: (1) attempt to achieve goals considered to require human mental capabilities (artificial intelligence); (2) model highly organized intellectual activity (simulation of cognitive behavior); and (3) describe purposeful behavior of living organisms or artifacts (self-organizing systems). Courses in this area are often taught with few prerequisites, but by requiring some or all of the prerequisites listed here this course could be taught at a more advanced level.

Course A9. Artificial Intelligence and Heuristic Programming (3-0-3)

Prerequisites: Courses I1, A4 (desirable), and M7 (desirable); and some knowledge of experimental and theoretical psychology would also be useful.

Definition of heuristic versus algorithmic methods, rationale of heuristic approach, description of cognitive processes, and approaches to mathematical invention. Objectives of work in artificial intelligence, simulation of cognitive behavior, and self-organizing systems. Heuristic programming techniques including the use of list processing languages. Survey of examples from representative application areas. The mind-brain problem and the nature of intelligence. Class and individual projects to illustrate basic concepts.

4. Undergraduate Programs

As indicated in the Introduction, there has been considerable discussion on the desirability of undergraduate degree programs in computer science. Many who favor these programs believe that an undergraduate computer science "major" is as natural today as a major in established fields such as mathematics, physics, or electrical engineering. Many who oppose these programs feel that, although undergraduate courses in computer science should be available for support of work in other areas, to offer an undergraduate degree in computer science may encourage too narrow a specialization at the expense of breadth. They point out that the lack of such breadth may be a serious handicap to a student desiring to do graduate work in computer science, and they contend that it would be better for the student to major in some established discipline while taking a number of computer science courses as supporting work. To meet these objections the Committee has made every effort to present a curriculum which includes a broad representation of basic concepts and an adequate coverage of professional techniques.

The number of undergraduate degree programs now in existence or in the planning stages—approximately one third of all Ph.D. granting institutions in the United States either have such computer science programs now or expect to have them by 1970 [5]—indicates that a discussion of the desirability of such programs is much less relevant than the early development of guidelines and standards for them. The Committee feels strongly, however, that schools should exercise caution against the premature establishment of undergraduate degree programs. The pressures created by large numbers of students needing to take courses required for the degree could easily result in a general lowering of standards exactly when it is vital that such programs be established and maintained only with high standards.

The variation of undergraduate program requirements among and within schools dictates that this Committee's recommendations must be very general. It is fully expected that each individual school will modify these recommendations to meet its specific circumstances, but it is hoped that these modifications will be expansions of or changes in the emphasis of the basic program proposed, rather than reductions in quantity or quality. The requirements recommended herein have been kept to a minimum in order to allow the student to obtain a "liberal education" and to enable individual programs to add additional detailed requirements. Since the liberal education requirements of each school are already well established, the Committee has not considered making recommendations on such requirements.

The Committee's recommendations for an undergraduate computer science curriculum are stated in terms of computer science course work, programming experience, mathematics course work, technical electives, and possible areas of specialization. Some suggestions are also given as to how the courses might fit chronologically into a semester-by-semester schedule.

Computer Science Courses. The basic and intermediate course requirements listed below emphasize the first two "major subject divisions"—namely, "information structures and processes" and "information processing systems"—described in Section 2 of this report. These courses should give the student a firm grounding in the fundamentals of computer science.

The major in computer science should consist of at least 30 semester hours including the courses:

- B1. Introduction to Computing
- B2. Computers and Programming
- B3. Introduction to Discrete Structures
- B4. Numerical Calculus
- I1. Data Structures
- I2. Programming Languages
- I3. Computer Organization
- I4. Systems Programming

and at least two of the courses:

- I5. Compiler Construction
- I6. Switching Theory
- I7. Sequential Machines
- I8. Numerical Analysis I
- I9. Numerical Analysis II

Programming Experience. Developing programming skill is by no means the main purpose of an undergraduate program in computer science; nevertheless, such skill is an important by-product. Therefore such a program should insure that the student attains a reasonable level of programming competence. This can be done in part by including computer work of progressive complexity and diversity in the required courses, but it is also desirable that each student participate in a "true-to-life" programming project. This might be arranged through summer employment, a cooperative work-study program, part-time employment in computer centers, special project courses, or some other appropriate means.

Mathematics Courses. The Committee feels that an academic program in computer science must be well based in mathematics since computer science draws so heavily upon mathematical ideas and methods. The recommendations for required mathematics courses given below should be regarded as minimal; obviously additional course work in mathematics would be essential for students specializing in numerical applications.

The supporting work in mathematics should consist of at least 18 hours including the courses:

- M1. Introductory Calculus
- M2. Mathematical Analysis I
- M2P. Probability
- M3. Linear Algebra

and at least two of the courses:

- M4. Mathematical Analysis II
- M5. Advanced Multivariate Calculus
- M6. Algebraic Structures
- M7. Probability and Statistics

Technical Electives. Assuming that a typical four-year curriculum consists of 124 semester hours, a number of technical electives beyond the requirements listed above should be available to a student in a computer science program. Some of these electives might be specified by the program to develop a particular orientation or minor. Because of the temptation for the student to overspecialize, it is suggested that a limit be placed on the number of computer science electives a student is allowed to take—for example, three such courses might be permitted. For many students it will be desirable to use the remaining technical electives to acquire a deeper knowledge of mathematics, physical science, electrical engineering, or some other computer-related field.

Students should be carefully advised in the choice of their electives. In particular, those preparing for graduate school must insure that they will be qualified for admission into the program of their choice. Those seeking a more "professional" education can specialize to some extent through the proper choice of electives.

Areas of Specialization. Although undue specialization is not appropriate at the undergraduate level, the technical electives may be used to orient undergraduate programs in a number of different directions. Some of the possible orientations, along with appropriate courses (of Section 3) and subject areas (of Section 2) from which the optional and elective courses might be taken, are given below.

APPLIED SYSTEMS PROGRAMMING

Optional courses

- I5. Compiler Construction
- I6. Switching Theory

Electives from courses

- A2. Advanced Computer Organization
- A5. Information Organization and Retrieval
- A6. Computer Graphics

Electives from areas

- IV.8 Combinatorial Mathematics
- IV.9 Mathematical Logic
- IV.11 Probability and Statistics
- IV.12 Operations Analysis

COMPUTER ORGANIZATION AND DESIGN

Optional courses

- I6. Switching Theory
- I7. Sequential Machines

Electives from courses

- A2. Advanced Computer Organization
- A4. System Simulation
- A8. Large-scale Information Processing Systems

Electives from areas

- IV.3 Differential Equations
- V.2 Basic Electronics
- V.6 Digital and Pulse Circuits
- V.7 Coding and Information Theory

SCIENTIFIC APPLICATIONS PROGRAMMING

Optional courses

- I8. Numerical Analysis I
- I9. Numerical Analysis II

Electives from courses

- A3. Analog and Hybrid Computing
- A4. System Simulation
- A5. Information Organization and Retrieval
- A6. Computer Graphics

Electives from areas

- IV.3 Differential Equations
- IV.7 Optimization Theory
- V.4 Thermodynamics and Statistical Mechanics
- V.5 Field Theory

DATA PROCESSING APPLICATIONS PROGRAMMING

Optional courses

- I5. Compiler Construction
- I6. Switching Theory

Electives from courses

- A4. System Simulation
- A5. Information Organization and Retrieval
- A8. Large-scale Information Processing Systems

Electives from areas

- IV.7 Optimization Theory
- IV.11 Probability and Statistics
- IV.12 Operation Analysis
- V.7 Coding and Information Theory

Semester Chronology. Any institution planning an undergraduate program based on the recommendations of this report should work out several complete four-year curricula to insure that the required courses mesh in an orderly manner with electives and with the "general education" requirements of the institution. This will help the school to take into account local circumstances such as having very few entering freshmen who can begin college mathematics with the calculus.

Table I gives some examples of how a student in computer science might be scheduled for the minimum set of courses recommended for all majors.

TABLE I

Year	*Semester*	*First example*	*Second example*	*Third example*
Freshman	First	M1, B1	Basic Math.	Basic Math.
	Second	M2, B2	M1, B1	Basic Math.
Sophomore	First	M3, B3	M2, B2	M1, B1
	Second	M4, B4	M3, B3	M2, B2
Junior	First	M2P, I1	M4, B4	M2P, B3, B4
	Second	M5, I2	M2P, I1	M3, I1, I2
Senior	First	I3, I8	M7, I2, I3	M6, I3, I6
	Second	I4, I9	I4, I5, I6	M7, I4, I7

5. Master's Degree Programs

The recommendations given in this section concern undergraduate preparation for graduate study in computer science, requirements for a Master of Science degree in computer science, and some possible areas of concentration for students who are at the master's degree level.

Undergraduate Preparation. The recommended preparation for graduate study in computer science consists of three parts as listed below. The course work which would provide this background is indicated in parentheses.

a. Knowledge of computer science including algorithmic processes, programming, computer organization, discrete structures, and numerical mathematics. (Courses B1, B2, B3, and B4 or I8 of Section 3.)

b. Knowledge of mathematics, including the calculus and linear algebra, and knowledge of probability and statistics. (Courses M1, M2, M3, M4, M2P, M7 of CUPM.)

c. Additional knowledge of some field such as computer science, mathematics, electrical engineering, physical science, biological science, linguistics, library science, or management science which will contribute to the student's graduate study in computer science. (Four appropriate courses on an intermediate level.)

A student with a bachelor's degree in computer science, such as recommended in Section 4, can have taken all these prerequisites as basic and supporting courses and can also have taken further work which overlaps with some of the subject matter to be treated at the master's level. Although such a student will be able to take more advanced graduate work in computer science to satisfy his master's requirements, he may need to take more supporting work than a student whose undergraduate degree was in some other field. A student with an undergraduate degree in mathematics, physical science, or electrical engineering can easily qualify for such a program if he has taken adequate supporting courses in computer science. Other applicants should have no more than a few deficiencies in order to qualify.

In the near future many of the potential students, because of having completed their undergraduate work some time ago, will not have had the opportunity to meet these requirements. Liberal policies should therefore be established so that promising students can make up deficiencies.

Degree Requirements. Each student's program of study for the master's degree should have both breadth and depth. In order to obtain breadth, the student should take course work from each of the three subject divisions of computer science described in Section 2. To obtain depth, he should develop an area of concentration in which he would write a master's thesis or complete a master's project (if required).

The master's degree program in computer science should consist of at least nine courses. Normally at least two courses—each in a different subject area—should be taken from each of the following subject divisions of computer science:

I. Information Structures and Processes
II. Information Processing Systems
III. Methodologies

Sufficient other courses in computer science or related areas should be taken to bring the student to the forefront of some area of computer science.

In order that the student may perform in his required course work at the graduate level he must acquire a knowledge of related areas, such as mathematics and the physical sciences, either as part of his undergraduate preparation or as part of his graduate program. Computer science as a discipline requires an understanding of mathematical methods and an ability to use mathematical techniques beyond the specific undergraduate preparation in mathematics recommended above. Hence, a student who does not have a "strong" mathematics background should take either further courses in mathematics, or he should take computer science courses which contain a high mathematical content.

If Courses I1, I2, I3, and I4 of Section 3 are taught at a sufficiently high level, they can be used to satisfy the "breadth" requirements for the first two subject divisions listed above. In any case, the student who has taken such courses as part of his undergraduate program could take more advanced courses in these areas so that the requirement for two courses in each subject division might be relaxed somewhat. This might permit such a student to take more supporting work outside computer science.

Areas of Concentration. The "depth" requirement will often involve courses from fields other than computer science, so that a student may have to take additional courses in these fields just to meet prerequisites unless he has anticipated this need in his undergraduate preparation. In any event, the particular courses a student selects from each of the three subject divisions of computer science should be coordinated with his area of concentration. To illustrate how this might be done, six possible concentrations are shown below together with lists of the subject areas (of Section 2) from which appropriate courses might be selected for each of the concentrations. The characterization of courses in terms of subject areas instead of explicit content effectively gives a list of suggested topics which can be drawn upon in designing master's level courses suited to the needs of individual institutions.

THEORETICAL COMPUTER SCIENCE

- I.1 Data Structures
- I.2 Programming Languages
- I.3 Models of Computation
- III.3 Symbol Manipulation
- III.8 Artificial Intelligence
- IV.8 Combinatorial Analysis
- IV.9 Mathematical Logic
- V.7 Coding and Information Theory

APPLIED SOFTWARE

- I.1 Data Structures
- I.2 Programming Languages
- II.1 Computer Design and Organization
- II.2 Translators and Interpreters
- II.3 Computer and Operating Systems
- III.3 Symbol Manipulation
- III.6 Simulation
- IV.7 Optimization Theory
- IV.9 Mathematical Logic

APPLIED HARDWARE

- I.1 Data Structures
- I.3 Models of Computation
- II.1 Computer Design and Organization
- II.3 Computer and Operating Systems
- III.5 Computer Graphics
- IV. 7 Optimization Theory
- IV. 9 Mathematical Logic
- V.6 Digital and Pulse Circuits
- V.7 Coding and Information Theory

NUMERICAL MATHEMATICS

- I.1 Data Structures
- I.2 Programming Languages
- II.1 Computer Design and Organization
- II.3 Computer and Operating Systems
- III.1 Numerical Mathematics
- III.6 Simulation
- IV.5 Theoretical Numerical Analysis
- IV.6 Methods of Applied Mathematics
- IV.7 Optimization Theory

INSTRUMENTATION

- I.1 Data Structures
- I.2 Programming Languages
- II.1 Computer Design and Organization
- II.4 Special Purpose Systems
- III.6 Simulation
- III.9 Process Control
- IV.6 Methods of Applied Mathematics
- IV.7 Optimization Theory
- V.8 Communication and Control Theory

INFORMATION SYSTEMS

- I.1 Data Structures
- I.2 Programming Languages
- II.1 Computer Design and Organization
- II.3 Computer and Operating Systems
- III.2 Data Processing and File Management
- III.4 Text Processing
- III. 7 Information Retrieval
- IV.7 Optimization Theory
- IV.9 Mathematical Logic

The requirement of a master's thesis or other project has been left unspecified since general institutional requirements will usually determine this. It is strongly recommended, however, that a master's program in computer science contain some formal provision for insuring that the student gains or has gained project experience in computer applications. This could be effected by requiring that students carry out either individually or cooperatively a substantial assigned task involving analysis and programming, or better, that students be involved in an actual project on campus or in conjunction with other employment.

This proposed program embodies sufficient flexibility to fulfill the requirements of either an "academic" degree obtained in preparation for further graduate study or a terminal "professional" degree. Until clearer standards both for computer science research and the computing profession have emerged, it seems unwise to attempt to distinguish more definitely between these two aspects of master's degree programs.

6. Doctoral Programs

Academic programs at the doctoral level reflect the specific interests of the faculty and, hence, vary from university to university. Therefore, the Committee cannot expect to give recommendations for such doctoral programs in as great a detail as has been done for the undergraduate and master's degree programs. The large number of institutions planning such programs and the variety of auspices under which they are being sponsored, however, suggest that a need exists for guidelines as to what constitutes a "good" doctoral program. While recommendations on doctoral programs will not be given at this time, the problem of how to obtain such guidelines has been of considerable interest to the Committee.

One possible source of such guidelines is the existing doctoral programs. A description of the program at Stanford University [15] has already been published in *Communications of the ACM* and descriptions of many other programs are available from the universities concerned. Information based on a number of such programs is contained in the report of the June 1967, Stony Brook Conference [11]. This report also contains a list of thesis topics currently being pursued or recently completed. In the future the Curriculum Committee hopes to encourage wide dissemination of the descriptions of existing programs and research topics. Perhaps it can take an active role in coordinating the interchange of such information.

In 1966 Professor Thomas Hull was asked by ACM to examine the question of doctoral programs in computer science. After discussion with the members of this Committee and with many other interested persons, Professor Hull decided to solicit a series of articles on the research and teaching areas which might be involved in doctoral programs. Each article is to be written by an expert in the particular subject area, such as programming languages, systems programming, computer organization, numerical mathematics, automata theory, large systems, and artificial intelligence. Each article is to attempt to consider all aspects of the subject area which might be helpful to those developing a graduate program, including as many of the following topics as possible:

a. Definition of the subject area, possibly in terms of an annotated bibliography.
b. Prerequisites for work in the area at the doctoral level.
c. Outlines of appropriate graduate courses in the area.
d. Examples of questions for qualifying examinations in the area.
e. Indication of suitable thesis topics and promising directions for research in the area.
f. The extent to which the subject area ought to be required of all doctoral students in computer science.

These articles are scheduled for publication in *Communications of the ACM* and it is hoped that they will stimulate further articles on doctoral programs.

7. Service Courses, Minors, and Continuing Education

Though it is now generally recognized that a significant portion of our undergraduate students needs some knowledge of computing, the amount and type of computing knowledge necessary for particular areas of study are still subject to considerable discussion. The Pierce Report [7] estimates that about 75 percent of all college undergraduates are enrolled in curricula where some computer training would be useful. This estimate, based on figures compiled by the US Office of Education, involves dividing the undergraduate student population into three groups. The first group, about 35 percent of all undergraduates, consists of those in scientific or professional programs having a substantial quantitative content (e.g. mathematics, physics, and engineering). At least some introductory knowledge of computing is already considered highly desirable for almost all of these students. The second group, some 40 percent, is made up of those majoring in fields where an understanding of the fundamentals of computing is steadily becoming more valuable (e.g. business, behavioral sciences, education, medicine, and library science). Many programs in these areas are already requiring courses in computing, and most are expected to add such requirements in the future. The third group, roughly 25 percent, comprises those undergraduates who are majoring in areas which do not necessarily depend on the use of computers (e.g. music, drama, literature, foreign languages, liberal arts, and fine arts). There are many persons who maintain that even these students could benefit from a course which would give them an appreciation of this modern technology and its influence on the structure of our society.

The extent and nature of the courses on computing needed for these three groups of students should be given further careful study, but the existence of a substantial need for service courses in computer science seems undeniable. Students in the more quantitative fields are usually well-equipped to take the basic courses designed for the computer science major. In particular, Course B1 should serve as an excellent introductory course for these students and, depending upon their interests, Course B2 or B4 might serve as a second course. When these students develop a greater interest in computing, they should normally be able to select an appropriate "minor" program of study from the courses described in Section 3. In developing a minor program careful consideration should be given to the comparative values of each course in the development of the individual student.

Some special provisions appear to be necessary for students in the second and third groups described above. A special version of Course B1 which would place more emphasis on text processing and other nonnumeric applications might be more appropriate for students in the second group. However, it is important that this course provides adequate preparation for such courses as B2 and B3, since many of these students might be expected to take further courses in computer science. It may also be desirable to develop courses giving primary emphasis to the economic, political, sociological, and other implications of the growing use of computer technology. Such courses would not be considered substitutes for basic technical courses such as B1, but they could serve the needs of the third group of students.

Professional programs at all levels offer limited opportunity for courses outside their highly structured curricula, and they also present special problems. In some cases it may be necessary to develop special courses for students in such programs or to integrate work on computing into existing courses. Those preparing for graduate professional programs will often find it desirable to include some of the basic computer science courses in their undergraduate work.

The responsibility for developing and conducting the basic service courses in computer science should be concentrated within the academic structure and combined with the operation of educational programs in computer science. By properly aggregating students from similar fields, those responsible for planning academic courses can make them more generally applicable and broadly directed. Under this arrangement teachers can be used more effectively and course content can more easily be kept current with the rapidly moving developments in the field. Also, students who find a need or a desire to delve further into computer science are more likely to have the necessary background to take advanced courses. On the other hand, it must be recognized that some departments will have many situations where special applications of the computer can best be introduced in their own courses. Certainly those responsible for the basic computer science service courses must be sensitive to the needs of the students for whom these courses are intended.

Finally, the need for continuing education in computer science must be recognized. Much of the course material discussed in this report did not exist ten or fifteen years ago, and practically none of this material was available to students until the last few years. Anyone who graduated from college in the early 1960's and whose "major" field of study is related to computing is already out-of-date unless he has made a determined effort to continue his education. Those responsible for academic programs in computer science and those agencies which help to direct and support continuing education should be especially alert to these needs in this unusually dynamic and important field.

8. Implementation

In educational institutions careful consideration should be given to the problems of implementing a computer-related course of study—be it a few introductory or service courses, an undergraduate degree program, or a graduate degree program. Some of these problems involve organization, staff requirements, and physical facilities (including computing services). Although individual ways of providing a favorable environment for computer science will be found in each school, the following discussion is intended to call attention to the extent of some of these problems.

Organization for Academic Programs. It should be realized that the demands for education in computer science are strong. If some suitable place in the institutional structure is not provided for courses and programs in computer science to be developed, they will spring up within a number of existing departments and a possible diffusion of effort will result as has been experienced with statistics in many universities.

If degree programs in computer science are to be offered, it is desirable to establish an independent academic unit to administer them. Such a unit is needed to provide the appropriate mechanisms for faculty appointments and promotions, for attention to continuing curriculum development, and for the allocation of resources such as personnel, budget, space, and equipment. This academic unit should also be prepared to provide general service courses and to cooperate in developing computer-oriented course work in other departments and professional schools.

Many universities have established departments of computer science as part of their colleges of arts and sciences, and some have established divisions of mathematical sciences, which include such departments as mathematics, applied mathematics, statistics, and computer science. Other institutions have located computer science departments in colleges of engineering and applied science. Academic units in computer science have also been affiliated with a graduate school, associated with more than one college, or even established independent of any college in a university.

The organizational problems for this new field are serious, and their solution will inevitably require new budget commitments from a university. However, failure to come to grips with the problem will probably prove more costly in the long run; duplicated courses and programs of diluted quality may result, and a major upheaval may eventually be required for reorganization.

Staff Requirements. Degree programs in computer science require a faculty dedicated to this discipline—that is, individuals who consider themselves computer scientists regardless of their previous academic training. Although graduate programs in computer science are now producing a limited number of potential faculty members, the demand for such people in industry and government and the competition for faculty among universities are quite intense. Hence educational institutions will have to obtain most of their computer science faculty from other sources—at least for the immediate future. Many faculty members in other departments of our universities have become involved with computing and have contributed to its development to the point that they are anxious to become part of a computer science program. Within industry and government there are also people with the necessary academic credentials who are willing to teach the technology they have helped develop. Thus, extensive experience and academic work in computer science, accompanied by academic credentials in a related area such as mathematics, electrical engineering, or other appropriate disciplines, can serve as suitable qualifications for staff appointments in a computer science program. Joint appointments with other academic departments or with the computing center can help fill some of the need, but it is desirable that a substantial portion of the faculty be fully committed to computer science. Moreover, there is some critical size of faculty—perhaps the equivalent of five full-time positions—which is needed to provide a reasonable coverage of the areas of computer science discussed in Section 2.

Since relatively few good textbooks are available in the computer sciences, the computer science faculty will need to devote an unusually large part of its time to searching the literature and developing instructional materials. This fact should be taken into consideration in determining teaching loads and staff assignments.

Physical Facilities. Insofar as physical facilities are concerned, computer science should generally be included among the laboratory sciences. Individual faculty members may need extra space to set up and use equipment, to file cards and voluminous computer listings, and otherwise to carry out their teaching and research. In addition to normal library facilities, special collections of material, such as research reports, computer manuals, and computer programs, must be obtained and facilities made available for their proper storage and effective use. Space must also be provided for keypunches, remote consoles to computers, and any other special equipment needed for education and/or research. Laboratory-type classrooms must be available to allow students, either as individuals or as groups, to spread out and study computer listings.

It is no more conceivable that computer science courses—let alone degree programs—can exist without a computer available to students than that chemistry and physics offerings can exist without the associated laboratory equipment. Degree programs require regular access to at least a medium-sized computer system of sufficient complexity in configuration to require the use of an operating system. The total operating costs of such systems are at least $20,000 per month. In terms of hours per month, the machine requirements of computer science degree programs will vary according to the number of students enrolled, the speed of the computer and the efficiency of its software, and the philosophy of the instructors. It is entirely possible that an undergraduate degree program might require as much as four hours of computing on a medium-sized computer per class day.

Space for data and program preparation and program checking must be provided, and the logistics of handling hundreds and possibly thousands of student programs per day must be worked out so that each student has frequent access to the computer with a minimum of waiting and confusion. Although many of these same facilities must be provided for students and faculty other than those in computer science, the computer science program is particularly dependent on these services. It is simply false economy to hamper the use of expensive computing equipment by crowding it into unsuitable space or in some other way making it inaccessible.

The study and development of systems programs will require special forms of access to at least medium-scale computing systems. This will place an additional burden on the computer center and may possibly require the acquisition of completely separate equipment for educational and research purposes. In advanced programs it is likely that other specialized equipment will be necessary to handle such areas as computer graphics, numeric control of machines, process control, simulation, information retrieval systems, and computer-assisted instruction.

Although assistance in financing computer services and equipment can be obtained from industry and from federal and state governments, the Committee feels that universities should provide for the costs of equipment and services for computer science programs just as they provide for costs of other laboratory sciences. Based on its knowledge of costs at a number of schools the Committee estimates that computer batch processing of student jobs for elementary courses presently costs an average of about $30 per semester hour per student, whereas the Pierce Report [7] estimates that it costs colleges about $95 per chemistry student per year for a single chemistry laboratory course. Although computer costs are decreasing relative to capacity, it is expected that students will be able to use more computer time effectively in the future as computers become more accessible through the use of such techniques as time-sharing. On the basis of these estimates and expectations, future computer costs for academic programs may well approach faculty salary costs.

Relation of the Academic Program to the Computing Center. As indicated above, the demands which an academic program in computer science places on a university computing center are more than routine. Computer and programming systems must be expanded and modified to meet the growing and varied needs of these programs as well as the needs of the other users. The service function of a computer center must therefore be enhanced by an activity which might be described as "applied computer science." In a complementary way, it is appropriate for a computer science faculty to be deeply involved in the application of computers, particularly in the development of programming systems. For these reasons, the activities of a computer center and a computer science department should be closely coordinated. The sharing of staff through joint appointments helps facilitate such cooperation, and it is almost necessary to provide such academic appointments in order to attract and retain certain essential computer center personnel.

It should be realized, however, that the basic philosophies of providing services and of pursuing academic ends differ to such an extent that conflicts for attention may occur. At one extreme, the research of a computer science faculty may so dominate the activities of a computer center that its service to the academic community deteriorates. At the other extreme, the routine service demands of a computer center may inhibit the faculty's ability to do their own research, or the service orientation of a center may cause the educational program to consist of mere training in techniques having only transient value. Considerable and constant care must be taken to maintain a balance between these extremes.

REFERENCES

1. Association for Computing Machinery, Curriculum Committee on Computer Science. An undergraduate program in computer science—preliminary recommendations. *Comm. ACM 8*, 9 (Sept. 1965), 543–552.
2. NEWELL, A., PERLIS, A. J., AND SIMON, H. A. Computer science. (Letter to the Editor). *Science 157*, 3795 (22 Sept. 1967), 1373–1374.
3. University of Chicago. Graduate programs in the divisions, announcements 1967–1968. U. of Chicago, Chicago, pp. 167–169.
4. GORN, S. The computer and information sciences: a new basic discipline. *SIAM Review 5*, 2 (Apr. 1963), 150–155.
5. HAMBLEN, J. W. Computers in higher education: expenditures, sources of funds, and utilization for research and instruction 1964–65, with projections for 1968–69. (A report on a survey supported by NSF). Southern Regional Education Board, Atlanta, Ga., 1967.
6. ROSSER, J. B., ET AL. Digital computer needs in universities and colleges. Publ. 1233, National Academy of Sciences-National Research Council, Washington, D. C., 1966.
7. President's Science Advisory Committee. Computers in higher education. The White House, Washington, D. C., Feb. 1967.
8. Mathematical Association of America, Committee on the Undergraduate Program in Computer Science (CUPM). Recommendations on the undergraduate mathematics program for work in computing. CUPM, Berkeley, Calif., May 1964.
9. Commission on Engineering Education, COSINE Committee. Computer sciences in electrical engineering. Commission in Engineering Education, Washington, D. C., Sept. 1967.
10. British Computer Society, Education Committee. Annual education review. *Comput. Bull. 11*, 1 (June 1967), 3–73.
11. FINERMAN, A. (Ed.) *University Education in Computing Science*. (Proceedings of the Graduate Academic Conference in Computing Science, Stony Brook, New York, June 5–8, 1967) ACM Monograph, Academic Press, New York, 1968.
12. Mathematical Association of America, Committee on the Undergraduate Program in Mathematics (CUPM). A general curriculum in mathematics for colleges. CUPM, Berkeley, Calif., 1965.
13. ——. Recommendations in the undergraduate mathematics program for engineers and physicists. CUPM, Berkeley, Calif., 1967.
14. ——. A curriculum in applied mathematics. CUPM, Berkeley, Calif., 1966.
15. FORSYTHE, G. E. A university's education program in computer science. *Comm. ACM 10*, 1 (Jan. 1967), 3–11.

Acknowledgments

The following people have served as consultants to the Committee on one or more occasions or have given considerable other assistance to our work.

Richard V. Andree, University of Oklahoma
Robert L. Ashenhurst, University of Chicago
Bruce H. Barnes, Pennsylvania State University
Robert S. Barton, University of Utah
J. Richard Buchi, Purdue University
Harry Cantrell, General Electric Company
Mary D'Imperio, Department of Defense
Arthur Evans, Massachusetts Institute of Technology
David C. Evans, University of Utah
Nicholas V. Findler, State University of New York at Buffalo
Patrick C. Fischer, University of British Columbia
George E. Forsythe, Stanford University
Bernard A. Galler, University of Michigan
Saul Gorn, University of Pennsylvania
Preston C. Hammer, Pennsylvania State University
Richard W. Hamming, Bell Telephone Laboratories
Harry D. Huskey, University of California at Berkeley
Peter Z. Ingerman, Radio Corporation of America
Donald E. Knuth, California Institute of Technology
Robert R. Korfhage, Purdue University
Donald J. Laird, Pennsylvania State University
George E. Lindamood, University of Maryland
William C. Lynch, Case Institute of Technology
M. Douglas McIlroy, Bell Telephone Laboratories
Robert McNaughton, Rensselaer Polytechnic Institute
Michel Melkanoff, University of California at Los Angeles
William F. Miller, Stanford University
Anthony G. Oettinger, Harvard University
Elliott I. Organick, University of Houston
Robert H. Owens, University of Virginia
Charles P. Reed, Jr., Georgia Institute of Technology
Saul Rosen, Purdue University
Daniel Teichroew, Case Institute of Technology
Andries van Dam, Brown University
Robert J. Walker, Cornell University
Peter Wegner, Cornell University

Written comments on the Committee's work, contributions to course outlines, and other assistance have been rendered by the following:

Bruce W. Arden, University of Michigan
John E. Bakken, Midwest Oil Corporation
Larry L. Bell, Auburn University
Robert D. Brennan, International Business Machines Corp.
Yaohan Chu, University of Maryland
Charles H. Davidson, University of Wisconsin
Harold P. Edmundson, University of Maryland
Charles W. Gear, University of Illinois
Robert T. Gregory, University of Texas
Keith Hastings, University of Toronto
Carl F. Kossack, University of Georgia
Ralph E. Lee, University of Missouri at Rolla
George Mealy, Massachusetts Institute of Technology
Harlan D. Mills, International Business Machines Corp.
Jack Minker, University of Maryland and Auerbach Corp.
Jack Noland, General Electric Company
James C. Owings, Jr., University of Maryland
David L. Parnas, Carnegie-Mellon University
Charles R. Pearson, J. P. Stevens and Co.
Tad Pinkerton, University of Michigan
Roland L. Porter, Los Angeles, California
Anthony Ralston, State University of New York at Buffalo
Roy F. Reeves, Ohio State University
John R. Rice, Purdue University
Gerard Salton, Cornell University
Gordon Sherman, University of Tennessee
Vladimir Slamecka, Georgia Institute of Technology
Joseph F. Traub, Bell Telephone Laboratories

Numerous other people have contributed to the work of the Committee through informal discussions and other means. The Committee is grateful for all of the assistance it has received and especially for the cooperative spirit in which it has been given.

Appendix. Course Outlines and Bibliographies

For each of the twenty-two courses described in Section 3, this Appendix contains a brief discussion of the approach to teaching the course, a detailed outline of the content of the course, and a bibliography listing material which should be useful to the teacher and/or the student in the course. The amount of attention which might be devoted to the various topics in the content of some of the courses is indicated by percentage or by number of lectures. Whenever possible, each bibliographic entry is followed by a reference to its review in *Computing Reviews*. The format used for these references is CR-xyvi-n, where xy indicates the year of the review, v the volume number, i the issue number, and n the number of the review itself. Most of the bibliographic entries are followed by a brief annotation which is intended to indicate the way in which the item would be useful and perhaps to clarify the subject of the item. In some cases the title is sufficient for this purpose, and no annotation is given. In other cases the items are simply keyed in various ways to the sections of the content to which they apply. Although an effort has been made to cite a wide variety of texts and reference materials for each course, space and other considerations have prevented the listing of all books and papers which might bear on the topics treated.

Course B1. Introduction to Computing (2-2-3)

APPROACH

This first course in computing concentrates on the solution of computational problems through the introduction and use of an algorithmic language. A single such language should be used for most of the course so that the students may master it well enough to attack substantial problems. It may be desirable, however, to use a simple second language of quite different character for a problem or two in order to demonstrate the wide diversity of the computer languages available. Because of its elegance and novelty, SNOBOL can be used quite effectively for this purpose. In any case, it is essential that the student be aware that the computers and languages he is learning about are only particular instances of a widespread species.

The notion of an algorithm should be stressed throughout the course and clearly distinguished from that of a program. The language structures should be carefully motivated and precisely defined using one or more of the formal techniques available. Every effort should be made to develop the student's ability to analyze complex problems and formulate algorithms for their solution. Numerous problems should be assigned for computer solution, beginning early in the course with several small projects to aid the student in learning to program, and should include at least one major project, possibly of the student's own choosing. Careful verification of program operation and clear program documentation should be emphasized.

CONTENT

This outline reflects an order in which the material might be presented; however, the order of presentation will be governed by the choice of languages and texts as well as individual preferences. In particular, the treatment of some of the topics listed below might be distributed throughout the course. Although not specifically listed in the following outline, programming and computer projects should constitute an important part of the content of this course.

1. *Algorithms, Programs, and Computers.* The concept and properties of algorithms. Flowcharts of algorithms and the need for precise languages to express algorithms. The concept of a program, examples of simple programs, and description of how computers execute programs. Programming languages including the description of their syntax and semantics. (10%)

2. *Basic Programming.* Constants, identifiers, variables, subscripts, operations, functions, and expressions. Declarations, substitution statements, input-output statements, conditional statements, iteration statements, and complete programs. (10%)

3. *Program Structure.* Procedures, functions, subroutine calling, and formal-actual parameter association. Statement grouping, nested structure of expressions and statements, local versus global variables, run-time representation, and storage allocation. Common data, segmenting, and other structural features. (10%)

4. *Programming and Computing Systems.* Compilers, libraries, loaders, system programs, operating systems, and other information necessary for the student to interact with the computer being used. (5%)

5. *Debugging and Verification of Programs.* Error conditions and messages, techniques of debugging, selection of test data, checking of computer output, and programming to guard against errors in data. (5%)

6. *Data Representation.* Systems of enumeration and binary codes. Representation of characters, fixed and floating-point numbers, vectors, strings, tables, matrices, arrays, and other data structures. (10%)

7. *Other Programming Topics.* Formatted input and output. Accuracy, truncation, and round-off errors. Considerations of efficiency. Other features of language(s) being considered. (10%)

8. *Organization and Characteristics of Computers.* Internal organization including input-output, memory-storage, processing and control. Registers, arithmetic, instruction codes, execution of instruction, addressing, and flow of control. Speed, cost and characteristics of various operations and components. (10%)

9. *Analysis of Numerical and Nonnumerical Problems.* Applications of algorithm development and programming to the solution of a variety of problems (distributed throughout the course). (15%)

10. *Survey of Computers, Languages, Systems, and Applications.* The historical development of computers, languages, and systems including recent novel applications of computers, and new developments in the computing field. (10%)

11. *Examinations.* (5%)

ANNOTATED BIBLIOGRAPHY

In addition to the materials listed here, there are numerous books and manuals on specific computer languages which would be appropriate as part of the textual material for this course. Very few books, however, place sufficient emphasis on algorithms and provide the general introductory material proposed for this course.

1. ARDEN, B. W. *An Introduction to Digital Computing.* Addison-Wesley, Reading, Mass., 1963, 389 pp. CR-6345-4551.

This text uses MAD and emphasizes the solution of numerical problems, although other types of problems are discussed. Numerous examples and exercises.

2. FORTE, A. *SNOBOL3 Primer*. M.I.T. Press, Cambridge, Mass., 1967, 107 pp.

   An elementary exposition of SNOBOL3 which might well be used to introduce a "second" language. Many exercises and examples. (SNOBOL4 is now becoming available.)

3. GALLER, B. A. *The Language of Computers*. McGraw-Hill, New York, 1962, 244 pp. CR-6341-3574.

   Emphasizes "discovering" the structure of algorithms needed for the solution of a varied set of problems. The computer language features necessary to express these algorithms are carefully motivated. The language introduced is primarily based on MAD, but FORTRAN and ALGOL are also discussed.

4. GRUENBERGER, F. The teaching of computing (Guest editorial). *Comm. ACM 8*, 6 (June 1965), 348 and 410. CR-6565-8074.

   Conveys eloquently the philosophy which should be used in developing and teaching an introductory computing course.

5. GRUENBERGER, F. AND JAFFRAY, G. *Problems for Computer Solution*. Wiley, New York, 1965, 401 pp. CR-6671-8757.

   Contains a collection of problems appropriate for computer solution by students. Student is guided into the analysis of the problems and the development of good computational solutions, but actual computer programs for the solutions are not given.

6. HULL, T. E. *Introduction to Computing*. Prentice-Hall, Englewood Cliffs, N. J., 1966, 212 pp.

   Text on fundamentals of algorithms, basic features of stored-program computers, and techniques involved in implementing algorithms on computers. Presents a complete description of FORTRAN IV with examples of numerical methods, nonnumerical applications, and simulations. Numerous exercises.

7. MARCOVITZ, A. B. AND SCHWEPPE, E. J. *An Introduction to Algorithmic Methods Using the MAD Language*. Macmillan, New York, 1966, 433 pp. CR-6781-11,199.

   Emphasizes algorithms and their expression as programs, characteristics of computers and computer systems, formal definition of computer languages, and accuracy and efficiency of programs. Numerous examples and exercises.

8. PERLIS, A. J. Programming for digital computers. *Comm. ACM 7*, 4 (Apr. 1964), 210–211.

   Description of course developed by Perlis at Carnegie Institute of Technology which has strongly influenced the course proposed here.

9. RICE, J. K. AND RICE, J. R. *Introduction to Computer Science: Problems, Algorithms, Languages and Information*, Preliminary edition. Holt, Rinehart and Winston, New York, 1967, 452 pp.

   Presentation revolves around the theme of "problem solving," emphasizing algorithms, languages, information representations, and machines necessary to solve problems. Problem solution methods classified, and many sample problems included. The nature of errors and uncertainty is considered. Detailed appendix on FORTRAN IV by E. Desautels.

10. School Mathematics Study Group. *Algorithms, Computation and Mathematics*, rev. ed. Stanford University, Stanford, Calif., 1966. *Student Text*, 453 pp., *Teacher's Commentary*, 301 pp.; *Algol Supplement: Student Text*, 133 pp., *Teacher's Commentary*, 109 pp.; *Fortran Supplement: Student Text*, 132 pp., *Teacher's Commentary*, 102 pp. Available from A. C. Vroman, Inc., 367 South Pasadena, Pasadena, Calif. *A MAD Language Supplement* by E. I. Organick is available from Ulrich's Book Store, 549 E. University Avenue, Ann Arbor, Mich.

    Although developed for high school students and teachers, this work contains much material appropriate for this course. Develops an understanding of the relationship between mathematics, computing, and problem solving. Basic text uses English and flow charts to describe algorithms; supplements introduce the computer language and give these algorithms in ALGOL, FORTRAN, and MAD.

Course B2. Computers and Programming (2-2-3)

APPROACH

This course is designed to introduce the student to basic computer organization, machine language programming, and the use of assembly language programming systems. A particular computer, machine language and programming system should be used extensively to illustrate the concepts being taught and to give the student actual experience in programming. However, it is important that the course not degenerate into mere training in how to program one machine. Alternative machine languages, machine organization, and programming systems should be discussed and compared. Emphasis should be placed on the overall structure of the machines and programming techniques considered. A "descriptive" presentation of various computer features and organizations may be very effective; nevertheless, it is recommended that a precise language be introduced and used to describe computer organizations and instruction execution (as the Iverson notation has been used to describe the IBM System/360).

CONTENT

The following outline indicates a possible order in which the material for this course might be taught, but other arrangements might be equally suitable depending upon the choice of text, availability of computing facilities, and preferences of the instructor. Computer projects—although not specifically listed below—should be an essential part of the course content.

1. *Computer Structure and Machine Language.* Organization of computers in terms of input-output, storage, control, and processing units. Register and storage structures, instruction format and execution, principal instruction types, and machine language programming. Machine arithmetic, program control, input-output operations, and interrupts. Characteristics of input-output and storage devices. (10%)

2. *Addressing Techniques.* Absolute addressing, indexing, indirect addressing, relative addressing, and base addressing. Memory mapping functions, storage allocation, associative addressing, paging, and machine organization to facilitate modes of addressing. (5%)

3. *Digital Representation of Data.* Bits, fields, words, and other information structures. Radices and radix conversion, representation of integer, floating-point, and multiple-precision numbers in binary and decimal form, and round-off errors. Representation of strings, lists, symbol tables, arrays and other data structures. Data transmission, error detection and correction. Fixed versus variable word lengths. (10%)

4. *Symbolic Coding and Assembly Systems.* Mnemonic operation codes, labels, symbolic addresses and address expressions. Literals, extended machine operations, and pseudo operations. Error flags and messages, updating, and program documentation. Scanning of symbolic instructions and symbol table construction. Overall design and operation of assemblers. (10%)

5. *Selected Programming Techniques (chosen from among the following).* Techniques for sorting, searching, scanning, and converting data. String manipulation, text editing, and list processing. Stack management, arithmetic expression recognition, syntactic recognition, and other compilation techniques. (10%)

6. *Logic Design, Micro-programming, and Interpreters.* AND, OR, and NOT elements, design of a half-adder and an adder, storage and delay elements, and design of an arithmetic unit. Parallel versus serial arithmetic, encoding and decoding logic, and micro-programming. Interpreters, simulation, and emulation. Logical equivalence between hardware and software. (5%)

7. *Macros.* Definition, call, and expansion of macros. Nested and recursive macro calls and definitions. Parameter handling, conditional assembly, and assembly time computations. (10%)

8. *Program Segmentation and Linkage.* Subroutines, coroutines, and functions. Subprogram loading and linkage, common data linkage, transfer vectors, and parameters. Dynamic storage allocation,

overlays, re-entrant subprograms, and stacking techniques. Linkage using page and segment tables. (10%)

9. *Computer Systems Organization.* Characteristics and use of tapes, disks, drums, cores, data-cells, and other large-volume devices in storage hierarchies. Processing unit organization, input-output channels and devices, peripheral and satellite processors, multiple processor configurations, computer networks, and remote access terminals. (10%)

10. *Systems and Utility Programs.* Loaders, input-output systems, monitors, and accounting programs. Program libraries. Organization, documentation, dissemination, and maintenance of system programs. (10%)

11. *Recent Developments.* Selected topics in computer organization, technology, and programming systems. (5%)

12. *Examinations.* (5%)

ANNOTATED BIBLIOGRAPHY

Whereas many of the books on "computer programming" might seem to be appropriate texts or references for this course, only a few even begin to approach the subject as proposed for this course. Most books deal with specific machines, actual or hypothetical, but very few discuss computer organization from any general point of view or consider the techniques of symbolic programming by any method other than examples. A few of the many books which deal with specific machines have been included in this list, but no manufacturers' manuals have been listed even though they may be used effectively as supplemental material.

1. BROOKS, F. P., JR., AND IVERSON, K. E. *Automatic Data Processing.* Wiley, New York, 1963, 494 pp. CR-6673-9523.

   On computing fundamentals, machine language organization and programming using IBM 650 as the principal example.

2. DAVIS, G. B. *An Introduction to Electronic Computers.* McGraw-Hill, New York, 1965, 541 pp.

   Informally written text containing a general introduction to computing, rather complete coverage of FORTRAN and COBOL, and considerable material on machines and machine language programming.

3. FISCHER, F. P., AND SWINDLE, G. F. *Computer Programming Systems.* Holt, Rinehart and Winston, New York, 1964, 643 pp. CR-6455-6299.

   Part I is concerned with machine oriented programming and programming systems using IBM 1401 as the illustrative computer.

4. FLORES, I. *Computer Programming.* Prentice-Hall, Englewood Cliffs, N. J., 1966, 386 pp. CR-6674-10,060.

   Covers machine language and software techniques using the Flores Assembly Program (FLAP) for illustrative purposes.

5. HASSITT, A. *Computer Programming and Computer Systems.* Academic Press, New York, 1967, 374 pp. CR-6784-12,355.

   Discusses various features of computer organization and programming languages using examples from a number of machines including IBM 1401, 1620, 7090 and System/360, and CDC 1604 and 3600.

6. IVERSON, K. E. *A Programming Language.* Wiley, New York, 1962, 286 pp. CR-6671-9004.

   Introduces a language used extensively for description of computers as well as for description of computer programs. Contains material on machine organization, sorting and data structures.

7. STARK, P. A. *Digital Computer Programming.* Macmillan, New York, 1967, 525 pp.

   Presents machine language and symbolic programming for a 24-bit computer.

8. STEIN, M. L., AND MUNRO, W. D. *Computer Programming: A Mixed Language Approach.* Academic Press, New York, 1964, 459 pp. CR-6455-6140.

   A text on computer organization and assembly language programming using CDC 1604 as the basic computer.

9. WEGNER, P. *Programming Languages, Information Structures and Machine Organization.* McGraw-Hill, New York, 1968, about 410 pp.

   Covers machine languages, multiprogramming, assembler construction and procedure-oriented languages. Programming languages are treated as information structures.

Course B3. Introduction to Discrete Structures (3-0-3)

APPROACH

The theoretical material should be introduced in a mathematically precise manner with all concepts and results being amply motivated and being illustrated with examples from computer science. The student should be given extensive homework assignments of both a theoretical and a programming nature which further the understanding of the applications of the concepts in computer science.

CONTENT

Since the material listed below is more than can normally be offered in a one-semester three-credit course on this level, care must be taken to select those topics which will support the more advanced courses as they are developed at each particular school. The description in each of the four sections is divided into two parts labeled (a) Theory and (b) Applications, but in practice the material in both parts would be intermixed.

1. *Basic Set Algebra.*

a. Theory: Sets and basic set algebra. Direct products. Mappings, their domains and ranges, and inverse mappings. Finite and denumerable sets. Relations including order relations. Set inclusion as partial ordering. Equivalence relations, equivalence classes, partition of sets, congruences. The preservation of relations under mappings. Finite sets and their subsets. Permutations, combinations, and related combinatorial concepts.

b. Applications: Examples of sets. The Peano axioms for the set of integers. Congruences and ordering relations over the integers. Relations over the integers defined by arithmetic operations. The set of all subsets of an n-element set and the set of all n-digit binary numbers. The set of all strings over a finite alphabet. Languages over an alphabet as subsets of the set of all strings over the alphabet. Algorithms for listing combinations, compositions, or partitions. Algorithms for ranking combinations.

2. *Basic Algebraic Structures.*

a. Theory: Operations on a set. Algebraic structures as sets with particular functions and relations defined on it. Groups, subgroups, cyclic groups, and other examples of groups. The concepts of homomorphism and isomorphism on a set with operations. Semigroups and semigroups of transformations. Definition and general discussion of examples of structures with several operations, e.g. fields and possibly lattices.

b. Applications: Computer use for working group theoretic problems, e.g. with permutation groups as they occur as input transformation in switching networks. The semigroup of all words over a fixed finite alphabet under the operation of concatenation. The letters of the alphabet as generators. Pair algebra.

3. *Boolean Algebra and Propositional Logic.*

a. Theory: The axioms of set algebra. Axiomatic definition of Boolean algebras as algebraic structures with two operations. Duality. Basic facts about Boolean functions. Propositions and propositional functions. Logical connectives. Truth values and truth tables. The algebra of propositional functions. The Boolean algebra of truth values. Conjunctive and disjunctive normal forms.

b. Applications: Boolean algebra and switching circuits. Basic computer components. Decision tables.

4. *Graph Theory.*

a. Theory: Directed and undirected graphs. Subgraphs, chains, circuits, paths, cycles, connectivity, trees. Graphs and their relation to partial orderings. Graph isomorphisms. Cyclomatic and chromatic numbers. The adjacency and the incidence matrices. Minimal paths. Matchings of bipartite graphs. Elements of transport networks.

b. Applications: Flow charts and state transition graphs. Connectivity in flow charts. Syntactic structure of arithmetic expressions as trees. Graph theoretic examples in coding theory. Algorithms for determining cycles and minimal paths. Basic elements of list structures. Accessing problems. Graphs of a game. Matching algorithms and some related applications.

ANNOTATED BIBLIOGRAPHY

1. BECKENBACH, E. F. (Ed.) *Applied Combinatorial Mathematics*. Wiley, New York, 1964, 608 pp.

   A collection of articles on a broad spectrum of topics. Not directly suitable as a text, but an excellent source of ideas and an important reference.

2. BERGE, C. *Theory of Graphs and Its Applications*. Wiley, New York, 1962, 244 pp.

   A good presentation of directed and undirected graph theory, with some attention to algorithms. The work suffers from many misprints and errors which have been carried over into the English translation. A general reference text for this course.

3. BIRKHOFF, G., AND BARTEE, T. *Modern Applied Algebra*, Preliminary edition, *Parts I and II*. McGraw-Hill, New York, 1967.

   Preliminary edition available only in limited quantities, but the full text expected by the fall of 1968. Appears to be very close in spirit to the material proposed for this course, but the content is more algebraically oriented and includes little on graphs.

4. BUSACKER, R., AND SAATY, T. *Finite Graphs and Networks: An Introduction with Applications*. McGraw-Hill, New York, 1965, 294 pp.

   A good work on graph theory with a very nice collection of applications. Useful as source and reference for the graph theory part of this course.

5. GROSSMAN, I., AND MAGNUS, W. *Groups and Their Graphs*. Random House, New York, 1965, 195 pp. CR-6564-8003.

   An elementary but very well written discourse on basic connections between group and graph theory.

6. HARARY, F., NORMAN, R. Z., AND CARTWRIGHT, D. *Structural Models: An Introduction to the Theory of Directed Graphs*. Wiley, New York, 1965, 415 pp. CR-6566-8421.

   Excellent on directed graphs and probably the best source book on that field. Should be an important reference for the corresponding portion of this course.

7. HOHN, F. *Applied Boolean Algebra*, 2nd ed. Macmillan, New York, 1966, 273 pp.

   Very good introduction to basic facts of Boolean algebra and especially its applications in electrical engineering. Important reference for the corresponding portion of this course.

8. KEMENY, J., MIRKIL, H., SNELL, J., AND THOMPSON, G. *Finite Mathematical Structures*. Prentice-Hall, Englewood Cliffs, N. J., 1959, 487 pp.

   A text for physical science and engineering students who have completed the calculus. First two chapters on compound statements, sets, and functions should be particularly useful.

9. KEMENY, J., SNELL, J., AND THOMPSON, G. *Introduction to Finite Mathematics*, 2nd ed. Prentice-Hall, Englewood Cliffs, N. J., 1966, 352 pp.

   Freshman-sophomore level text designed primarily for students in biological and social sciences. Follows CUPM recommendations for the mathematical education of such students. First three chapters on compound statements, sets and subsets, partitions, and counting cover similar material as proposed for this course.

10. KORFHAGE, R. *Logic and Algorithms: With Applications to the Computer and Information Sciences*. Wiley, New York, 1966, 194 pp. CR-6782-11,339.

    A fine new text introducing those basic topics from mathematical logic important in computer science—for instance Boolean algebra, Turing machines, and Markov algorithms. Written in the spirit which should pervade this course.

11. LEDERMAN, W. *Introduction to the Theory of Finite Groups*. Interscience, New York, 1953, 160 pp.

    A very readable introduction to finite groups. Particularly interesting to this course is the chapter on permutation groups.

12. MACLANE, S., AND BIRKHOFF, G. *Algebra*. Macmillan, New York, 1967, 598 pp.

    A substantially revised and updated version of *A Survey of Modern Algebra*, which has been a classic text on modern algebra. Should be one of the main references for the algebraic parts of this course.

13. ORE, O. *Graphs and Their Uses*. Random House, New York, 1963, 131 pp.

    An introduction to the elementary concepts of graph theory. Very pleasant to read.

14. RIORDAN, J. *An Introduction to Combinatorial Analysis*. Wiley, New York, 1958, 244 pp.

    One of the best source books on enumerative combinatorial analysis. However, it is too advanced for use as a text in a course of this type.

15. RYSER, H. *Combinatorial Mathematics*. Wiley, New York, 1963, 154 pp. CR-6562-7371.

    An excellent introduction to such topics as (0,1) matrices, Latin-squares, and block-design, but containing almost no graph theory.

16. WHITESITT, J. E. *Boolean Algebra and Its Applications*. Addison-Wesley, Reading, Mass., 1961, 182 pp.

    An introductory text designed for readers with a limited mathematical background.

Course B4. Numerical Calculus (2-2-3)

APPROACH

In this course the emphasis is placed upon building algorithms for the solution of numerical problems, the sensitivity of these algorithms to numerical errors, and the efficiency of these algorithms. In the laboratory portion of the course the student is to complete a substantial number of computational projects using a suitable procedure-oriented language.

CONTENT

1. *Basic Concepts of Numerical Error*. Significant digit arithmetic rounding procedures. Classification of error, evaluation of expressions and functions.

2. *Interpolation and Quadrature*. Polynomial interpolation, elements of difference calculus, Newton and Lagrange formulas, Aitken's interpolation method, quadrature formulas, Romberg integration, numerical differentiation, and the inherent error problems.

3. *Solution of Nonlinear Equations*. Bisection method, successive approximations including simple convergence proofs, linearization and Newton's method, method of false-position. Applications to polynomial equations. Generalization to iterative methods for systems of equations.

4. *Linear Systems of Equations*. Solution of linear systems and determinant evaluation by elimination procedures. Roundoff errors and ill-conditioning. Iterative methods.

5. *Numerical Solution of Ordinary Differential Equations*. Euler's method, modified Euler's method, simplified Runge-Kutta.

ANNOTATED BIBLIOGRAPHY

Listed below are some of the books which might be used as texts and/or references for this course. Most of the books cover the following topics: solution of polynomial and other nonlinear equations;

interpolation, numerical quadrature, and numerical differentiation; ordinary differential equations; and linear algebra. Significant deviations from these topics are indicated by the annotation.

1. CONTE, S. D. *Elementary Numerical Analysis: An Algorithmic Approach.* McGraw-Hill, New York, 1965, 278 pp.

   Designed as a text for a one-semester, three-hour course for engineering and science undergraduate students. Machine-oriented treatment with many illustrative examples including flow charts and FORTRAN programs. Except for the chapter on differential equations, a knowledge of basic calculus and of programming in a procedure-oriented language is sufficient background. Numerous exercises.

2. JENNINGS, W. *First Course in Numerical Methods.* Macmillan, New York, 1964, 233 pp. CR-6671-9036.

   Designed as a text for a one-semester course for advanced undergraduate students in science and engineering. Brief treatment of the standard topics. Presupposes calculus, differential equations, some experience with the computer, and, for later chapters, matrices. Some exercises.

3. MACON, N. *Numerical Analysis.* Wiley, New York, 1963, 161 pp.

   Designed as a text for a one-semester first course in numerical analysis. Emphasis is more on the mathematical aspects rather than the computational aspects although there is an introductory chapter on the elements of computing, flow charting, and FORTRAN programming. For the early chapters calculus provides sufficient background. For later chapters an elementary knowledge of matrix theory, differential equations, and advanced calculus is recommended. Examples and exercises.

4. MCCORMICK, J. M., AND SALVADORI, M. G. *Numerical Methods in FORTRAN.* Prentice-Hall, Englewood Cliffs, N.J., 1964, 324 pp. CR-6676-10,883.

   Designed as a text either for an elementary course in numerical analysis at the junior-senior level or for a course in programming. First part presents the methods without reference to programming techniques. There are 320 examples and problems. The last part contains 53 completely worked illustrative FORTRAN programs. Presupposes beginning analysis.

5. MCCRACKEN, D., AND DORN, W. S. *Numerical Methods and FORTRAN Programming.* Wiley, New York, 1964, 457 pp. CR-6562-7107.

   Designed as a text for a four semester-hour course in science or engineering at the sophomore-senior level. Emphasis on practical methods—for example, the treatment of simultaneous linear algebraic equations does not make use of matrices. Chapters on various aspects of FORTRAN are interspersed with chapters on numerical methods. Includes a brief chapter on partial differential equations. Presupposes beginning analysis. Examples and exercises.

6. MILNE, W. E. *Numerical Calculus.* Princeton University Press, Princeton, N. J., 1949, 393 pp.

   Written in 1949 in the early days of computing, this is a very useful reference even though the treatment is oriented toward manual computation and though some of the methods have been superseded. Presupposes a knowledge of calculus and differential equations. Examples and exercises.

7. NIELSEN, K. L. *Methods in Numerical Analysis,* 2nd ed. Macmillan, New York, 1956 and 1964, 382 pp. CR-6455-6333.

   Designed as a textbook for a practical course for engineers. Primary emphasis on the use of desk calculators and tables. Presupposes calculus. Examples and exercises.

8. PENNINGTON, R. H. *Introductory Computer Methods and Numerical Analysis.* Macmillan, New York, 1965, 452 pp. CR-6565-8060.

   Designed as a text for a one-year elementary course for scientists and engineers to be taken immediately after integral calculus. The first part treats digital computers and programming. Numerical methods are then discussed from a computer viewpoint with the aid of flow diagrams. Little knowledge of computing is assumed. For some of the topics a knowledge of matrices and ordinary differential equations would be helpful. Many examples and exercises.

9. SINGER, J. *Elements of Numerical Analysis.* Academic Press, New York, 1964, 395 pp. CR-6561-6959.

   Designed as a text for junior undergraduate students in mathematics. Treatment geared more to manual computation than to the use of computers. Presupposes beginning analysis and, for some parts, differential equations and advanced calculus. Examples and exercises.

10. STIEFEL, E. L. *An Introduction to Numerical Mathematics,* transl. by W. C. and C. J. Rheinboldt. Academic Press, New York, 1963, 286 pp. CR-6455-6335.

    Appropriate for a junior-senior level course in mathematics, science, and engineering. Emphasis is on the algorithmic approach, although there are only a few flow charts and specific references to programs. A wide variety of topics and methods is treated. Basic calculus is required for the early chapters, but for later chapters familiarity with ordinary differential equations is desirable. Examples are given. There is a separate problem supplement with 36 exercises.

Course I1. Data Structures (3-0-3)

APPROACH

This course is intended to present the data structures which may be used in computer storage to represent the information involved in solving problems. However, emphasis should be placed on treating these data structures independently of the applications in which they are embedded. Each data structure should be motivated carefully in terms of the operations which may conveniently be performed, and illustrated with examples in which the structure is useful. The identification of the natural relations between entities involved in problems and alternate representations of information should be stressed. Computer storage structures should also be described and classified according to their characteristics, and the interaction between data structures and storage structures should be studied.

The student should be required to apply the techniques presented to problems which illustrate a wide variety of data structures. Solutions to a number of these problems should be programmed and run on a computer.

CONTENT

More material is listed here than can normally be covered in a one-semester course. The instructor should carefully select material which gives the student a broad introduction to this subject, but which fits together pedagogically. It may be desirable to develop an advanced course to cover some of these topics more completely.

1. *Basic Concepts of Data.* Representation of information as data inside and outside the computer. Bits, bytes, fields and data items. Records, nodes and data elements. Data files and tables. Names, values, environments, and binding times of data. Use of pointer or linkage variables to represent data structure. Identifying entities about which data is to be maintained, and selecting data nodes and structures which are to be used in problem solution. Storage media, storage structures, encoding of data and transformations from one medium and/or code to another. Alternative representations of information and data. Packing, unpacking, and compression of data. Data formats, data description languages, and specification of data transformations.

2. *Linear Lists and Strings.* Stacks, last-in-first-out, first-in-first-out, double-ended, and other linear lists. Sequential versus linked storage allocation. Single versus double linkage. Circular lists. Character strings of variable length. Word packing, part-word addressing, and pointer manipulation. Insertion, deletion and accessing of list elements.

3. *Arrays and Orthogonal Lists.* Storage of rectangular arrays in one-dimensional media. Storage mapping functions, direct and in-

direct address computation, space requirements, set-up time, accessing time, and dynamic relocation time. Storage and accessing triangular arrays, tetrahedral arrays, and sparse matrices.

4. *Tree Structures.* Trees, subtrees, ordered trees, free trees, oriented trees and binary trees. Representation of trees using binary trees, sequential techniques, or threaded lists. Insertion, deletion, and accessing elements of trees. Relative referencing, finding successors and predecessors, and walking through trees. Examples of tree structures such as algebraic formulas, arrays, and other hierarchic data structures (PL/I and COBOL).

5. *Storage Systems and Structures.* Behavioral properties of unit record (card), random access (core), linear (tape), and intermediate (disk, drum, etc.) storage media and devices including cost, size, speed, reusability, inherent record and file structure, and deficiencies and interrelation of these properties. Influence of machine structure—in particular addressing—on data structuring. Hierarchies of storage, virtual memory, segmentation, paging, and bucketing. Influence of data structures and data manipulation on storage systems. Associative structures, both hardware and software.

6. *Storage Allocation and Collection.* Static versus dynamic allocation. Sequential versus linked allocation. Last-in-first-out data versus data of unrelated life times. Uniform block size and available space lists. Variable block size and stratified available space lists. Explicit release of available storage. Coalescing adjacent free space and compacting occupied space or data. Accessing disciplines for movable data, unmovable anchors, and updating of pointers. Reference counts and list borrowing. Garbage collection by surveying active data.

7. *Multilinked Structures.* Use of different types of data nodes or elements. Use of different types of linkage to sequence, adjoin, or associate data elements and to build hierarchies of data structures. Sublists, list names, list heads, and attribute lists. Multidimensional linked lists and mixed list structures. Accessing, insertion, deletion and updating. Relative referencing, finding successors and predecessors, and walking through structures. Representation of graphs and networks. Structures used for string manipulation and list processing languages.

8. *Sorting (Ordering) Techniques.* Radix sorting, radix exchange sorting, merge sorting, bubble sorting, address table sorting, topological sorting and other sorting methods. Comparative efficiency of sorting techniques. Effect of data structures and storage structures on sorting techniques.

9. *Symbol Tables and Searching.* Linear, stack, tree and scatter structured tables, and table lookup techniques. Hash code algorithms. Use of index lists and associative techniques. Comparison of search strategies in terms of speed and cost. Batching and ordering of requests to remote storage to minimize number of accesses. TRIE memory as an example of structure organized for searching.

10. *Data Structures in Programming Languages.* Compile-time and run-time data structures needed to implement source language data structures of programming languages. Linkage between partially executed procedures, data structures for coroutines, scheduled procedures, and other control structures, and storage management of data structures in procedure-oriented languages. Examples of higher level languages which include list processing and other data structuring features.

11. *Formal Specification of Data Structures.* Specification of syntax for classes of data structures. Predicate selectors and constructors for data manipulation, data definition facilities, programs as data structures, computers as data structures and transformations, formal specification of semantics, and formal systems viewed as data structures.

12. *Generalized Data Management Systems.* Structures of generalized data management systems: directory maintenance, user languages (query), data description maintenance, and job management. Embedding data structures in generalized data management systems. Examples of generalized data management systems and comparison of system features.

ANNOTATED BIBLIOGRAPHY

Although a great deal of material is available in this area, very little of it is appropriate for classroom use.

1. Association for Computing Machinery. ACM sort symposium, Nov. 29–30, 1962, Princeton, N. J. *Comm. ACM 6*, 5 (May 1963), 194–272.

   Seventeen papers on various aspects of sorting.

2. Association for Computing Machinery. Papers presented at the ACM Storage Allocation Symposium, June 23–24, 1961, Princeton, N. J. *Comm. ACM 4*, 10 (Oct. 1961), 416–464.

   Eleven papers on various techniques of storage allocation.

3. Association for Computing Machinery. Proceedings of the ACM Symposium on Symbolic and Algebraic Manipulation, Washington, D. C., Mar. 29–31, 1966. *Comm. ACM 9*, 8 (Aug. 1966), 547–643.

   Eleven papers some of which discuss applications of data structuring techniques. One paper by Knowlton describes the list language L^6.

4. CLIMENSON, W. D. File organization and search techniques. In C. A. Cuadra (Ed.), *Annual Review of Information Science and Technology, Vol. 1*, (Amer. Doc. Inst., Ann. Rev. ser.), Interscience, New York, 1966, pp. 107–135. CR-6783-11,900.

   Surveys file organizations and data structures with particular emphasis on developments during 1965. Provides framework for some of the material covered by this course. An extensive bibliography.

5. COHEN, J. A use of fast and slow memories in list-processing languages. *Comm. ACM 10*, 2 (Feb. 1967), 82–86.

   Describes a paging scheme which keeps the "most often called pages in the fast memory" and involves a slow down of 3 to 10 as compared with in-core operations.

6. Control Data Corporation. *3600/3800 INFOL Reference Manual.* Publication No. 60170300, CDC, Palo Alto, Calif., July 1966.

   Describes the *INF*ormation *O*riented *L*anguage which is designed for information storage and retrieval applications.

7. DAHL, O.-J., AND NYGAARD, K. SIMULA—an ALGOL-based simulation language. *Comm. ACM 9*, 9 (Sept. 1966), 671–678.

   Contains interesting data and control structures.

8. D'IMPERIO, M. Data structures and their representation in storage. In M. Halpern (Ed.), *Annual Review in Automatic Programming, Vol. 5*, Pergamon Press, New York, spring 1968.

   Defines certain basic concepts involved in the representation of data and processes to be performed on data. Analyzes a problem and describes nine different solutions involving different data structures. Discusses ten list processing languages and gives examples of their data and storage structures.

9. FITZWATER, D. R. A storage allocation and reference structure. *Comm. ACM 7*, 9 (Sept. 1964), 542–545. CR-6561-6933.

   Describes a method of structuring and referencing dynamic structures in AUTOCODER for the IBM 7070/72/74.

10. General Electric Company. *Integrated Data Store—A New Concept in Data Management.* Application Manual AS-CPB-483A, Revision of 7-67, GE Computer Division, Phoenix, Ariz., 1967.

    Describes a sophisticated data management system which uses paging and chaining to develop complex data structures.

11. GRAY, J. C. Compound data structures for computer-aided design: a survey. Proc. ACM 22nd Nat. Conf., 1967, Thompson Book Co., Washington, D. C., pp. 355–365.

    Considers requirements of a data structure software package and surveys a number of such packages.

12. HELLERMAN, H. Addressing multidimensional arrays. *Comm. ACM 5*, 4 (Apr. 1962), 205–207. CR-6235-2619.

    Surveys direct and indirect methods for accessing arrays.

13. IVERSON, K. E. *A Programming Language.* Wiley, New York, 1962, 286 pp. CR-6671-9004.

Contains considerable material on data structures, graphs, trees, and sorting, as well as a language for describing these.

14. KLEIN, M. M. Scheduling project networks. *Comm. ACM 10*, 4 (Apr. 1967), 225–234. CR-6784-12,275.

Discusses project networking and describes the C-E-I-R critical path algorithm.

15. KNUTH, D. E. *The Art of Computer Programming, Vol. 1, Fundamental Algorithms*. Addison-Wesley, Reading, Mass., 1968, 634 pp.

Chap. 2 on "Information Structures" contains the first comprehensive classification of data structures to be published. Each structure considered is carefully motivated and generously illustrated. Includes a brief history of data structuring and an annotated bibliography.

16. LANDIN, P. J. The mechanical evaluation of expressions. *Comput. J. 6*, 4 (Jan. 1964), 308–320. CR-6456-6677.

Presents a mathematical language based on Church's λ-notation and uses it to describe computational structures such as expressions and lists.

17. LAWSON, H. W., JR. PL/I list processing. *Comm. ACM 10*, 6 (June 1967), 358–367.

Discusses the list processing facilities in PL/I.

18. MADNICK, S. E. String processing techniques. *Comm. ACM 10*, 7 (July 1967), 420–424.

Presents and evaluates six techniques for string data storage structures. One of these techniques is used for an implementation of SNOBOL on an IBM System/360.

19. MARRON, B. A., AND DE MAINE, P. A. D. Automatic data compression. *Comm. ACM 10*, 11 (Nov. 1967), 711–715.

Describes a three-part compressor which can be used on "any" body of information to reduce slow external storage requirements and to increase the rate of information transmission through a computer.

20. MEALY, G. H. Another look at data. Proc. AFIPS 1967 Fall Joint Comput. Conf., Vol. 31, Thompson Book Co., Washington, D. C., pp. 525–534.

Sketches a theory of data based on relations. Includes some rather precise definitions of concepts such as data structure, list processing, and representation.

21. MINKER, J., AND SABLE, J. File organization and data management. In C. A. Cuadra (Ed.), *Annual Review of Information Science and Technology, Vol. 2*, (Amer. Doc. Inst., Ann. Rev. ser.). Interscience, New York, 1967, pp. 123–160.

Surveys file organizations and generalized data management systems developed during 1966. Describes linkage types, data structures, storage structures, and how data structures have been mapped into storage structures. Extensive bibliography.

22. MORRIS, R. Scatter storage techniques. *Comm. ACM 11*, 1 (Jan. 1968), 38–44.

Surveys hashing schemes for symbol table algorithms.

23. ROSEN, S. (Ed.) *Programming Languages and Systems*. McGraw-Hill, New York, 1967, 734 pp.

Part 4 of this collection contains papers on IPL-V, COMIT, SLIP, SNOBOL, LISP and a comparison of list-processing computer languages.

24. ROSS, D. T. The AED free storage package. *Comm. ACM 10*, 8 (Aug. 1967), 481–492.

Describes a storage allocation and management system for the mixed n-component elements ("beads") needed for "plex programming."

25. SALTON, G. Data manipulation and programming problems in automatic information retrieval. *Comm. ACM 9*, 3 (Mar. 1966), 204–210. CR-6674-10,078.

Describes a variety of representations for tree structured data and examines their usefulness in retrieval applications.

26. SAVITT, D. A., LOVE, H. H., JR., AND TROOP, R. E. ASP: a new concept in language and machine organization. Proc. 1967 Spring Joint Comput. Conf., Vol. 30, Thompson Book Co., Washington, D. C., pp. 87–102.

Describes the data bases used in the "Association-Storing Processor." These structures are complex in organization and may vary dynamically in both organization and content.

27. SCHORR, H., AND WAITE, W. M. An efficient machine-independent procedure for garbage collection in various list structures. *Comm. ACM 10*, 8 (Aug. 1967), 501–506.

Reviews and compares past garbage collection methods and presents a new algorithm.

28. STANDISH, T. A. A data definition facility for programming languages. Ph.D. Thesis, Carnegie Institute of Technology, Pittsburgh, Pa., 1967.

Presents a descriptive notation for data structures which is embedded in a programming language.

29. WEGNER, P. (Ed.) *Introduction to Systems Programming*. Academic Press, New York, 1965, 316 pp. CR-6455-6300.

Contains a collection of papers of which the following are of special interest for this course: Iliffe, pp. 256–275; Jenkins, pp. 283–293; and Burge, pp. 294–312.

30. WEGNER, P. *Programming Languages, Information Structures, and Machine Organization*. McGraw-Hill, New York, 1968, about 410 pp.

Introduces information structures and uses them in describing computer organization and programming languages.

Course I2. Programming Languages (3-0-3)

APPROACH

This course is intended to survey the significant features of existing programming languages with particular emphasis on the underlying concepts abstracted from these languages. The relationship between source programs and their run-time representation during evaluation will be considered, but the actual writing of compilers is to be taught in Course I5.

CONTENT

There are four basic parts of this course: the structure of simple statements; the structure of algorithmic languages; list processing and string manipulation languages; and topics in programming languages.

Part A. Structure of Simple Statements. (10 lectures)

1. Informal syntax and semantics of arithmetic expressions and statements, translation between infix, prefix, and postfix notation, and the use of pushdown stores for translation and execution of arithmetic expressions and statements. Precedence hierarchy of arithmetic operations, relational operators, and Boolean operators. Backus normal form representation of syntax of arithmetic statements and the semantics of arithmetic statements. (6 lectures)

2. Precedence relations, precedence grammars, and syntactic analysis of precedence grammars. Application to arithmetic expressions, code generation, error diagnostics and error correction for syntactic arithmetic expression compilation. (4 lectures)

Part B. Structure of Algorithmic Languages. (20 lectures)

3. Review of program constituents, branching statements and loops. (2 lectures)

4. Grouping of statements, declarations, "types" of program constituents, nomenclature, scopes, local and nonlocal quantities, independent blocks (FORTRAN), and nested blocks (ALGOL). (2 lectures)

5. Function and statement type procedures, formal parameters and actual parameters, and call by value, name and reference. Binding time of program constituents, recursive procedures, and side effects during execution of procedures. (3 lectures)

6. Storage allocation for independent blocks (FORTRAN) and storage allocation for nested blocks and procedures using a run-time

pushdown store. Overall structure of an ALGOL-style compiler. (3 lectures)

7. Coroutines, tasks, interrupt specification, and classification of control structures in procedure-oriented languages. (2 lectures)

8. Syntactic specification of procedures, blocks and statements. Formal semantics corresponding to syntactic specification. Survey of principal concepts of syntactic analysis. (5 lectures)

9. Generalized arrays. Data definition facilities, pointer-valued variables, and list creation and manipulation using pointer-valued variables. Templates and controlled storage allocation. Distinction between data specification by a data template and the creation of instances of a specified data structure. (3 lectures)

Part C. List Processing and String Manipulation Languages. (7 lectures)

10. List structures, basic operations on list structures, LISP-like languages, machine-oriented list processing languages (IPL-V), embedding of list operations in algorithmic languages (SLIP), dynamic storage allocation for list languages, and garbage collection. (5 lectures)

11. String structures, operations on strings, and functions which have strings as arguments and strings as their values (SNOBOL). (2 lectures)

Part D. Topics in Programming Languages. (8 lectures)

12. Additional features of programming languages, simulation languages, algebraic manipulation languages, and languages with parallel programming facilities. (2–6 lectures)

13. Formal description of languages and their processors. The work of Floyd, Wirth, and others. (2–6 lectures)

14. Other topics selected by the instructor.

ANNOTATED BIBLIOGRAPHY

1. American Standards Association X3.4.1 Working Group. Toward better documentation of programming languages. *Comm. ACM 6*, 3 (Mar. 1963), 76–92.

   A series of papers describing the documentation of significant current programming languages.

2. Association for Computing Machinery. Proceedings of the ACM programming languages and pragmatics conference, San Dimas, Calif., August 8–12, 1965. *Comm. ACM 9*, 3 (Mar. 1966), 137–232.

   Includes a number of papers applicable to this course.

3. Association for Computing Machinery. Proceedings of the ACM symposium on symbolic and algebraic manipulation, Washington, D. C., March 29–31, 1966. *Comm. ACM 9*, 8 (Aug. 1966), 547–643.

   A number of languages for symbolic and algebraic manipulation are described in this special issue.

4. DAHL, O.-J., AND NYGAARD, K. SIMULA—an ALGOL-based simulation language. *Comm. ACM 9*, 9 (Sept. 1966), 671–678.

   Describes a language encompassing ALGOL, but having many additional features including those needed for simulation.

5. GALLER, B. A., AND PERLIS, A. J. A proposal for definitions in ALGOL. *Comm. ACM 10*, 4 (Apr. 1967), 204–219.

   Describes a generalization of ALGOL which allows new data types and operators to be declared.

6. GOODMAN, R. (Ed.) *Annual Review in Automatic Programming, Vols. 1, 2, 3, 4.* Pergamon Press, New York, 1960 to 1965. CR-6123-0811, CR-6235-2602, and CR-6564-7901.

   These volumes contain several papers which are applicable to this course.

7. HALSTEAD, M. H. *Machine-Independent Computer Programming.* Spartan Books, New York, 1962.

   Contains both internal and external specifications of the NELIAC programming language.

8. IEEE Computer Group. The special issue on computer languages. *IEEE Trans. EC-13*, 4 (Aug. 1964), 343–462.

   Contains articles on ALGOL, FORTRAN, FORMAC, SOL and other computer languages.

9. International Business Machines. PL/I Language Specification. Form C28-6571-4, IBM System/360 Operating System, IBM Corporation, White Plains, N. Y., 1967.

   A specification of the PL/I language.

10. International Standards Organization Technical Committee 97, Subcommittee 5. Survey of programming languages and processors. *Comm. ACM 6*, 3 (Mar. 1963), 93–99.

    An international survey of current and imminent programming languages.

11. KNUTH, D. E. The remaining trouble spots in ALGOL 60. *Comm. ACM 10*, 10 (Oct. 1967), 611–618.

    This paper lists the ambiguities which remain in ALGOL 60 and which have been noticed since the publication of the Revised ALGOL 60 Report in 1963.

12. MARKOWITZ, H. M., KARR, H. W., AND HAUSNER, B. *SIMSCRIPT: A Simulation Programming Language.* Prentice-Hall, Englewood Cliffs, N. J., 1963, 138 pp.

    A description of the SIMSCRIPT simulation language. There is a new SIMSCRIPT 1.5 supplement now available which describes a generalization of the original language.

13. MOOERS, C. N. TRAC, a procedure-describing language for the reactive typewriter. *Comm. ACM 9*, 3 (Mar. 1966), 215–219. CR-6674-10,079.

    Describes a language for the manipulation of text from an on-line typewriter.

14. NAUR, P. (Ed.) Revised report on the algorithmic language, ALGOL 60. *Comm. ACM 6*, 1 (Jan. 1963), 1–17. CR-6016-0323.

    The Backus normal form notation was developed to help describe the syntax of ALGOL in the original version of this report (*Comm. ACM 3*, 5 (May 1960), 299–314).

15. PERLIS, A. J. The synthesis of algorithmic systems—first annual A. M. Turing lecture. *J. ACM 14*, 1 (Jan. 1967), 1–9. CR-6782-11,512.

    A stimulating talk on the nature of programming languages and the considerations which should underlie their future development.

16. ROSEN, S. (Ed.) *Programming Systems and Languages.* McGraw-Hill, New York, 1967, 734 pp.

    This collection of papers contains many of the important references for this course. In particular, Parts 1 and 2 of the collection are useful for Parts A and B of the course and Part 4 of the collection is useful for Part C of the course.

17. SHAW, C. J. A comparative evaluation of JOVIAL and FORTRAN IV. *Automatic Programming Inf., No. 22.* Technical College, Brighton, England, Aug. 1964, 15 pp. CR-6562-7265.

    A descriptive point-by-point comparison of these two languages. Concerned mainly with the features of the languages rather than their processors.

18. SHAW, C. J. A programmer's look at JOVIAL, in an ALGOL perspective. *Datamation 7*, 10 (Oct. 1961), 46–50. CR-6233-1933.

    An interesting article showing how ALGOL and JOVIAL evolved from ALGOL 58 and how they differ.

19. USA Standards Institute. Standards X3.9-1966, FORTRAN and X3.10-1966, Basic FORTRAN. USASI, 10 East 40th Street, New York, N. Y. 10016, 1966.

    Standard definitions of essentially FORTRAN II and FORTRAN IV. These also appeared in almost final form in *Comm. ACM 7*, 10 (Oct. 1964), 591–625.

20. WEGNER, P. *Programming Languages, Information Structures, and Machine Organization.* McGraw-Hill, New York, 1968, about 410 pp.

    Develops a unified approach to the study of programming languages emphasizing the treatment of such languages as information structures. First two chapters devoted to machine organization, machine language, and assembly language, but much of Chap. 3 and essentially all of Chap. 4 devoted to the topics of this course.

21. WIRTH, N. A generalization of ALGOL. *Comm. ACM 6*, 9 (Sept. 1963), 547–554. CR-6451-5030.

    Proposes a generalization of ALGOL which involves the elimination of "type" declarations and the replacement of procedure declarations by an assignment of a so-called "quotation."

22. WIRTH, N., AND WEBER, H. EULER—a generalization of ALGOL and its formal definition, Parts I and II. *Comm. ACM 9*, 1 (Jan. 1966), 13–23, and 2 (Feb. 1966), 89–99.

    Develops a method for defining programming languages which introduces a rigorous relationship between structure and meaning. The structure of a language is defined by a phrase structure syntax and the meaning is defined in terms of the effects which the execution of a sequence of interpretation rules has upon a fixed set of variables called the "environment."

Course I3. Computer Organization (3-0-3) or (3-2-4)

APPROACH

This course is intended to introduce the student to the basic ideas of computer elements and logic design techniques and to the principles of computer systems organization. Emphasis should be placed on the various alternative possibilities which must be considered in arriving at a computer design; choices such as character or word organized data, serial or parallel data transmission, synchronous or asynchronous control should be compared and evaluated.

In addition to using block diagrams, it is recommended that a formal descriptive language for computer specification be introduced and used to provide a uniform method for the presentation of much of the material. The student should carry out a detailed computer design project and evaluate his design by simulation, if possible. A laboratory in which simple logic elements may be combined to perform digital functions is also desirable.

CONTENT

The following topics are to be covered, although not necessarily in the order listed.

1. *Basic Digital Circuits.* Switches, relays, transistors, diodes, magnetic cores, circuits of individual elements, and integrated circuits. (These topics may be spread throughout the course.) (5%)

2. *Boolean Algebra and Combinational Logic.* Boolean values, variables, operations, expressions and equations. Logic elements such as AND, OR, NOT, NAND and NOR. Correspondence between Boolean functions and combinations of logic elements. (5%)

3. *Data Representation and Transfer.* Flip-flops, registers, core storage, and other memory elements. Review of number representations, binary versus binary-coded decimal representation, and integer versus floating-point representation. Weighted and nonweighted codes, redundancy, and coding of character information. Coders and decoders. Clearing, gating and other transfer considerations. (10%)

4. *Digital Arithmetic.* Counters, comparators, parity checkers, and shift registers. Half and full adders. Serial versus parallel adders. Subtraction and signed magnitude versus complemented arithmetic. Multiplication and division algorithms. Integer versus floating-point arithmetic. Double precision arithmetic. Elementary speed-up techniques for arithmetic. (10%)

5. *Digital Storage and Accessing.* Structure of core memory, memory control, data buses, and address buses. Addressing and accessing methods including index registers, indirect addressing, base registers, and other techniques. Overlapping, interleaving, protection, dynamic relocation, and memory segmentation methods. Characteristics of drum, disk, tape, and other surface recording media and devices. Data flow in multimemory systems and hierarchies of storage. (10%)

6. *Control Functions.* Synchronous versus asynchronous control. Time pulse distributors, controlled delay techniques, and Gray code control sequencers. Instruction repertoire, decoding networks, and sequencing methods. Centralized, decentralized, and micro-programmed control units. Internal, external and trapping interrupts. Interrupt sensing, priority, selection, recognition, and processing. Input-output control. (10%)

7. *Input-Output Facilities.* Characteristics of input-output devices and their controllers. Relationship between input-output devices, main storage, auxiliary storage, buffers, data channels, and multiplexers. Serial versus parallel transmission. Low speed, high speed, and burst mode data flow. (10%)

8. *System Organization.* Overall organization of modules into a system. Interface between modules. Word-oriented versus character-oriented machines. Simplex and multiprocessor machines. Special purpose computers. Relationship between computer organization and software. (15%)

9. *Reliability.* Error detection and correction. Diagnostics and preventive maintenance. Start-up, power-down, and recovery procedures. (5%)

10. *Description and Simulation Techniques.* Definition of a formal computer description language which would be used in discussing most of the other topics listed for the course. Use of a computer simulator to design and test simple computers or computer modules. (10%)

11. *Selected Topics.* Multiple arithmetic units, instruction overlapping, and look-ahead techniques. Discussion of alternate organizations including highly parallel machines. (5%)

12. *Examinations.* (5%)

ANNOTATED BIBLIOGRAPHY

As indicated, several of the books listed below might possibly be used as texts for this course, but it probably would be good to supplement any of them with additional material. Only a few of the many references on computer description languages and programs for simulating computer designs are listed; no annotations are given for these.

General textbooks

1. BARTEE, T. C. *Digital Computer Fundamentals.* McGraw-Hill, New York, 1960, 1966, 401 pp. CR-6676-10,647.

   Not advanced enough but a very useful supplement for circuits and equipment.

2. BARTEE, T. C., LEBOW, I. L., AND REED, I. S. *Theory and Design of Digital Systems.* McGraw-Hill, New York, 1962, 324 pp. CR-6344-4416.

   Very mathematical and somewhat out-of-date. An interesting reference.

3. BRAUN, E. L. *Digital Computer Design—Logic, Circuitry, and Synthesis.* Academic Press, New York, 1963, 606 pp. CR-6453-5484.

   Somewhat out-of-date for a text but useful as a reference.

4. BUCHHOLZ, W. *Planning a Computer System.* McGraw-Hill, New York, 1962, 336 pp. CR-6346-4786.

   Good reference on systems concepts but somewhat dated.

5. Burroughs Corporation. *Digital Computer Principles.* McGraw-Hill, New York, 1962, 507 pp.

   Restricted scope (engineering oriented) and dated, but could be used as a reference.

6. CHU, Y. *Digital Computer Design Fundamentals.* McGraw-Hill, New York, 1962, 481 pp. CR-6343-4198.

   Good reference which contains a wealth of material on logic design.

7. FLORES, I. *Computer Logic.* Prentice-Hall, Englewood Cliffs, N. J., 1960, 458 pp. CR-6122-0641 and CR-6124-0936.

   Dated and unorthodox but possibly useful for supplementary reading.

8. FLORES, I. *The Logic of Computer Arithmetic.* Prentice-Hall,

Englewood Cliffs, N. J., 1963, 493 pp. CR-6452-5458.

Very detailed, unorthodox treatment of computer arithmetic.

9. GSCHWIND, H. W. *Design of Digital Computers.* Springer-Verlag, New York, 1967.

A possible text.

10. HELLERMAN, H. *Digital Computer System Principles.* McGraw-Hill, New York, 1967, 424 pp.

A possible text. Uses Iverson notation throughout. Would have to be supplemented on circuits and equipment as well as novel organizations.

11. MALEY, G. A., AND SKIKO, E. J. *Modern Digital Computers.* Prentice-Hall, Englewood Cliffs, N. J., 1964, 216 pp. CR-6561-7081.

A possible reference. Somewhat dated but contains a good description of the IBM 7090 and 7080 machines.

12. MURTHA, J. C. Highly parallel information processing systems. In F. L. Alt (Ed.), *Advances in Computers, Vol. 7.* Academic Press, New York, 1966, pp. 1-116. CR-6782-11,678.

A useful reference on highly parallel systems.

13. PHISTER, M., JR. *Logical Design of Digital Computers.* Wiley, New York, 1958, 408 pp.

Somewhat dated. Relies heavily on sequential circuit theory and concentrates on serial, clocked machines.

14. RICHARDS, R. K. *Arithmetic Operations in Digital Computers.* D. Van Nostrand, Princeton, N. J., 1955, 397 pp.

Somewhat dated but still a good reference for arithmetic.

15. RICHARDS, R. K. *Electronic Digital Systems.* Wiley, New York, 1966, 637 pp. CR-6676-10,649.

An interesting reference for reliability and design automation. Discusses telephone systems and data transmission.

References on computer description languages

16. CHU, Y. An ALGOL-like computer design language. *Comm. ACM 8,* 10 (Oct. 1965), 607-615. CR-6672-9315.

17. FALKHOFF, A. D., IVERSON, K. E., AND SUSSENGUTH, E. H. A formal description of System /360. *IBM Syst. J. 3,* 3 (1964), 198-263.

18. GORMAN, D. F., AND ANDERSON, J. P. A logic design translator. Proc. AFIPS 1962 Fall Joint Comput. Conf., Vol. 22, Spartan Books, New York, pp. 251-261.

19. IVERSON, K. E. *A Programming Language.* Wiley, New York, 1962, 286 pp. CR-6671-9004.

20. MCCLURE, R. M. A programming language for simulating digital systems. *J. ACM 12,* 1 (Jan. 1965), 14-22. CR-6563-7634.

21. PARNAS, D. L., AND DARRINGER, J. A. SODAS and a methodology for system design. Proc. AFIPS 1967 Fall Joint Comput. Conf., Vol. 31, Thompson Book Co., Washington, D. C., pp. 449-474.

22. WILBER, J. A. A language for describing digital computers. M.S. Thesis, Report No. 197, Dept. of Comput. Sci., U. of Illinois, Urbana, Ill., Feb. 15, 1966.

Course I4. Systems Programming (3-0-3)

APPROACH

This course is intended to bring the student to grips with the actual problems encountered in systems programming. To accomplish this it may be necessary to devote most of the course to the study of a single system chosen on the basis of availability of computers, systems programs, and documentation.

The course should begin with a thorough review of "batch" processing systems programming, emphasizing loading and subroutine linkage. The limitations of these systems should be used to motivate the more complex concepts and details of multiprogramming and multiprocessor systems. The theoretical concepts and practical techniques prescribed in Course I1 should be used to focus on the data bases, their design for the support of the functions of the key system components (hardware and software), and the effective interrelation of these components. Problem assignments should involve the design and implementation of systems program modules; the design of files, tables or lists for use by such modules; or the critical use and evaluation of existing system programs. Other problems might involve the attaching or accessing of procedure or data segments of different "ownership" that are resident in a single file system or the development of restricted accessing methods (i.e. privacy schemes) and other such techniques.

CONTENT

This description has been written with MULTICS in mind as the system chosen for central study, but the description can be modified to fit any reasonably comprehensive system. There is considerably more material listed here than can normally be covered in one semester, so that careful selection of topics should be made or the course should be extended to two semesters.

1. *Review of Batch Process Systems Programs.* Translation, loading, and execution. Loader languages. Communication between independent program units. Limitations imposed by binding at pre-execution times. Incremental linkage.

2. *Multiprogramming and Multiprocessor Systems.* General introduction to the structure of these systems, the techniques involved in their construction and some of the problems involved in their implementation.

3. *Addressing Techniques.* Review of indexing and indirect addressing. Relocation and base registers. Two-dimensional addressing (segmentation). Segmented processes. Concepts of virtual memory. Effective address computation. Modes of access control. Privileged forms of accessing. Paging. Physical register (address) computation, including use of associative memories.

4. *Process and Data Modules.* Concept of a process as a collection of procedure and data components (segments). Process data bases. Controlled sharing of segments among two or more processes. Intersegment linking and segment management. Interprocedure communication. Process stacks. Levels of isolation within a process (rings of protection).

5. *File System Organization and Management.* File data bases and their storage structures. Accessing, protection and maintenance of files. Storage and retrieval of segments and/or pages from files in secondary storage (segment and page control, directory control, and core management). Search strategies.

6. *Traffic Control.* State words. Running, ready, blocked, and inactive processes. Process switching. Priority control of waiting processes. Scheduling algorithms. Pseudo processes. System tables for process management.

7. *Explicit Input-Output References.* Auxiliary (secondary) memory references. Communication with peripheral devices. Management of input-output and other request queues. Effects of data rates on queue management.

8. *Public and Private Files.* On line and off line memory. Automatic shifting of data among devices in the storage hierarchy and "flushing" of online memory, i.e. multilevel storage management. File backup schemes and recovery from system failures.

9. *Other Topics.* Some of the following topics may be studied if time permits. They might also be covered in subsequent seminars.

a. System accounting for facilities employed by the user. Special hardware features for metering different uses. Accounting for system overhead. Factors which determine system overhead.

b. Characteristics of large systems. Overall discussion of large system management including effect of binding times for system and user process variables. Other selected topics on large systems such as the effect of new hardware components (e.g. mass memories) on the overall system design.

c. Foreground and background processes. Foreground-initiated background processes. Remote job control. Hierarchical job control. Broadcasting.

d. Microprogramming as an equivalent of various hardware and/or software component subprograms in a computing system.

e. Command languages. Commands of a multiprogramming system. Command language interpreters.

f. Provisions for dynamic updating of the operating system without shutdown.

g. Operating behavior, e.g. system startup, (graceful) degradation, and shutdown.

ANNOTATED BIBLIOGRAPHY

In addition to the following sources of information, there are many manuals available from manufacturers which describe specific systems programs for a wide range of computers.

1. CHOROFAS, D. N. *Programming Systems for Electronic Computers.* Butterworths, London, 1962, 188 pp. CR-6566-8553.

   Chapters 14, 15, and 16 contain a general discourse on the control and diagnostic functions of operating systems.

2. CLARK, W. A., MEALY, G. H., AND WITT, B. I. The functional structure of OS/360. *IBM Syst. J. 5*, 1 (1966), 3–51.

   A general description in three parts of the operating system for the IBM System/360. Part I (Mealy), Introductory Survey; Part II (Witt), Job and Task Management; and Part III (Clark), Data Management.

3. DESMONDE, W. H. *Real-Time Data Processing Systems. Introductory Concepts.* Prentice-Hall, Englewood Cliffs, N. J., 1964, 192 pp. CR-6562-7236.

   An elementary survey of the design and programming of real-time data processing systems based on three IBM systems: Sabre, Mercury, and Gemini.

4. ERDWINN, J. D. (Ch.) Executive control programs—Session 8. Proc. AFIPS 1967 Fall Joint Comput. Conf., Vol. 31, Thompson Book Co., Washington, D. C., pp. 201–254.

   Five papers on control programs for a variety of circumstances.

5. FISCHER, F. P., AND SWINDLE, G. F. *Computer Programming Systems.* Holt, Rinehart and Winston, New York, 1964, 643 pp. CR-6455-6299.

   Sets out to "discuss the entire field of computer programming systems," but in reality considers primarily the systems programs for the IBM 1401; "other computer systems are mentioned only where a particular characteristic of a programming system, found on that computer, warrants discussion." Only IBM computer systems and (with a very few exceptions) only IBM literature are referenced.

6. FLORES, I. *Computer Software.* Prentice-Hall, Englewood Cliffs, N. J., 1965, 464 pp. CR-6671-8995.

   Elementary and conversational text primarily concerned with assembly systems using FLAP (Flores Assembly Program) as its example. Some material on service programs, supervisors and loaders.

7. GLASER, E. (Ch.) A new remote accessed man-machine system—Session 6. Proc. AFIPS 1965 Fall Joint Comput. Conf., Vol. 27, Pt. 1, Spartan Books, New York, pp. 185–241. (Reprints available from the General Electric Company.)

   Six papers on the MULTICS system.

8. HEISTAND, R. E. An executive system implemented as a finite-state automaton. *Comm. ACM 7*, 11 (Nov. 1964), 669–677. CR-6562-7282.

   Describes the executive system for the 473L command and control system. The system was considered as a finite automaton and the author claims this approach forced a modularity on the resulting program.

9. LEONARD, G. F., AND GOODROE, J. R. An environment for an operating system. Proc. ACM 19th Nat. Conf., 1964, Association for Computing Machinery, New York, pp. E2.3-1 to E2.3-11. CR-6561-6546.

   An approach to computer utilization involving the extension of the operations of a computer with software so as to provide a proper environment for an operating system.

10. MARTIN, J. *Design of Real-Time Computer Systems.* Prentice-Hall, Englewood Cliffs, N. J., 1967, 629 pp.

    A general text covering many aspects of real-time data processing systems including design, applications, management, and operation.

11. MARTIN, J. *Programming Real-Time Computer Systems.* Prentice-Hall, Englewood Cliffs, N. J., 1965, 386 pp.

    Based on some of the early systems such as Sage, Project Mercury, Sabre, and Panamac. A general coverage designed for managers, systems analysts, programmers, salesmen, students.

12. MILLER, A. E. (Ch.) Analysis of time-shared computer system performance—Session 5. Proc. ACM 22nd Nat. Conf., 1967, Thompson Book Co., Washington, D. C., pp. 85–109.

    Three papers on measurement of time-shared system performance.

13. M.I.T. Computation Center. *Compatible Time-Sharing System: A Programmer's Guide*, 2nd ed. M.I.T. Press, Cambridge, Mass., 1965.

    A handbook on the use of CTSS which contains valuable information and guidelines on the implementation of such systems.

14. Project MAC. *MULTICS System Programmer's Manual.* Project MAC, M.I.T., Cambridge, Mass., 1967, (limited distribution).

    A description of and guide to systems programming for MULTICS.

15. ROSEN, S. (Ed.) *Programming Systems and Languages.* McGraw-Hill, New York, 1967, 734 pp.

    Collection of important papers in the area of which Part 5 (Operating Systems) is particularly relevant to this course.

16. ROSENBERG, A. M. (Ch.) Program structures for the multiprogramming environment—Session 6A. Proc. ACM 21st Nat. Conf., 1966, Thompson Book Co., Washington, D. C., pp. 223–239.

    Two papers: one on program behavior under paging; the other on analytic design of look-ahead and program segmenting systems.

17. ROSENBERG, A. M. (Ch.) Time-sharing and on-line systems—Session 7. Proc. ACM 22nd Nat. Conf., 1967, Thompson Book Co., Washington, D. C., pp. 135–175.

    Three papers on various topics related to the subject.

18. SALTZER, J. H. Traffic control in a multiplexed computer system. M.I.T. Ph.D. Thesis, June 1966. (Also available as Project MAC publication MAC-TR-30.)

    On traffic control in the MULTICS system.

19. SMITH, J. W. (Ch.) Time-shared scheduling—Session 5A. Proc. ACM 21st Nat. Conf., 1966, Thompson Book Co., Washington, D. C., pp. 139–177.

    Four papers on time-sharing which are more general than the session title indicates.

20. THOMPSON, R. N., AND WILKINSON, J. A. The D825 automatic operating and scheduling program. Proc. AFIPS 1963 Spring Joint Comput. Conf., Vol. 23, Spartan Books, New York, pp. 41–49. CR-6453-5699.

    A general description of an executive system program for handling a multiple computer system tied to an automatic input-output exchange containing a number of input-output control modules. Discusses many of the problems encountered in such systems and the general plan of attack in solving these problems.

21. WEGNER, P. (Ed.) *Introduction to System Programming.* Academic Press, New York, 1965, 316 pp. CR-6455-6300.

    Contains a collection of papers of which the following are of special interest for this course: Gill, pp. 214–226; Howarth, pp. 227–238; and Nash, pp. 239–249.

Course I5. Compiler Construction (3-0-3)

APPROACH

This course is to emphasize the techniques involved in the analysis of source language and the generation of efficient object code. Although some theoretical topics must be covered, the course should have the practical objective of teaching the student how compilers may be constructed. Programming assignments should consist of implementations of components of a compiler and possibly the design of a simple but complete compiler as a group project.

CONTENT

There is probably more material listed here than can reasonably be covered, so some selection will be necessary.

1. Review of assembly techniques, symbol table techniques, and macros. Review of syntactic analysis and other forms of program recognition. Review of compilation, loading, and execution with emphasis on the representation of programs in the loader language.
2. One-pass compilation techniques. Translation of arithmetic expressions from postfix form to machine language. Efficient use of registers and temporary storage.
3. Storage allocation for constants, simple variables, arrays, temporary storage. Function and statement procedures, independent block structure, nested block structure, and dynamic storage allocation.
4. Object code for subscripted variables, storage mapping functions, and dope vectors. Compilation of sequencing statements.
5. Detailed organization of a simple complete compiler. Symbol tables. Lexical scan on input (recognizer), syntax scan (analyzer), object code generators, operator and operand stacks, output subroutines, and error diagnostics.
6. Data types, transfer functions, mixed mode expressions and statements.
7. Subroutine and function compilation. Parameters called by address, by name and by value. Subroutines with side effects. Restrictions required for one pass execution. Object code for transmission of parameters. Object code for subroutine body.
8. Languages designed for writing compilers: TMG (McClure), COGENT (Reynolds), GARGOYLE (Garwick), META II (Schorre), and TGS-II (Cheatham).
9. Bootstrapping techniques. Discussion of a meta-compiler in its own language.
10. Optimization techniques. Frequency analysis of use of program structures to determine most important features for optimization.
11. Local optimization to take advantage of special instructions. Loading registers with constants, storing zeros, changing sign, adding to memory, multiplication or division by two, replacement of division with multiplication by a constant, squaring, raising to integer powers, and comparing to zero. Subscript optimization.
12. Expression optimization. Identities involving minus signs, common subexpression evaluation and other techniques. Minimization of temporary storage and the number of arithmetic registers in multiple register machines.
13. Optimization of loops. Typical loops coded several ways. Index register optimization in the innermost loop. Classification of loops for optimization purposes.
14. Problems of global optimization. Determination of flowchart graph of program. Analysis of program graphs. Rearrangement of computation to do as little as possible in innermost loop. Factoring of invariant subexpressions. Object code for interfaces between flow blocks.

ANNOTATED BIBLIOGRAPHY

1. ACM Compiler Symposium. Papers presented at the ACM Compiler Symposium, November 17–18, 1960, Washington, D. C., *Comm. ACM 4*, 1 (Jan. 1961), 3–84.

   Contains a number of relevant papers including one by R. W. Floyd entitled "An Algorithm for Coding Efficient Arithmetic Operations" and one by P. Z. Ingerman on "Thunks."

2. Arden, B. W., Galler, B. A., and Graham, R. M. An algorithm for translating Boolean expressions. *J. ACM 9*, 2 (Apr. 1962), 222–239. CR-6341-3567.

   Description of code generation in the Mad Compiler.

3. Brinch-Hansen, P., and House, R. The COBOL compiler for the Siemens 3003. *BIT 6*, 1 (1966), 1–23.

   Describes the design of a ten-pass compiler with extensive error detection.

4. Cheatham, T. E., Jr. The TGS-II translator generator system. Proc. IFIP Congress, New York, 1965, Vol. 2, Spartan Books, New York, pp. 592–593.

   A report on the "current position" of Computer Associates "translator generator system."

5. Cheatham, T. E., Jr. *The Theory and Construction of Compilers*. Document CA-6606-0111, Computer Associates, Inc., Wakefield, Mass., June 2, 1966, limited distribution.

   Notes for course AM 295 at Harvard, fall 1967.

6. Cheatham, T. E., Jr., and Sattley, K. Syntax-directed compiling. Proc. AFIPS 1964 Spring Joint Comput. Conf., Vol. 25, Spartan Books, New York, pp. 31–57. CR-6455-6304.

   An introduction to top-down syntax directed compilers.

7. Conway, M. E. Design of a separable transition-diagram compiler. *Comm. ACM 6*, 7 (July 1963), 396–408. CR-6451-5024.

   Describes the organization of a Cobol compiler. The methods are largely applicable to construction of compilers for other languages such as Algol.

8. Conway, R. W., and Maxwell, W. L. CORC—the Cornell computing language. *Comm. ACM 6*, 6 (June 1963), 317–321.

   Description of a language and compiler which are designed to provide extensive error diagnostics and other aids to the programmer.

9. Ershov, A. P. ALPHA—an automatic programming system of high efficiency. *J. ACM 13*, 1 (Jan. 1966), 17–24. CR-6673-9720.

   Describes a compiler for a language which includes most of Algol as a subset. Several techniques for optimizing both the compiler and the object code are presented.

10. Ershov, A. P. *Programming Programme for the BESM computer*, transl. by M. Nadler. Pergamon Press, New York, 1959, 158 pp. CR-6235-2595.

    One of the earliest works on compilers. Introduced the use of stacks and the removal of common subexpressions.

11. Ershov, A. P. On programming of arithmetic operations. *Comm. ACM 1*, 8 (Aug. 1958), 3–6 and 9 (Sept. 1958), 16.

    Gives an algorithm for creating rough machine language instructions in pseudoform and then altering them into a more efficient form.

12. Freeman, D. N. Error correction in CORC. Proc. AFIPS 1964 Fall Joint Computer Conf., Vol. 26, Part I, Spartan Books, New York, pp. 15–34.

    Discusses techniques of correcting errors in programs written in the Cornell computing language.

13. Garwick, J. V. GARGOYLE, a language for compiler writing. *Comm. ACM 7*, 1 (Jan. 1964), 16–20. CR-6453-5675.

    Describes an Algol-like language which uses syntax-directed methods.

14. Gear, C. W. High speed compilation of efficient object code. *Comm. ACM 8*, 8 (Aug. 1965), 483–488. CR-6671-9000.

    Describes a three-pass compiler which represents a compromise between compilation speed and object code efficiency. Primary attention is given to the optimization performed by the compiler.

15. GRIES, D., PAUL, M., AND WIEHLE, H. R. Some techniques used in the ALCOR ILLINOIS 7090. *Comm. ACM 8*, 8 (Aug. 1965), 496–500. CR-6566-8556.

Describes portions of an ALGOL compiler for the IBM 7090.

16. HAWKINS, E. N., AND HUXTABLE, D. H. R. A multipass translation scheme for ALGOL 60. In R. Goodman (Ed.), *Annual Review in Automatic Programming, Vol. 3*, Pergamon Press, New York, 1963, pp. 163–206.

Discusses local and global optimization techniques.

17. HORWITZ, L. P., KARP, R. M., MILLER, R. E., AND WINOGRAD, S. Index register allocation. *J. ACM 13*, 1 (Jan. 1966), 43–61. CR-6674-10,068.

A mathematical treatment of the problem. Useful in compiler writing.

18. International Computation Centre (Eds.) *Symbolic Languages in Data Processing*, Proceedings of the Symposium in Rome, March 26–31, 1962. Gordon and Breach, New York, 1962, 849 pp.

The twelve papers listed under "Construction of Processors for Syntactically Highly Structured Languages" in this volume are particularly of interest for this course.

19. KNUTH, D. E. A history of writing compilers. *Comput. Autom. 11*, 12 (Dec. 1962), 8–18.

Describes some of the early techniques used in writing American compilers.

20. MCCLURE, R. M. TMG—a syntax directed compiler. Proc. ACM 20th Nat. Conf., 1965, Association for Computing Machinery, New York, pp. 262–274.

The compiler writing system described in this paper was designed to facilitate the construction of simple one-pass translators for some specialized languages. It has features which simplify the handling of declarative information and errors.

21. NAUR, P. The design of the GIER ALGOL compiler. In R. Goodman (Ed.), *Annual Review in Automatic Programming, Vol. 4*, Pergamon Press, New York, 1964, pp. 49–85. CR-6564-7904.

Describes a multipass compiler written for a computer with a small high-speed memory.

22. RANDELL, B., AND RUSSELL, L. J. *ALGOL 60 Implementation*. Academic Press, New York, 1964, 418 pp. CR-6565-8246.

Contains a survey of ALGOL implementation techniques and a description of an error-checking and debugging compiler for the KDF9 computer.

23. REYNOLDS, J. C. An introduction to the COGENT programming system. Proc. ACM 20th Nat. Conf., 1965, Association for Computing Machinery, New York, pp. 422–436.

Describes the structure and major facilities of a compiler-compiler system which couples the notion of syntax-directed compiling with that of recursive list processing.

24. ROSEN, S. (Ed.) *Programming Systems and Languages*. McGraw-Hill, New York, 1967, 734 pp.

A collection of papers of which the following are of special interest for this course: Backus, et al., pp. 29–47; Bauer and Samelson, pp. 206–220; Dijkstra, pp. 221–227; Kanner, Kosinski, and Robinson, pp. 228–252; Rosen, Spurgeon, and Donnelly, pp. 264–297; and Rosen, pp. 306–331.

25. SCHORRE, D. V. META II, a syntax-oriented compiler writing language. Proc. ACM 19th Nat. Conf., 1964, Association for Computing Machinery, New York, pp. D1.3-1 to D1.3-11. CR-6561-6943.

Describes a compiler writing language in which its own compiler can be written.

26. WEGNER, P. (Ed.) *Introduction to System Programming*. Academic Press, New York, 1965, 316 pp. CR-6455-6300.

Contains a collection of papers of which the following are of special interest for this course: Pyle, pp. 86–100; Wegner, pp. 101–121; Randell, pp. 122–136; Huxtable, pp. 137–155; Hoare, pp. 156–165; and d'Agapeyeff, pp. 199–214.

Course I6. Switching Theory (3-0-3) or (2-2-3)

APPROACH

This course should present the theoretical foundations and mathematical techniques concerned with the design of logical circuits. Examples should be chosen to illustrate the applicability to computers or other digital systems whenever possible. Facility with Boolean algebra and appreciation for the effects of delays should be developed. Some laboratory experiments are highly desirable.

CONTENT

1. Review of nondecimal number systems. Introduction to unit-distance, error-correcting, and other codes.
2. Development of switching algebra and its relation to Boolean algebra and propositional logic. Brief discussion of switching elements and gates. Analysis of gate networks. Truth tables and completeness of connectives.
3. Simplification of combinational networks. Use of map and tabular techniques. The prime implicant theorem. Threshold logic.
4. Different modes of sequential circuit operation. Flow table, state diagram, and regular expression representations. Clocked circuits. Flip-flop and feedback realizations.
5. Synthesis of sequential circuits. State minimization and internal variable assignments for pulse and fundamental mode circuits. Race considerations. Iterative and symmetric networks.
6. Effects of delays. Static, dynamic, and essential hazards.

ANNOTATED BIBLIOGRAPHY

As is indicated, several of the books listed below could be used as texts for this course, but it probably would be desirable to supplement any of them with additional material.

General textbooks

1. CALDWELL, S. H. *Switching Circuits and Logical Design*. Wiley, New York, 1958, 686 pp.

The classic book on relay-oriented switching theory.

2. HARRISON, M. A. *Introduction to Switching and Automata Theory*. McGraw-Hill, New York, 1965, 499 pp. CR-6671-9109.

A mathematical and abstract reference for advanced topics.

3. HIGONNET, R. A., AND GREA, R. A. *Logical Design of Electrical Circuits*. McGraw-Hill, New York, 1958, 220 pp.

Almost exclusively devoted to relay networks.

4. HUMPHREY, W. S., JR. *Switching Circuits with Computer Applications*. McGraw-Hill, New York, 1958, 264 pp.

A somewhat out-of-date undergraduate level text.

5. KRIEGER, M. *Basic Switching Circuit Theory*. Macmillan, New York, 1967, 256 pp. CR-6784-12,510.

Basic elementary treatment which does not discuss hazards or codes.

6. MCCLUSKEY, E. J., JR. *Introduction to the Theory of Switching Circuits*. McGraw-Hill, New York, 1965, 318 pp. CR-6673-9834.

A possible text for this course.

7. MCCLUSKEY, E. J., JR., AND BARTEE, T. C. (Eds.) *A Survey of Switching Circuit Theory*. McGraw-Hill, New York, 1962, 205 pp. CR-6342-3958.

A collection of papers. Weak as a text since there are no problems. Possibly of some value as reading to illustrate different approaches.

8. MALEY, G. A., AND EARLE, J. *The Logic Design of Transistor Digital Computers*. Prentice-Hall, Englewood Cliffs, N. J., 1963, 322 pp. CR-6345-4582.

Despite its title, this book covers a considerable amount of switching theory. Emphasis is on NOR circuits and asynchronous systems, and on techniques rather than theorems. Numerous examples.

9. Marcus, M. P. *Switching Circuits for Engineers.* Prentice-Hall, Englewood Cliffs, N. J., 1962, 296 pp. CR-6341-3681.

Broad but not too mathematical coverage of switching theory.

10. Miller, R. E. *Switching Theory, Vol. 1, Combinational Circuits.* Wiley, New York, 1965, 351 pp. CR-6565-8369.

Highly mathematical and somewhat advanced for an undergraduate course. Interesting discussion of the effects of delays.

11. Prather, R. E. *Introduction to Switching Theory: A Mathematical Approach.* Allyn and Bacon, Boston, 1967, 496 pp.

A highly mathematical and broad coverage of both combinatorial switching theory and sequential machine theory.

12. Torng, H. C. *Introduction to the Logical Design of Switching Systems.* Addison-Wesley, Reading, Mass., 1965, 286 pp. CR-6456-6806.

General elementary coverage including a discussion of switching elements and magnetic logic. Outmoded discussion of iterative (cascaded) networks. Many computer-related examples.

13. Warfield, J. N. *Principles of Logic Design.* Ginn and Co., Boston, 1963, 291 pp. CR-6451-5136.

Covers some elementary switching theory in the context of computer logic.

More specialized books

14. Curtis, V. A. *A New Approach to the Design of Switching Circuits.* D. Van Nostrand, Princeton, N. J., 1962, 635 pp. CR-6346-4818.

Devoted mainly to decomposition theory for combinational circuits. Useful as a reference in this area and as a source of examples since it contains many detailed sample problems.

15. Dertouzos, M. L. *Threshold Logic: A Synthesis Approach.* M.I.T. Press, Cambridge, Mass., 1965, 256 pp. CR-6676-10,929.

Concentrates on the characterization and application of threshold elements in terms of logical design.

16. Hu, S. T. *Threshold Logic.* University of California Press, Berkeley, Calif., 1965, 338 pp.

A comprehensive reference which also contains some of the author's original research.

17. Lewis, P. M., and Coates, C. L. *Threshold Logic.* Wiley, New York, 1967, 483 pp.

Emphasizes single and multigate networks for controlled sensitivity.

18. Phister, M., Jr. *Logical Design of Digital Computers.* Wiley, New York, 1958, 401 pp.

Covers the application of sequential circuit theory to design of computer logic. Considers only clocked circuits and (for the most part) serial operation.

Course I7. Sequential Machines (3-0-3)

APPROACH

This is to be a rigorous theoretical course. The material is about evenly devoted to three major points of view: the structural aspects of sequential machines, the behavioral aspects of sequential machines, and the variants of finite automata. Machines with unbounded storage such as Turing machines and pushdown-store automata are to be covered in course A7.

CONTENT

1. Definition of finite automata and sequential machines. Various methods of representing automata including state tables, state diagrams, set theoretic methods, and sequential nets. (3 lectures)

2. Equivalent states and equivalent machines. Reduction of states in sequential machines. (3 lectures)

3. Right-invariant and congruence relations. The equivalence of nondeterministic and deterministic finite automata. Closure properties of languages definable by finite automata and the Kleene-Myhill theorem on regular languages. (4 lectures)

4. Decision problems of finite automata. Testing equivalence, acceptance of a nonempty set, acceptance of an infinite set. (3 lectures)

5. Incomplete sequential machines. Compatible states and algorithms for constructing minimal state incomplete sequential machines. (3 lectures)

6. The state assignment problem. Series-parallel decompositions. Coordinate assignments. (2 lectures)

7. Algebraic definition of a sequential machine. Homomorphisms of monoids. (2 lectures)

8. Partitions with the substitution property. Homomorphism decompositions into a series-composition. (2 lectures)

9. Decomposition of permutation automata. (1 lecture)

10. The decomposition of finite-state automata into a cascade of permutation-reset automata using the method of set systems (covers). (2 lectures)

11. Final series-parallel decomposition into a cascade of two-state automata and simple-group automata. (2 lectures)

12. Brief introduction to undecidability notions. The halting problem. (2 lectures)

13. Multitape nonwriting automata. (4 lectures)

14. Generalized sequential machines. (2 lectures)

15. Subsets of regular languages. Group-free automata. (3 lectures)

16. Regular expressions. Algebra, derivatives and star height. (5 lectures)

17. Probabilistic automata. (3 lectures)

ANNOTATED BIBLIOGRAPHY

Except for two survey articles, only books are included in the following list. Since this field has developed within the last fifteen years, much of the material is still in the periodical literature.

1. Caianiello, E. R. (Ed.) *Automata Theory.* Academic Press, New York, 1966, 343 pp. CR-6676-10,935.

A collection of research and tutorial papers on automata, formal languages, graph theory, logic, algorithms, recursive function theory, and neural nets, which, because of varying interest and difficulty, might be useful for supplementary reading by ambitious students.

2. Fischer, P. C. Multitape and infinite-state automata—a survey. *Comm. ACM 8*, 12 (Dec. 1965), 799–805. CR-6675-10,561.

A survey of machines which are more powerful than finite automata and less powerful than Turing machines. Also an extensive bibliography.

3. Gill, A. *Introduction to the Theory of Finite-State Machines.* McGraw-Hill, New York, 1962, 207 pp. CR-6343-4207.

An automata theory approach to finite-state machines which is somewhat engineering oriented and written at a fairly elementary level.

4. Ginsburg, S. *An Introduction to Mathematical Machine Theory.* Addison-Wesley, Reading, Mass., 1962, 137 pp. CR-6452-5431.

A text on the behavior of the sequential machines of Huffman-Moore-Mealy, abstract machines of Ginsburg, and tape recognition devices of Rabin and Scott.

5. Glushkov, V. M. *Introduction to Cybernetics*, transl. by Scripta Technica, Inc. Academic Press, New York, 1966, 324 pp.

A translation of the Russian text which assumes only a limited background. Approaches subject from somewhat different point of view than most Western texts. Contains much relevant material.

6. Harrison, M. *Introduction to Switching and Automata Theory*, McGraw-Hill, New York, 1965, 499 pp. CR-6671-9109.

This text for engineers and mathematicians develops the foundations of both switching and automata theory in abstract mathematical terms. Emphasis is on switching theory. Coverage includes sequential machines, regular events, definite events, probabilistic machines, and context-free languages.

7. HARTMANIS, J., AND STEARNS, R. E. *Algebraic Structure Theory of Sequential Machines.* Prentice-Hall, Englewood Cliffs, N. J., 1966, 211 pp. CR-6782-11,635.

   The first thorough treatment of the structure theory of sequential machines and its applications to machine synthesis and machine decomposition. A research monograph selected from a series of papers by the authors and not written as a text. Practically no exercises.

8. HENNIE, F. C., III. *Iterative Arrays of Logical Circuits.* M.I.T. Press, Cambridge, Mass., and Wiley, New York, 1961, 242 pp. CR-6232-1733.

   Currently the most complete treatise on iterative arrays.

9. KAUTZ, W. H. (Ed.) *Linear Sequential Switching Circuits—Selected Technical Papers.* Holden-Day, San Francisco, 1965, 234 pp. CR-6674-10,205.

   A collection of papers on linear sequential machines.

10. MCNAUGHTON, R. The theory of automata—a survey. In F. L. Alt (Ed.), *Advances in Computing, Vol. 2,* Academic Press, New York, 1961, pp. 379–421. CR-6342-3920.

    Most of the areas of automata theory are included with the exception of switching theory and other engineering topics.

11. MILLER, R. E. *Switching Theory, Vol. 2, Sequential Circuits and Machines.* Wiley, New York, 1965, 250 pp. CR-6783-12,120.

    Highly mathematical and somewhat advanced as a text for an undergraduate course.

12. MINSKY, M. *Computation: Finite and Infinite Machines.* Prentice-Hall, Englewood Cliffs, N. J., 1967, 317 pp.

    The concept of an "effective procedure" is developed in this text. Also treats algorithms, Post productions, regular expressions, computability, infinite and finite-state models of digital computers, and computer languages.

13. MOORE, E. F. (Ed.) *Sequential Machines: Selected Papers.* Addison-Wesley, Reading, Mass., 1964, 266 pp.

    This collection of classical papers on sequential machines includes an extensive bibliography by the editor.

14. PRATHER, R. E. *Introduction to Switching Theory: A Mathematical Approach.* Allyn and Bacon, Boston, 1967, 496 pp.

    A mathematical and broad treatment of both combinatorial switching theory and sequential machines.

15. SHANNON, C. E., AND MCCARTHY, J. (Eds.) *Automata Studies.* Princeton University Press, Princeton, N. J., 1956, 285 pp.

    A collection of many of the early papers on finite automata, Turing machines, and synthesis of automata which stimulated the development of automata theory. Philosophical papers, in addition to mathematical papers, are included, since the aim of the collection is to help explain the workings of the human mind.

Courses I8 and I9. Numerical Analysis I and II (3-0-3) and (3-0-3)

APPROACH

The numerical methods presented in these courses are to be developed and evaluated from the standpoint of efficiency, accuracy, and suitability for high-speed digital computing. While other arrangements of the material in these courses are possible, the ones suggested here do allow the two courses to be taught independently of one another.

CONTENT OF COURSE I8

1. *Solution of Equations.* Newton's method and other iterative methods for solving systems of equations. Aitken's δ^2 process. Newton-Bairstow method. Muller's method and Bernoulli's method for polynomial equations. Convergence conditions and rates of convergence for each method.

2. *Interpolation and Approximation.* Polynomial interpolation. Lagrange's method with error formula. Gregory-Newton and other equal interval interpolation methods. Systems of orthogonal polynomials. Least-squares approximation. Trigonometric approximation. Chebyshev approximation.

3. *Numerical Differentiation and Quadrature.* Formulas involving equal intervals. Romberg integration. Extrapolation to the limit. Gaussian quadrature.

4. *Solution of Ordinary Differential Equations.* Runge-Kutta methods. Multistep methods. Predictor-corrector methods. Stability.

CONTENT OF COURSE I9

5. *Linear Algebra.* Rigorous treatment of elimination methods and their use to solve linear systems, invert matrices, and evaluate determinants. Compact schemes. Methods for solving the eigenvalue-eigenvector problem including the power method, the inverse power method, Jacobi's method, Givens' method and Householder's method. Roundoff analysis and conditioning.

6. *Numerical Solution of Boundary Value Problems in Ordinary Differential Equations.*

7. *Introduction to the Numerical Solution of Partial Differential Equations.* Computational aspects of finite difference methods for linear equations. Determination of grids. Derivation of difference equations. Solution of large linear systems by iterative methods such as simultaneous displacements, successive displacements, and successive overrelaxation.

ANNOTATED BIBLIOGRAPHY

Listed below are some but by no means all of the books which could be used as texts and/or references for these courses. The more general texts normally include solution of polynomial and other nonlinear equations; interpolation, numerical quadrature, and numerical differentiation; ordinary differential equations; and linear algebra. Significant deviations from these are indicated by the annotations.

Besides listing books which might be used as texts for part or all of these courses, the following includes books for those desiring to go deeper into the various areas. In particular, Refs. 1, 3, 10, 17, and 18 have been included for linear algebra; Refs. 2 and 16 for partial differential equations; Ref. 15 for the solution of nonlinear equations; and Ref. 7 for ordinary differential equations.

1. FADDEEV, D. K., AND FADDEEVA, V. N. *Computational Methods of Linear Algebra,* transl. by R. C. Williams. W. H. Freeman, San Francisco, 1963, 621 pp. CR-6016-0374.

   An excellent reference on the theory of computational methods in linear algebra. Does not treat the theory of computational errors. Introductory chapter could serve as a text for a course in linear algebra. Beginning analysis and an elementary knowledge of complex variables is assumed. Examples but no exercises.

2. FORSYTHE, G. E., AND WASOW, W. R. *Finite-Difference Methods for Partial Differential Equations.* Wiley, New York, 1960, 444 pp.

   A fundamental reference on the numerical solution of partial differential equations by finite-difference methods. Provides a thorough treatment of hyperbolic, parabolic, and elliptic equations. Orientation is toward the use of high-speed computers, but it is not intended as a guide for programmers. For most of the book, advanced calculus and linear algebra provide sufficient background. Previous knowledge of partial differential equations not required. Some illustrative examples but no exercises.

3. FOX, L. *An Introduction to Numerical Linear Algebra.* Oxford University Press, New York, 1964, 295 pp. CR-6456-6723.

   A basic reference on computational methods in linear algebra. Designed for engineers and scientists as well as mathematicians. Emphasis on the principles involved rather than the details of applications to computers. Intended to prepare the reader for a more advanced book such as Wilkinson's *The Algebraic Eigenvalue Problem.* Introductory chapter on matrix algebra. Illustrative examples and exercises.

4. FRÖBERG, C. E. *Introduction to Numerical Analysis.* Addison-Wesley, Reading, Mass., 1965, 340 pp. CR-6671-9037.

   Designed as a text for an undergraduate numerical analysis course. Includes, in addition to the standard topics, partial differential equations (briefly), approximation by Chebyshev polynomials and other functions, Monte Carlo methods, and linear programming. Emphasis on modern methods well-adapted for computers. Mathematically rigorous treatment with detailed error analysis given in typical cases. Presupposes differential and integral calculus and differential equations. Illustrative examples and exercises.

5. HAMMING, R. W. *Numerical Methods for Scientists and Engineers.* McGraw-Hill, New York, 1962, 411 pp. CR-6236-3367.

   Excellent as a reference. Provides interesting and different point of view. Treats interpolation and approximation; numerical differentiation and integration; and ordinary differential equations by polynomial and other methods such as Fourier methods, and exponentials. Brief treatments of nonlinear equations and linear algebra, simulation, and Monte Carlo methods. Presupposes beginning analysis, Fourier series, mathematical statistics, feed-back circuits, noise theory. Illustrative examples and exercises.

6. HENRICI, P. *Elements of Numerical Analysis.* Wiley, New York, 1964, 328 pp.

   Designed as a text for a one-semester course in numerical analysis. Covers the standard topics except linear algebra. Emphasis on numerical analysis as a mathematical discipline. A distinction is made between algorithms and theorems. Introductory chapters on complex variables and difference equations. Beginning analysis (12 semester hours) and ordinary differential equations are assumed. Illustrative examples and exercises.

7. HENRICI, P. *Discrete Variable Methods in Ordinary Differential Equations.* Wiley, New York, 1962, 407 pp. CR-6341-3733.

   A basic reference on the numerical methods for solving ordinary differential equations. Designed as a text for a senior-level course on ordinary differential equations. Includes a mathematically rigorous treatment of various methods. Emphasis is on the study of discretization errors and round-off errors. Presupposes differential equations, advanced calculus, linear algebra, and elementary complex variables (though large parts of the book do not require all of these topics). Illustrative examples and exercises.

8. HILDEBRAND, F. B. *Introduction to Numerical Analysis.* McGraw-Hill, New York, 1956, 511 pp.

   A good book for supplementary reading though written in 1956. Gives primary emphasis to methods adapted for desk calculators. Includes standard topics except for linear algebra. Separate chapters on least-squares, polynomial approximation, Gaussian quadrature, and approximation of various types. Beginning analysis sufficient background for most of the book. An extensive set of exercises.

9. HOUSEHOLDER, A. S. *Principles of Numerical Analysis.* McGraw-Hill, New York, 1953, 274 pp.

   Good for supplementary reading. Designed as mathematical textbook rather than a compendium of computational rules. Published in 1953, the book includes many methods applicable only to hand computation though it was written with computers in mind. Includes the standard topics except ordinary differential equations. Presupposes beginning analysis plus some knowledge of probability and statistics. Some exercises.

10. HOUSEHOLDER, A. S. *The Theory of Matrices in Numerical Analysis.* Blaisdell, New York, 1964, 257 pp.

    Good for supplementary reading. Considers the development and appraisal of computational methods in linear algebra from the theoretical point of view. Does not develop specific computer flowcharts or programs. Presupposes a knowledge of matrix algebra. Illustrative examples and exercises.

11. ISAACSON, E., AND KELLER, H. B. *Analysis of Numerical Methods.* Wiley, New York, 1966, 541 pp. CR-6783-11,966.

    A very well written and rather comprehensive text presenting a careful analysis of numerous important numerical methods with a view toward their applicability to computers. With an appropriate selection of material the book lends itself well to use as a text; otherwise, it is an excellent reference.

12. MILNE, W. E. *Numerical Solution of Differential Equations.* Wiley, New York, 1953, 275 pp.

    Since it was written in 1953, much of this material has been superseded by more recent work; yet it remains very suitable for supplemental reading. Ordinary and partial differential equations are treated as well as some problems in linear algebra. Many of the methods are adapted for hand computation rather than for computers. Beginning analysis should provide sufficient background for most of the book. Illustrative examples and some exercises.

13. RALSTON, A. *A First Course in Numerical Analysis.* McGraw-Hill, New York, 1965, 578 pp. CR-6671-9035.

    Designed as a text for a one-year course in numerical analysis (though not all of the material could be covered) to be taken by graduate students and advanced undergraduate students, primarily in mathematics. Although numerical analysis is treated as a full-fledged branch of applied mathematics, orientation is toward the use of digital computers. Basic topics in numerical analysis covered thoroughly. Separate chapters devoted to functional approximation by least-squares techniques and by minimum-maximum error techniques. Presupposes beginning analysis, advanced calculus, orthogonal polynomials, and complex variables. A course in linear algebra is assumed for the chapters in that area. An extensive set of illustrative examples and exercises.

14. TODD, J. (Ed.) *A Survey of Numerical Analysis.* McGraw-Hill, New York, 1962, 589 pp. CR-6236-3368.

    Written by a number of authors. Some of the early chapters have been used in connection with introductory courses. Because of its breadth of coverage it is especially suited as a reference for these courses. Besides the usual topics, there are separate chapters on orthogonalizing codes, partial differential equations, integral equations, and problems in number theory. The prerequisites vary with the chapters but for early chapters beginning analysis and linear algebra would suffice. Exercises given in some of the early chapters.

15. TRAUB, J. F. *Iterative Methods for the Solution of Equations.* Prentice-Hall, Englewood Cliffs, N. J., 1964, 310 pp. CR-6672-9339.

    A good reference on the numerical solution of equations and (briefly) systems of equations by iteration algorithms. The methods are treated with rigor, though rigor in itself is not the main object. Contains a considerable amount of new material. Many illustrative examples.

16. VARGA, RICHARD. *Matrix Iterative Analysis.* Prentice-Hall, Englewood Cliffs, N. J., 1962, 322 pp. CR-6343-4236.

    An excellent reference giving theoretical basis behind methods for solving large systems of linear algebraic equations which arise in the numerical solution of partial differential equations by finite-difference methods. Designed as a text for a first-year graduate course in mathematics.

17. WILKINSON, J. H. *Rounding Errors in Algebraic Processes.* Prentice-Hall, Englewood Cliffs, N. J., 1964, 161 pp. CR-6455-6341.

    Studies the cumulative effect of rounding errors in computations involving large numbers of arithmetic operations performed by digital computers. Special attention given to problems involving polynomials and matrices. A very important reference for a computer-oriented course in numerical analysis.

18. WILKINSON, J. H. *The Algebraic Eigenvalue Problem.* Clarendon Press, Oxford, England, 1965, 662 pp.

    A basic reference on computational methods in linear algebra. Provides a thorough treatment of those methods with which the author has had direct numerical experience on the computer. Treats the methods theoretically and also from the standpoint of rounding errors. Presupposes beginning analysis, linear algebra, and elementary complex variables. Illustrative examples but no exercises.

Course A1. Formal Languages and Syntactic Analysis (3-0-3)

APPROACH

This course combines the theoretical concepts which arise in formal language theory with their practical application to the syntactic analysis of programming languages. The objective is to build a bridge between theory and practical applications, so that the mathematical theory of context-free languages becomes meaningful to the programmer and the theoretically oriented student develops an understanding of practical applications. Assignments in this course should include both computer programming assignments and theorem proving assignments.

CONTENT

The following topics should be covered, but the organization of the material and relative emphasis on individual topics is subject to individual preference.

1. Definition of a formal grammar as notation for specifying a subset of the set of all strings over a finite alphabet, and of a formal language as a set specified by a formal grammar. Production notation for specifying grammars. Recursively enumerable, context-sensitive, context-free, and finite-state grammars. Examples of languages specified by grammars such as $a^n b^n$, $a^n b^n c^n$.

2. Specification of arithmetic expressions and arithmetic statements as context-free grammars. Use of context-free grammars as recognizers. Use of recognizers as a component in compilation or interpretive execution of arithmetic statements.

3. Syntactic analysis, recognizers, analyzers and generators. Top-down and bottom-up algorithms. The backtracking problem and the reduction of backtracking by bounded context techniques. Theory of bounded context analysis and LR(k) grammars.

4. Precedence and operator precedence techniques. The algorithms of Floyd, Wirth and Weber, etc. Semantics of precedence grammars for arithmetic statements and simple block structure.

5. Top-down and bottom-up algorithms for context-free languages. The algorithms of Cheatham, Domolki, and others.

6. Languages for syntactic analysis and compilation such as COGENT and TMG. A simple syntactic compiler written in one of these languages.

7. Reductive grammars, Floyd productions, and semantics for arithmetic expressions. The work of Evans, Feldman, and others.

8. Theory of context-free grammars, normal forms for context-free grammars, elimination of productions of length zero and one. Chomsky and Greibach normal forms. Ambiguous and inherently ambiguous grammars. The characteristic sequence of a grammar. Strong equivalence, weak equivalence and equivalence with preservation of ambiguity. Asymptotic time and space requirements for context-free language recognition.

9. Combinatorial theorems for context-free grammars. Proof that $a^n b^n c^n$ cannot be represented by a context-free grammar. Linear and semilinear sets. Parikh's theorem.

10. Grammars and mechanical devices. Turing machines, linear bounded automata, pushdown automata, finite-state automata, and the corresponding grammars.

11. Properties of pushdown automata. Deterministic and nondeterministic automata and languages. Stack automata. Programming languages and pushdown automata.

ANNOTATED BIBLIOGRAPHY

1. BAR-HILLEL, Y., PERLES, M., AND SHAMIR, E. On formal properties of simple phrase structure grammars. *Zeitschrift für Phonetik, Sprachwissenschaft und Kommunikationsforschung 14* (1961), 143–172. (Reprinted in Y. Bar-Hillel (Ed.), *Languages and Information, Selected Essays*. Addison-Wesley, Reading, Mass., 1964. CR-6562-7178.)

   A well-written paper containing the first statement of many of the principal results of context-free languages.

2. BAUER, F. L., AND SAMELSON, K. Sequential formula translation. *Comm. ACM 3*, 2 (Feb. 1960), 76–83. CR-6015-0219.

   The first systematic paper on the translation of programming languages from left to right using precedence techniques.

3. BROOKER, R. A., AND MORRIS, D. A general translation program for phrase structure grammars. *J. ACM 9*, 1 (Jan. 1962), 1–10.

   Summarizes the design and machine-oriented characteristics of a syntax-directed compiler and describes both its syntactic and semantic features.

4. CHEATHAM, T. E., JR., AND SATTLEY, K. Syntax directed compiling. Proc. AFIPS 1964 Spring Joint Comput. Conf., Vol. 25, Spartan Books, New York, pp. 31–57. CR-6455-6304.

   A description of one of the earliest operational top-down syntax-directed compilers.

5. CHOMSKY, N. Formal properties of grammars. In R. R. Bush, E. H. Galanter, and R. D. Luce (Eds.), *Handbook of Mathematical Psychology, Vol. 2*, Wiley, New York, 1962, pp. 323–418. CR-6676-10,731.

   An excellent review of the work of both Chomsky and others in this field. Contains a good bibliography. See also the two companion chapters in this volume written by Chomsky and G. A. Miller.

6. EVANS, A. An ALGOL 60 compiler. In R. Goodman (Ed.), *Annual Review in Automatic Programming, Vol. 4*, Pergamon Press, New York, 1964, pp. 87–124. CR-6564-7905.

   The first compiler design application of a reductive syntax with labelled productions.

7. FELDMAN, J. A. A formal semantics for computer languages and its application in a compiler-compiler. *Comm. ACM 9*, 1 (Jan. 1966), 3–9. CR-6674-10,080.

   A description of a formal semantic language which can be used in conjunction with a language for describing syntax to specify a syntax-directed compiler.

8. FLOYD, R. W. A descriptive language for symbol manipulation. *J. ACM 8*, 4 (Oct. 1961), 579–584. CR-6234-2140.

   The first discussion of reductive grammars, including a reductive grammar from which the first example in Ref. 9 was derived. The association of semantics with syntactic recognition is directly illustrated.

9. FLOYD, R. W. Syntactic analysis and operator precedence. *J. ACM 10*, 3 (July 1963), 316–333.

   Defines the notions of operator grammars, precedence grammars (here called "operator precedence grammars"), precedence functions, and a number of other concepts. Examples of precedence grammars and nonprecedence grammars.

10. FLOYD, R. W. Bounded context syntactic analysis. *Comm. ACM 7*, 2 (Feb. 1964), 62–67. CR-6454-6074.

    Introduces the basic concepts of bounded context grammars and gives a set of conditions for testing whether a given grammar is of bounded context (m, n).

11. FLOYD, R. W. The syntax of programming languages—a survey. *IEEE Trans. EC-13*, 4 (Aug. 1964), 346–353.

    An expository paper which defines and explains such concepts as phrase-structure grammars, context-free languages, and syntax-directed analysis. Extensive bibliography.

12. GINSBURG, S. *The Mathematical Theory of Context-Free Languages*. McGraw-Hill, New York, 1966, 232 pp. CR-6783-12,074.

    Presents a rigorous discussion of the theory of context-free languages and pushdown automata.

13. GREIBACH, S. A. A new normal-form theorem for context-free phrase structure grammars. *J. ACM 12*, 1 (Jan. 1965), 42–52. CR-6564-7830.

    Shows that every grammar is equivalent with preservation of ambiguities to a grammar in the "Greibach Normal Form."

14. GRIFFITHS, T. V., AND PETRICK, S. R. On the relative efficiencies of context-free grammar recognizers. *Comm. ACM 8*, 5 (May 1965), 289–300. CR-6564-7999.

A comparative discussion of a number of syntactic analysis algorithms.

15. IEEE Computer Group, Switching and Automata Theory Committee. Conf. Rec. 1967 8th Ann. Symposium on Switching and Automata Theory. Special Publication 16 C 56, Institute of Electrical and Electronic Engineers, New York, 1967.

Contains a number of papers relevant to this course including those by: Rosenkrantz, pp. 14–20; Aho, pp. 21–31; Hopcroft and Ullman, pp. 37–44; Ginsburg and Greibach, pp. 128–139.

16. Irons, E. T. A syntax directed compiler for ALGOL 60. *Comm. ACM 4*, 1 (Jan. 1961), 51–55.

The first paper on syntactic compilation. It discusses both a top-down implementation of a syntactic compiler and the way in which semantics is associated with the generation steps of such a compiler.

17. Irons, E. T. Structural connections in formal languages. *Comm. ACM 7*, 2 (Feb. 1964), 67–72. CR-6455-6212.

The concept of structural connectedness defined is essentially the same as that of a bounded context grammar.

18. Knuth, D. E. On the translation of languages from left to right. *Inf. Contr. 8*, 6 (Dec. 1965), 607–639. CR-6674-10,162.

The concept of a grammar which permits translation from left to right with forward context k (LR(k) grammar) is developed and analyzed.

19. McClure, R. M. TMG—a syntax directed compiler. Proc. ACM 20th Nat. Conf., 1965, pp. 262–274.

A description of a compiler in which the syntax is specified by an ordered sequence of labeled productions and in which semantics can be explicitly associated with productions.

20. Naur, P. (Ed.) Revised report on the algorithmic language, ALGOL 60. *Comm. ACM 6*, 1 (Jan. 1963), 1–17. CR-6345-4540.

The first systematic application of context-free languages to the description of actual programming languages.

21. Reynolds, J. C. An introduction to the COGENT programming system. Proc. ACM 20th Nat. Conf., 1965, pp. 422–436.

Describes the structure and major facilities of a compiler-compiler system which couples the notion of syntax-directed compiling with that of recursive list processing.

22. Wirth, N., and Weber, H. EULER: a generalization of ALGOL, and its formal definition, Parts I & II. *Comm. ACM 9*, 1 (Jan. 1966), 13–23, and 2 (Feb. 1966), 89–99.

The first discussion of pure precedence grammars and their use in Algol-like languages. Many of the concepts introduced by other authors are discussed in an illuminating way.

Course A2. Advanced Computer Organization (3-0-3)

APPROACH

This title could label either a course in the organization of advanced computers or an advanced course in computer organization. It is meant to be primarily the latter, with some material on novel computer organizations included. The approach is that of "comparative anatomy": first, each of several organization and system design problems should be identified; then, a comparison of the solutions to the problem should be made for several different computers; next, the rationale of each solution should be discussed; and finally, an attempt should be made to identify the best solution. Students should prepare papers on designs used in other machines for several of the problem areas. These papers should include discussions of the circuit technology available at the time the machine was designed and the intended market for the machine, and they should compare the machine design with other designs.

CONTENT

The computer system design problem areas which should be covered in this course are listed below followed by a list of some of the machines which might be used to illustrate various solutions to these problems. Each major problem area should be discussed in general and at least three actual machine designs should be used to illustrate the widest possible range of solutions. A brief overall system description of each machine should be given before it is used to illustrate a particular design area.

Computer System Design Problem Areas

1. *Arithmetic Processing.* Integer and floating point representation, round-off and truncation, word and register lengths. Number and types of arithmetic units, malfunction detection and reaction, arithmetic abort detection, and reaction (overflow, etc.).

2. *Nonarithmetic Processing.* Addressable quanta and operation codes. Compatibility and interaction of nonarithmetic and arithmetic operands. Types of additional processing units.

3. *Memory Utilization.* Relationship between memory width and addressable quanta, memory block autonomy and phasing, memory access priorities (operands, instructions, input-output, etc.). Factoring of command-fetch processes (look-ahead).

4. *Storage Management.* Relocation, paging, and renaming. Storage protection. Hierarchy storage provisions and transfer mechanisms.

5. *Addressing.* Absolute addressing, indexing, indirect addressing, relative addressing, and base addressing.

6. *Control.* Clocking, interrupt processing, privileged mode operations, and autonomy of control functions.

7. *Input-Output.* Buffer facilities, channels (autonomy, interaction, interrupts), processing options (editing, formatting), input-output byte size versus memory width versus addressing quanta. Rate-matching (especially for input-output devices with inertia) and channel-sharing.

8. *Special System Designs.* Array or cellular computers, variable structure computers, and other advanced designs.

Illustrative Computers

ATLAS	one of the first machines to use paging
Bendix G-15	a bit serial machine with drum store
Burroughs B5000	a zero-address machine with stacks and Polish processing
CDC 6600	a very high-speed computer using look-ahead, instruction stacking and multiple peripheral processors
GIER (Denmark)	a machine which uses a small core storage with an auxiliary drum
IBM 701	a classic Von Neumann binary machine
IBM 1401	a serial character machine with peculiar addressing
IBM STRETCH	a machine which was intended to incorporate all state-of-the-art knowledge
IBM 360/ij	a series of machines which combine character and word handling capabilities
KDF-9	a computer using a nesting store
PB 440	a microprogrammable computer
SDS Sigma 7	a real-time time-sharing computer
UNIVAC I	a classic decimal machine

ANNOTATED BIBLIOGRAPHY

In addition to the references cited below, it is important that a collection of reference manuals for the actual computers be available to the student. These can be obtained from the computer manufacturers in most cases or from various reports such as the *Auerbach Standard EDP Reports*. In some cases where the title of the citation is self-explanatory, no annotation is given.

General references

1. Amdahl, G. M., Blaauw, G. A., and Brooks, F. P., Jr. Architecture of the IBM System/360. *IBM J. Res. Develop. 8*, 2 (Apr. 1964), 87–101. CR-6465-8374.

Although not a technical paper, it does give some insight into the decisions which determined many of the features of this family of computers.

2. Blaauw, G. A., et al. The structure of System/360. *IBM Syst. J. 3*, 2 (1964), 119–195.

   Describes the design considerations relating to the implementation, performance, and programming of the System/360 family of computers.

3. Boutwell, E. O., Jr., and Hoskinson, E. A. The logical organization of the PB 440 microprogrammable computer. Proc. AFIPS 1963 Fall Joint Comput. Conf., Vol. 24, Spartan Books, New York, pp. 201–213.

   Describes the use of a fast-read, slow-write memory for microprograms. The bus structure connecting the processing registers allows data transfers under control of the microprogram.

4. Buchholz, W. The system design of the IBM 701 computer. *Proc. IRE 41*, 10 (Oct. 1953), 1262–1274.

   Describes one of the first commercial binary computers.

5. Buchholz, W. (Ed.) *Planning A Computer System*. McGraw-Hill, New York, 1962, 336 pp. CR-6346-4786.

   Describes in reasonable detail a design philosophy and its bearing on specific design decisions for an entire computer system—in this case, Stretch.

6. Devonald, C. H., and Fotheringham, J. A. The ATLAS computer. *Datamation 7*, 5 (May 1961), 23–27. CR-6231-1405.

7. Digital Computer Laboratory, University of Illinois. *On the Design of a Very High Speed Computer*. Rep. No. 80, U. of Illinois, Urbana, Ill., 1957.

   A description of the first design for Illiac II.

8. Eckert, J. P., et al. The UNIVAC system. *Rev. of Elec. Dig. Comput.*, Proc. Joint IRE-AIEE Conf., Philadelphia, Pa., 10–12 Dec. 1951, pp. 6–14.

   A description of the Univac I computer.

9. Engineering Summer Conference, University of Michigan. Theory of computing machine design (course notes). U. of Michigan, Ann Arbor, Mich., 1960–1962. (Distribution of these notes was limited to participants.)

   Cover many aspects of design—from the applications of automata theory to the system design of parallel computers.

10. Fernbach, S. Very high-speed computers, 1964—the manufacturers' point of view. Proc. AFIPS 1964 Fall Joint Comput. Conf., Vol. 26, Pt. II, Spartan Books, New York, 1965, pp. 33–141.

    Contains detailed reports on the CDC 6600, the IBM System/360 Model 92, and a Philco multiprocessing system.

11. Gram, C., et al. GIER—a Danish computer of medium size. *IEEE Trans. EC-12*, 6 (Dec. 1963), 629–650.

    Gives an evaluation of the order structure and the hardware organization and describes the operating system and the Algol 60 system.

12. Gray, H. J. *Digital Computer Engineering*. McGraw-Hill, New York, 1963, 381 pp. CR-6341-3654.

    Chap. 1 discusses Eniac and Edvac as examples of parallel and serial organization. Chaps. 2–4 deal with organization problems.

13. Gschwind, H. W. *Design of Digital Computers*. Springer-Verlag, New York, 1967, 530 pp.

    A general reference.

14. Hellerman, H. *Digital Computer System Principles*. McGraw-Hill, New York, 1967, 424 pp.

    A possible text. A good reference.

15. Hollander, G. L. (Ch.) The best approach to large computing capacity—a debate. Proc. AFIPS 1967 Spring Joint Comput. Conf., Vol. 30, Thompson Book Co., Washington, D. C., pp. 463–485.

    Presents four approaches to achieving large computing capacity through: aggregation of conventional system elements (G. P. West); associative parallel processing (R. H. Fuller); an array computer (D. L. Slotnick); and the single-processor approach (G. M. Amdahl).

16. Mendelson, M. J., and England, A. W. The SDS Sigma 7: a real-time time-sharing system. Proc. AFIPS 1966 Fall Joint Comput. Conf., Vol. 29, Spartan Books, New York, pp. 51–64. CR-6700-0752.

    Discusses seven critical design problems—including interrupt processing, memory protection, space sharing, and recursive processing—and their solutions.

17. Richards, R. K. *Electronic Digital Systems*. Wiley, New York, 1966, 637 pp. CR-6676-10,649.

    Contains a good discussion of reliability and design automation.

18. Walz, R. F. Digital computers—general purpose and DDA. *Instrum. and Automat. 28*, 9 (Sept. 1955), 1516–1522.

    Describes the G-15 computer and the use of a digital differential analyzer (DDA) in general purpose digital systems.

19. Ware, W. H. *Digital Computer Technology and Design: Vol. I, Mathematical Topics, Principles of Operation and Programming; Vol. II, Circuits and Machine Design*. Wiley, New York, 1963, 237 pp. and 521 pp. CR-6562-7103 and 7104.

    Useful because of its coverage of early design techniques. Contains extensive bibliographies (at the end of each chapter), which refer to papers presenting the design features of numerous machines.

References on arithmetic and control

20. Blaauw, G. A. Indexing and control-word techniques. *IBM J. Res. Develop. 3*, 3 (July 1959), 288–301.

    Describes some of the control techniques used in the Stretch computer.

21. Beckman, F. S., Brooks, F. P., Jr., and Lawless, W. J., Jr. Developments in the logical organization of computer arithmetic and control units. *Proc. IRE 49*, 1 (Jan. 1961), 53–66. CR-6232-1680.

    Summarizes the developments in logical design and in arithmetic and control units through 1960. Contains a good bibliography.

22. Brooks, F. P., Jr., Blaauw, G. A., and Buchholz, W. Processing data in bits and pieces. *IEEE Trans. EC-8*, 3 (June 1959), 118–124. CR-6012-0035.

    Describes a data-handling unit which permits variable length binary or decimal arithmetic.

23. Sumner, F. H. The central control unit of the ATLAS computer. Proc. IFIP Congress, Munich, 1962, North-Holland Pub. Co., Amsterdam, pp. 292–296. CR-6342-3961.

References on storage management

24. Arden, B. W., Galler, B. A., O'Brien, T. C., and Westervelt, F. H. Program and addressing structure in a time-sharing environment. *J. ACM 13*, 1 (Jan. 1966), 1–16. CR-6781-11,210.

    Describes the hardware and software devices used to facilitate program switching and efficient use of storage in a time-sharing computer system.

25. Belady, L. A. A study of replacement algorithms for a virtual memory computer. *IBM Syst. J. 5*, 2 (1966), 78–101.

    Discusses several algorithms for automatic memory allocation and compares them using the results of several simulation runs.

26. Cocke, J., and Kolsky, H. G. The virtual memory in the STRETCH computer. Proc. AFIPS 1959 Eastern Joint Comput. Conf., Vol. 16, Spartan Books, New York, pp. 82–93.

27. Evans, D. C., and Leclerk, J. Y. Address mapping and the control of access in an interactive computer. Proc. AFIPS 1967 Spring Joint Comput. Conf., Vol. 30, Thompson Book Co., Washington, D. C., pp. 23–30.

    Describes the hardware implementation of a design based on separate program and data entities.

28. Gibson, D. H. Considerations in block-oriented systems design. Proc. AFIPS 1967 Spring Joint Comput. Conf., Vol. 30, Thompson Book Co., Washington, D. C., pp. 75–80.

    Analyzes block size, high-speed storage requirements, and job mix as they affect system design.

Reference on stack computers

29. ALLMARK, R. H., AND LUCKING, J. R. Design of an arithmetic unit incorporating a nesting store. Proc. IFIP Congress, Munich, 1962, North-Holland Pub. Co., Amsterdam, pp. 694–698. CR-6455-6460.

    Describes the arithmetic unit for the KDF-9 computer.

30. HALEY, A. C. D. The KDF-9 computer system. Proc. AFIPS 1962 Fall Joint Comput. Conf., Vol. 22, Spartan Books, New York, pp. 108–120. CR-6452-5466.

    Describes the stack register concept, the means used to communicate with it, and the use of zero-address instructions of variable length.

31. BARTON, R. S. A new approach to the functional design of a digital computer. Proc. AFIPS 1961 Western Joint Comput. Conf., Vol. 19, Spartan Books, New York, pp. 393–396. CR-6234-2158.

    The earliest published description of a Polish string processor—the B5000.

Parallel and variable structure organizations

32. ESTRIN, G. Organization of computer systems: the fixed plus variable structure computer. Proc. AFIPS 1960 Western Joint Comput. Conf., Vol. 17, Spartan Books, New York, pp. 33–40. CR-6235-2643.

33. ESTRIN, G., AND VISWANATHAN, C. R. Organization of a fixed plus variable structure computer for computation of eigenvalues and eigenvectors of real symmetric matrices. *J. ACM 9*, 1 (Jan. 1962), 41–60.

34. ESTRIN, G., AND TURN, R. Automatic assignment of computations in a variable structure computer system. *IEEE Trans. EC-12*, 6 (Dec. 1963), 755–773.

35. GREGORY, J., AND MCREYNOLDS, R. The SOLOMON computer. *IEEE Trans. EC-12*, 6 (Dec. 1963), 774–781.

    Presents the system organization, functional description, and circuit design from a total systems viewpoint.

36. HOLLAND, J. H. A universal computer capable of executing an arbitrary number of subprograms simultaneously. Proc. AFIPS 1959 Eastern Joint Comput. Conf., Vol. 16, Spartan Books, New York, pp. 108–113.

37. HOLLAND, J. H. Iterative circuit computers. Proc. AFIPS 1960 Western Joint Comput. Conf., Vol. 17, Spartan Books, New York, pp. 259–265.

38. SLOTNICK, D. L., BORCK, W. C., AND MCREYNOLDS, R. C. The SOLOMON computer. Proc. AFIPS 1962 Fall Joint Comput. Conf., Vol. 22, Spartan Books, New York, pp. 97–107.

    A general description of the philosophy and organization of a highly parallel computer design which is a predecessor of ILLIAC IV.

39. SCHWARTZ, J. Large parallel computers. *J. ACM 13*, 1 (Jan. 1966), 25–32.

    Considers various classes of machines incorporating parallelism, outlines a general class of large-scale multiprocessors, and discusses the problems of hardware and software implementation.

Course A3. Analog and Hybrid Computing (2-2-3)

APPROACH

This course is concerned with analog, hybrid, and related digital techniques for solving systems of ordinary and partial differential equations, both linear and nonlinear. A portion of the course should be devoted to digital languages for the simulation of continuous or hybrid systems (MIDAS, PACTOLUS, DSL/90, etc.). The course will have both lecture and laboratory sessions. The laboratory will allow the students to solve some problems on analog and/or hybrid computers and other problems through digital simulation of analog or hybrid computers. (Digital simulators of analog computers are now available for digital machines of almost any size [13-22]. Some simulators are written in problem oriented languages such as FORTRAN and may be adapted to almost any computer.)

CONTENT

1. *Basic Analog Components.* Addition, multiplication by a constant, integration, function generation, multiplication, division, square roots, noise generation, and other operations. Laboratory assignments are used to familiarize the student with the operation of the components. (15%)
2. *Solution of Differential Equations.* The block-oriented approach to the solution of linear, nonlinear, and partial differential equations. Magnitude and time scaling. Estimation of maximum values. Equations with forcing functions and variable coefficients. Simultaneous equations. Statistical problems. (20%)
3. *Analog Computer Hardware.* Description of various analog computers. Amplifiers, potentiometers, and other linear and nonlinear components. The patch board and the control panel. Recording and display equipment. Slow and repetitive operation. Several laboratory assignments to give the student "hands-on" experience with the available machines. (15%)
4. *Hybrid Computer Systems.* Different types of hybrid systems. Patchable logic and mode control. Comparators, switches, and different types of analog memories. Control of initial conditions or parameters. (15%)
5. *Analog and Digital Conversion.* Brief treatment of analog-to-digital and digital-to-analog conversion. Methods of conversion, sampling, interpolation, smoothing. Accuracy and speed considerations. Multiplexing of analog-to-digital converters. (10%)
6. *Digital Simulation of Analog and Hybrid Systems.* Comparison of available languages. (One language should be presented in detail. The students should compare some of the previous analog solutions to those obtained by simulation.) (20%)
7. *Exams.* (5%)

ANNOTATED BIBLIOGRAPHY

In the citations which follow, applicable chapters are sometimes indicated in parentheses after the annotation.

General textbooks or references for the major part of the course

1. ASHLEY, J. R., *Introduction to Analog Computation.* Wiley, New York, 1963, 294 pp.

    A compact textbook which stresses the use rather than the design aspects of analog computing. The text could be used for an undergraduate course, but hybrid computers would have to be covered from separate sources. (All chapters)

2. CARLSON, A., HANNAUER, G., CAREY, T., AND HOLSBERG, P. In *Handbook of Analog Computation.* Electronics Associates, Inc., Princeton, N. J., 1965.

    Although this manual is oriented to EAI equipment, it is a good basic reference and has an extensive bibliography on selected applications.

3. FIFER, S. *Analog Computation, Volumes I–IV.* McGraw-Hill, New York, 1961, 1,331 pp. CR-6126-1122.

    This series of four volumes contains a complete coverage of analog computers, including hardware and applications. It is a good source of problems and references up to 1961.

4. HUSKEY, H. D., AND KORN, G. A. (Eds.) *Computer Handbook.* McGraw-Hill, New York, 1962, 1,225 pp. CR-6234-2179.

    This comprehensive volume on both analog and digital computers is somewhat hardware-oriented although applications are also included.

5. JACKSON, A. S. *Analog Computation.* McGraw-Hill, New York, 1960, 652 pp. CR-6015-0190.

    Although now somewhat out-of-date, this is an excellent text for serious students in engineering, especially those with an interest in feedback-control theory. The text has many references and an appendix with problem sets. (Chaps. 2–5, 7, 8, 11, 14)

6. JENNESS, R. R. *Analog Computation and Simulation: Laboratory Approach.* Allyn and Bacon, Boston, 1955, 298 pp.

Two parts: the first introduces the analog computer; the second gives the solutions of 21 problems in great detail.

7. JOHNSON, C. L. *Analog Computer Techniques*, 2nd ed. McGraw-Hill, New York, 1963, 336 pp. CR-6451-5162.

The text assumes a knowledge of basic electrical and mathematical principles. Some parts require an understanding of servo-mechanism theory and the Laplace transform. Each chapter has references and problems. (Chaps. 1–3, 7, 10, 12)

8. KARPLUS, W. J. *Analog Simulation, Solution of Field Problems.* McGraw-Hill, New York, 1958, 434 pp. CR-6123-0729.

A reference on analog techniques for partial differential equations. Includes material on the mathematical background for analog study of field problems, a description of analog hardware, and a mathematical discussion of applications of analog techniques to different classes of differential equations. Problem-oriented. Extensive bibliographies.

9. KARPLUS, W. J., AND SOROKA, W. J. *Analog Methods*, 2nd ed. McGraw-Hill, New York, 1959, 496 pp.

Three parts: on indirect computing elements; on indirect computers; and on direct computers. Describes both electromechanical and electronic computers and covers applications comprehensively.

10. KORN, G. A., AND KORN, T. M. *Electronic Analog and Hybrid Computers.* McGraw-Hill, New York, 1963, 584 pp. CR-6562-7468.

This text covers the theory, design, and application of analog and hybrid computers and has one of the most complete bibliographies available. Its compactness makes it more suitable for an undergraduate text.

11. LEVINE, L. *Methods for Solving Engineering Problems Using Analog Computers.* McGraw-Hill, New York, 1964, 485 pp. CR-6455-6477.

One of the best available texts, but it needs supplementing on equipment. (Ref. 2 might be good for this purpose.) In addition to the usual topics, there are chapters on optimization techniques, estimation and testing of hypotheses, and applications in statistics. (Chaps. 1–7).

12. SMITH, G. W., AND WOOD, R. C. *Principles of Analog Computation.* McGraw-Hill, New York, 1959, 234 pp. CR-6121-0411.

Introduces analog computers and illustrates various programming techniques in simulation and computation.

Descriptions of digital simulators of continuous systems

13. BRENNAN, R. D., AND SANO, H. PACTOLUS—a digital analog simulator program for the IBM 1620. Proc. AFIPS 1964 Fall Joint Comput. Conf., Vol. 26, Spartan Books, New York, pp. 299–312. CR-6563-7630.

Well-written article describes a digital program for the simulation of an analog computer. The program is written in FORTRAN and may be adapted to most machines. It allows man-machine interaction.

14. FARRIS, G. J., AND BURKHART, L. E., The DIAN digital simulation program. *Simulation 6*, 5 (May 1966), 298–304.

Describes a digital computer program which has some of the features of a digital differential analyzer and which is particularly suitable for the solution of boundary value problems.

15. HARNETT, R. T., AND SANSOM, F. J. *MIDAS Programming Guide.* Report No. SEG-TDR-64-1, Analog Comput. Divn., Syst. Engng. Group, Res. and Techn. Divn., US Air Force Systems Command, Wright-Patterson Air Force Base, Ohio, Jan. 1964. CR-6672-9510.

This is the programming manual for the MIDAS simulation language. It is well-written and contains four examples complete with problem descriptions, block diagrams, coding sheets, and computed results.

16. JANOSKI, R. M., SCHAEFER, R. L., AND SKILES, J. J. COBLOC—a program for all-digital simulation of a hybrid computer. *IEEE Trans. EC-15*, 2 (Feb. 1966), 74–91.

COBLOC is a compiler which allows all-digital simulation of a hybrid computer having both analog and digital computation capability.

17. MORRIS, S. M., AND SCHIESSER, W. E. Undergraduate use of digital simulation. *Simulation 7*, 2 (Aug. 1966), 100–105. CR-6781-11,027.

Describes the LEANS (Lehigh Analog Simulator) program and shows the solution of a sample problem.

18. RIDEOUT, V. C., AND TAVERNINI, L. MADBLOC, a program for digital simulation of a hybrid computer. *Simulation 4*, 1 (Jan. 1965), 20–24.

Gives a brief description of the hybrid simulation language MADBLOC (one of the Wisconsin "BLOC" programs) which is written in the MAD language. Parameter optimization of a simple feedback system is given as an example.

19. STEIN, M. L., ROSE, J., AND PARKER, D. B. A compiler with an analog oriented input language. *Simulation 4*, 3 (Mar. 1965), 158–171.

Gives a description of a compiler program called "ASTRAL" which accepts analog oriented statements and produces FORTRAN statements. It is a reprint of the same paper from the Proc. of 1959 Western Joint Comput. Conf.

20. SYN, W. M., AND LINEBARGER, R. M. DSL /90—a digital simulation program for continuous system modeling. Proc. AFIPS 1966 Spring Joint Comput. Conf., Vol. 28, Spartan Books, New York, pp. 165–187. CR-6676-10,708.

A program which accepts block-oriented statements and compiles them into FORTRAN IV statements. Mixing of DSL /90 and FORTRAN statements is allowed. The program is available for the IBM 7090 /94 and 7040 /44.

Comparisons of digital simulators for continuous systems

21. LINEBARGER, R. N., AND BRENNAN, R. D. A survey of digital simulation: digital analog simulator programs. *Simulation 3*, 6 (Dec. 1964), 22–36. CR-6671-9009.

Gives a brief account of the following digital-analog simulation languages: SELFRIDE, DEPI, ASTRAL, DEPI4, DYSAC, PARTNER, DAS, JANIS, MIDAS, and PACTOLUS

22. LINEBARGER, R. N., AND BRENNAN, R. D. Digital simulation for control system design. *Instr. Contr. Syst. 38*, 10 (Oct. 1965), 147–152. CR-6675-10,425.

This paper has a very complete bibliography of digital simulators and a table classifying them.

Course A4. System Simulation (3-0-3)

APPROACH

This course can be taught from several different points of view: simulation can be treated as a tool of applied mathematics; it can be treated as a tool for optimization in operations research; or it can be treated as an example of the application of computer science techniques. Which orientation is used and the extent to which computer programs are an integral part of the course should depend upon the interests of the instructor and the students. Most instructors will find it useful to require several small programs and a term project. The availability of a simulation language for student use is desirable.

CONTENT

The numbers in square brackets refer to the items listed in the bibliography which follows.

1. *What is simulation?* (5%) [1, 2, 3]
   a. Statistical sampling experiment. [20]
   b. Comparison of simulation and other techniques. [7]
   c. Comparison of discrete, continuous, and hybrid simulation. [12, 21]
2. *Discrete Change Models.* (20%)
   a. Queueing models. [13]
   b. Simulation models. [1, 2, 3]

3. *Simulation languages.* (20%) [16, 21, 22]
4. *Simulation Methodology.* (20%) [1, 2, 3]
   a. Generation of random numbers and random variates. [14]
   b. Design of experiments and optimization. [6, 8, 9, 17]
   c. Analysis of data generated by simulation experiments. [10, 11, 15]
   d. Validation of models and results. [8, 19]
5. *Selected Applications of Simulation.* (10%) [4, 5]
   a. Business games.
   b. Operations research. [18]
   c. Artificial intelligence.
6. *Research Problems in Simulation Methodology.* (5%)
7. *Term Project.* (20%)

BIBLIOGRAPHY

Textbooks covering a number of the topics of this course

1. CHORAFAS, D. N. *Systems and Simulation.* Academic Press, New York, 1965, 503 pp.
2. NAYLOR, T. H., BALINTFY, J. L., BURDICK, D. S., AND CHU, K. *Computer Simulation Techniques.* Wiley, New York, 1966, 352 pp. CR-6781-11,103.
3. TOCHER, K. D. *The Art of Simulation.* D. Van Nostrand, Princeton, N. J., 1963, 184 pp. CR-6454-6091.

Bibliographies devoted to simulation

4. IBM Corporation. *Bibliography on Simulation.* Report 320-0924-0, 1966.
5. SHUBIK, M. Bibliography on simulation, gaming, artificial intelligence, and allied topics. *J. Amer. Statist. Assoc. 55,* 292 (Dec. 1960), 736–751. CR-6122-0581.

Other works on simulation (which also contain extensive bibliographies)

6. BURDICK, D. S., AND NAYLOR, T. Design of computer simulation experiments for industrial systems. *Comm. ACM 9,* 5 (May 1966), 329–338. CR-6783-11,714.
7. CONNORS, M. M., AND TEICHROEW, D. *Optimal Control of Dynamic Operations Research Models.* International Textbook Co., Scranton, Pa., 1967, 118 pp.
8. CONWAY, R. W. Some tactical problems in digital simulation. *Management 10,* 1 (Oct. 1963), 47–61.
9. EHRENFELD, S., AND BEN-TUVIA, S. The efficiency of statistical simulation procedures. *Technometrics 4,* 2 (May 1962), 257–276. CR-6341-3742.
10. FISHMAN, G. S. Problems in the statistical analysis of simulation experiments: The comparison of means and the length of sample records. *Comm. ACM 10,* 2 (Feb. 1967), 94–99. CR-6783-12,103.
11. FISHMAN, G. S., AND KIVIAT, P. J. The analysis of simulation-generated time series. *Mgmt. Sci. 13,* 7 (Mar. 1967), 525–557.
12. FORRESTER, J. W. *Industrial Dynamics.* M.I.T. Press, Cambridge, Mass., and Wiley, New York, 1961, 464 pp.
13. GALLIHER, H. Simulation of random processes. In *Notes on Operations Research,* Operations Research Center, M.I.T., Cambridge, Mass., 1959, pp. 231–250.
14. HULL, T. E., AND DOBELL, A. R. Random number generators. *SIAM Rev. 4,* 3 (July 1962), 230–254. CR-6341-3749.
15. JACOBY, J. E., AND HARRISON, S. Multivariable experimentation and simulation models. *Naval Res. Log. Quart. 9,* (1962), 121–136.
16. KRASNOW, H. S., AND MERIKALLIO, R. The past, present and future of general simulation languages. *Mgmt. Sci. 11,* 2 (Nov. 1964), 236–267. CR-6566-8521.
17. MCARTHUR, D. S. Strategy in research—alternative methods for design of experiments. *IRE Trans. Eng. Man. EM-8,* 1 (Jan. 1961), 34–40.
18. MORGENTHALER, G. W. The theory and application of simulation in operations research. In Russel L. Ackoff (Ed.), *Progress in Operations Research,* Wiley, New York, 1961, pp. 363–419.
19. SCHENK, H., JR. Computing "AD ABSURDUM." *The Nation 196,* 12 (June 15, 1963), 505–507.
20. TEICHROEW, D. A history of distribution sampling prior to the era of the computer and its relevance to simulation. *J. Amer. Statist. Assoc. 60,* 309 (Mar. 1965), 27–49. CR-6673-9823.
21. TEICHROEW, D. Computer simulation—discussion of the technique and comparison of languages. *Comm. ACM 9,* 10 (Oct. 1966), 723–741. CR-6782-11,466.
22. TOCHER, K. D. Review of simulation languages. *Oper. Res. Quart. 15,* 2 (June 1965), 189–218.

Course A5. Information Organization and Retrieval (3-0-3)

APPROACH

This course is designed to introduce the student to information organization and retrieval of natural language data. Emphasis should be given to the development of computer techniques rather than philosophical discussions of the nature of information. The applicability of the techniques developed for both data and document systems should be stressed. The student should become familiar not only with the techniques of statistical, syntactic and logical analysis of natural language for retrieval, but also with the extent of success or failure of these techniques. The manner in which the techniques may be combined into a system for use in an operational environment should be explored. In the event that a computer is available together with natural language text in a computer-readable form, programming exercises applying some of the techniques should be assigned. If this is not possible, the student should present a critique and in-depth analysis of an article selected by the instructor.

CONTENT

1. *Information Structures.* Graph theory, document and term-document graphs, semantic road maps, trees and lists, thesaurus and hierarchy construction, and multilists.

2. *Dictionary Systems.* Thesaurus look-up, hierarchy expansion, and phrase dictionaries.

3. *Statistical Systems.* Frequency counts, term and document associations, clustering procedures, and automatic classification.

4. *Syntactic Systems.* Language structure, automatic syntactic analysis, graph matching, and automatic tree matching.

5. *Vector Matching and Search Strategies.* Keyword matching, direct and inverted files, combined file systems, correlation functions, vector merging and matching, matching of cluster vectors, and user feedback systems.

6. *Input Specifications and System Organization.* Input options. Supervisory systems, their general organization, and operating procedures.

7. *Output Systems.* Citation indexing and bibliographic coupling. Secondary outputs including concordances, abstracts, and indexes. Selective dissemination. Catalog systems.

8. *Evaluation.* Evaluation environment, recall and precision, presentation of results, and output comparison.

9. *Automatic Question Answering.* Structure and extension of data bases, deductive systems, and construction of answer statements.

ANNOTATED BIBLIOGRAPHY

There is no one book currently available that could be used as a text for this course, so most of the material must be obtained from the literature. References 2 and 6 provide excellent state-of-the-art surveys and guides to the literature.

1. BECKER, J., AND HAYES, R. M. *Introduction to Information Storage and Retrieval: Tools, Elements, Theories.* Wiley, New York, 1963, 448 pp.

   A standard textbook, perhaps the best of those presently available.

2. CUADRA, C. (Ed.) *Annual Review of Information Science and Technology*. Interscience, New York, Vol. 1, 1966 and Vol. 2, 1967.

A survey and review publication.

3. HAYS, D. G. (Ed.) *Readings in Automatic Language Processing*. American Elsevier, New York, 1966.

Includes examples of text processing applications.

4. SALTON, G. Progress in automatic information retrieval. *IEEE Spectrum 2*, 8 (Aug. 1965), 90–103. CR-6675-10,409.

A survey of current capabilities in text processing.

5. SALTON, G. *Automatic Information Organization and Retrieval.* McGraw-Hill, New York, to be published in 1968.

A text concentrating on automatic computer-based information retrieval systems.

6. STEVENS, M. E. *Automatic Indexing: A State-of-the-Art Report*. Monograph 91, National Bureau of Standards, US Dept. of Commerce, Washington, D.C., March 30, 1965.

A survey article that covers the historical development of automatic indexing systems through 1964.

7. STEVENS, M. E., GIULIANO, V. E., AND HEILPRIN, L. B. (Eds.) *Statistical Association Methods for Mechanized Documentation*—Symposium Proceedings. Miscellaneous Publication 269, US Dept. of Commerce, Washington, D. C., 1964.

A collection of papers concerned with statistical association techniques.

Course A6. Computer Graphics (2-2-3)

APPROACH

Since this field is basically only a few years old, it is not surprising that no underlying theories are uniformly accepted by the researchers and implementers. Rather, the pertinent information exists as a number of loosely related project descriptions in conference proceedings and professional journals. This situation is similar to that in the information retrieval field, where those conducting courses at a number of major universities report on current accomplishments and research in an effort to coordinate and structure the mass of available information and to teach those techniques which have been found useful. Thus, for the present, this course probably should be taught as a seminar where the literature is read and perhaps reported by selected students. After some texts become available and after more experience has been gained, a more formal course atmosphere could be established.

Although the literature is plentiful, this course clearly assumes substantial value to the student only when it includes an intensive laboratory (hopefully using a display console) where the various algorithms can be tested, compared, and extended. The laboratory periods are meant to be used for explaining the details of algorithms or hardware and software that are not appropriate to a more formal lecture. A variety of programming projects in pattern recognition or display programming, for example, are within the scope of a one-semester course. The time spent on these projects would be in addition to the laboratory time.

CONTENT

The thread running through the topics listed below is the unit of information—the picture. The course should deal with common ways in which the picture is handled in a variety of hitherto largely unrelated disciplines. First hardware and then software topics should be considered, since the software today is still a function of present hardware.

The order and depth of coverage of the material suggested below is quite flexible—another sensible order of the material might be topics 1, 2, 6, 7, 8, and 3, 4, 5 optional, which would then constitute a course in displays. (In any case some material in Sections 6 and 7 would have to be covered briefly to prepare students for their projects.) Also an entire semester could be devoted to pattern recognition.

1. Motivation for graphical data processing and its history, particularly that of displays. (5%)

2. Brief introduction to psycho-physical photometry and display-parameters such as resolution and brightness. Block diagram of display systems and delineation of the functions of their components: the computer subsystem; buffer or shared memory; command decoder; display generator; and producer(s) of points, lines, vectors, conic sections, and characters. Extended capabilities such as subroutining, windowing, hardware matrix operations, and buffer manipulation. Comparison of various types of CRTs with other display producing techniques such as photochromics and electroluminescence. Brief discussion of passive graphics (output only) devices such as x-y plotters, and microfilm recorders. Interrupts, manual inputs and human interaction with active displays via light pens, voltage pens, function keys, tablets, wands, joy sticks, etc. Demonstration of equipment. (10%)

3. Contrast of information retrieval with document retrieval and definition of indexing and locating. Image recording parameters such as resolution, and their comparison with display parameters. Demonstration or discussion of microfilm and microfilm handling devices (manual and automated). Brief discussion of photochromics, thermoplastics and other nonconventional media. Brief discussion of electro-optical techniques for recording, modulating, and deflecting. (5%)

4. Scanning and digitizing of paper or film, and subsequent transmission of digitized information, including band-width /cost tradeoffs. Brief review of digital storage techniques and parameters, and discussion of tradeoffs in bulk digital versus image storage for pictorial and digital data. Introduction of the notion of a combination of a digital and an image system. (5%)

5. Digitizing as an input process for pattern description and recognition and preprocessing of this input (cosmetology and normalization). Contrast of symbol manipulative, linguistic, and mathematical techniques, such as gestalt, caricatures, features, moments, random nets, decision functions, syntax-directed techniques and real-time tracking techniques using scopes and tablets. Electro-optical techniques such as optical Fourier transforms may also be covered briefly. (20%)

6. Picture models and data structures. Geometry, topology, syntax, and semantics of pictures, stressing picture /subpicture hierarchy. The differences between block diagram, wire frame, and surface representations. Use of tables, trees, lists, plexes, rings, associative memory, and hashing schemes for data structures, and the data structure (or list processing) languages which create and manipulate them. Mathematics of constraint satisfaction, windowing, three-dimensional transformations and projections, and hidden-line problems. (25%)

7. Display software (probably specific to a given installation). Creation and maintenance of the display file, translations between the data structure and the display file, interrupt handling, pen pointing and tracking, and correlation between light pen detects and the data structure. Use of macros or compiler level software for standard functions. Software for multiconsole time-shared graphics with real-time interaction. (20%)

8. Selected applications: (10%)
   a. Menu programming and debugging
   b. Flowchart and block diagram processing
   c. Computer assisted instruction
   d. Computer aided design
   e. Chemical modeling
   f. Business
   g. Animated movies

ANNOTATED BIBLIOGRAPHY

This bibliography is not complete in its coverage and consists primarily of survey articles, as no textbooks exist. A number of the more detailed technical articles in the literature were omitted because they were concerned with specific situations or machines. Most of the survey articles listed have good bibliographies. A selection of topics from the outline above can thus be followed by a selection of appropriate research papers from the literature.

1. FETTER, W. A. *Computer Graphics in Communications*. McGraw-Hill, New York, 1965, 110 pp.

   This volume is strong on engineering applications and illustrations.

2. GRAY, J. C. Compound data structures for computer-aided design: a survey. Proc. ACM 22nd Nat. Conf., 1967, Thompson Book Co., Washington, D. C., pp. 355–366.

   A brief survey and comparison of various types of data structures currently in use.

3. GRUENBERGER, F. (Ed.) *Computer Graphics: Utility /Production /Art*. Thompson Book Co., Washington, D. C., 1967, 225 pp.

   Collection of survey papers, useful for orientation.

4. NARASIMHAN, R. Syntax-directed interpretation of classes of pictures. *Comm. ACM 9*, 3 (Mar. 1966), 166–173.

   An introduction to syntactic descriptive models for pictures, implemented using simulated parallel processing. This linguistic approach is also taken by Kirsch, Grenander, Miller, and others.

5. PARKER, D. B. Solving design problems in graphical dialogue. In W. J. Karplus (Ed.), *On-Line Computing*, McGraw-Hill, 1967, pp. 176–219.

   A software-oriented survey of display console features.

6. ROSS, D. G., AND RODRIGUEZ, J. E. Theoretical foundations for the computer-aided design system. Proc. AFIPS 1963 Spring Joint Comput. Conf., Vol. 23, Spartan Books, New York, pp. 305–322.

   Introduction of the "plex" as a compound list structure for both graphical and nongraphical entities. Outline of the AED philosophy and algorithmic theory of language.

7. SUTHERLAND, I. E. Sketchpad: a man-machine graphical communication system. Lincoln Lab. Tech. Rep. No. 296, M.I.T., Lexington, Mass., 1963, 91 pp.

   Presents the pace-setting Sketchpad system: its capabilities, data structure, and some implementation details.

8. SUTHERLAND, W. R. The on-line graphical specification of computer procedures. Ph.D. Dissertation, M.I.T., Cambridge, Mass., Jan. 1966, and Lincoln Lab. Tech. Rep. No. 405, May 1966.

   Describes a graphical language, executed interpretively, which avoids written labels and symbols by using data connections between procedure elements to determine both program flow and data flow.

9. VAN DAM, A. Bibliography on computer graphics. *ACM SIGGRAPHICS Newsletter 1*, 1 (Apr. 1967), Association for Computing Machinery, New York.

   This extensive bibliography is being kept up-to-date in successive issues of the *Newsletter*.

10. VAN DAM, A. Computer-driven displays and their uses in man/machine interaction. In F. L. Alt (Ed.), *Advances in Computers, Vol. 7*, Academic Press, New York, 1966, pp. 239–290.

    A hardware-oriented description of CRT console functions.

Course A7. Theory of Computability (3-0-3)

APPROACH

This is a theoretical course which should be taught in a formal and precise manner, i.e. definitions, theorems, and proofs. The theory of recursive functions and computability should, however, be carefully motivated and illustrated with appropriate examples.

CONTENT

More material is listed than can easily be covered in a three-hour one-semester course. The first three topics should definitely be covered, but the instructor can select material from the remaining topics.

1. Introduction to Turing machines (TM's) and the invariance of general computability under alterations of the model. Wang machines, Shepherdson-Sturgis machines, machines with only 2 symbols, machines with only 2 states, machines with nonerasing tapes, machines with multiple heads and multidimensional tapes. (4 lectures)

2. Universal Turing machines. (2 lectures)

3. Gödel numbering and unsolvability results, the halting problem, and Post's correspondence problem. (3 lectures)

4. Relative uncomputability, many-one reducibility and Turing reducibility, and the Friedberg-Muchnik theorem. (6 lectures)

5. TM's with restricted memory access, machines with one counter, pushdown automata and their relation to context-free languages. Universality of machines with two counters. (3 lectures)

6. TM's with limited memory, linear bounded automata and their relation to context-sensitive languages, and the Stearns-Hartmanis-Lewis hierarchy. (5 lectures)

7. TM's with limited computing time and the Hartmanis-Stearns time hierarchy. (5 lectures)

8. Models for real-time computation, TM's with many tapes versus 1 or 2 tapes, and TM's with many heads per tape versus 1 head per tape. (4 lectures)

9. Random-access stored-program machines, iterative arrays, general bounded activity machines, n-counter real-time machines, and other computing devices. (8 lectures)

10. Complexity classification by functional definition, primitive recursive functions, the Grzegorczyk hierarchy and its relation to ALGOL programming, real-time countability, and an algorithm for fast multiplication. (6 lectures)

ANNOTATED BIBLIOGRAPHY

1. AANDERAA, S., AND FISCHER, P. C. The solvability of the halting problem for 2-state Post machines. *J. ACM 14*, 4 (Oct. 1967), 677–682.

   A problem unsolvable for quintuple Turing machines is shown to be solvable for the popular quadruple version of Post.

2. CAIANIELLO, E. R. (Ed.) *Automata Theory*. Academic Press, New York, 1966, 342 pp. CR-6676-10,935.

   A collection of research and tutorial papers on automata, formal languages, graph theory, logic, algorithms, recursive function theory, and neural nets. Because of varying interest and difficulty, the papers might be useful for supplementary reading by ambitious students.

3. DAVIS, M. *Computability and Unsolvability*. McGraw-Hill, New York, 1958, 210 pp.

   Contains an introduction to the theory of recursive functions, most of Kleene's and Post's contributions to the field and some more recent work.

4. DAVIS, M. (Ed.) *The Undecidable—Basic Papers on Undecidable Propositions, Unsolvable Problems and Computable Functions*. Raven Press, Hewlett, New York, 1965, 440 pp. CR-6673-9790.

   An anthology of the fundamental papers of Church, Gödel, Kleene, Post, Rosser, and Turing on undecidability and unsolvability.

5. FISCHER, P. C. Multitape and infinite-state automata—a survey. *Comm. ACM 8*, 12 (Dec. 1965), 799–805. CR-6675-10,561.

   A survey of machines which are more powerful than finite automata and less powerful than Turing machines. Extensive bibliography.

6. FISCHER, P. C. On formalisms for Turing machines. *J. ACM 12*, 4 (Oct. 1965), 570–580. CR-6675-10,558.

Variants of one-tape Turing machines are compared and transformations from one formalism to another are analyzed.

7. FRIEDBERG, R. M. Two recursively enumerable sets of incomparable degrees of unsolvability (Solution of Post's Problem, 1944). *Proc. Nat. Acad. Sci. 43*, (1957), 236–238.

The "priority" method for generating recursively enumerable sets is introduced and used to solve this famous problem.

8. GINSBURG, S. *Mathematical Theory of Context-Free Languages*. McGraw-Hill, New York, 1966, 243 pp.

The first textbook on the theory of context-free languages. It gives a detailed mathematical treatment of pushdown automata, ambiguity, and solvability.

9. HARTMANIS, J., AND STEARNS, R. E. On the computational complexity of algorithms. *Trans. AMS 117*, 5 (May 1965), 285–306.

Turing computable sequences are classified in terms of the rate with which a multitape Turing machine can output the terms of the sequence, i.e. the "Hartmanis-Stearns time hierarchy."

10. HERMES, H. *Enumerability, Decidability, Computability*. Academic Press, New York, 1965, 245 pp. CR-6673-9781.

A systematic introduction to the theory of recursive functions, using Turing machines as a base.

11. KLEENE, S. C. *Mathematical Logic*. Wiley, New York, 1967, 398 pp.

A thorough yet elementary treatment of first-order mathematical logic for undergraduates. Contains much of the material of the author's graduate text, *Introduction to Metamathematics*, (D. Van Nostrand, Princeton, N. J., 1952, 550 pp.). The material has been updated and reorganized to be more suitable for the beginning student.

12. MCNAUGHTON, R. The theory of automata, a survey. In F. L. Alt (Ed.), *Advances in Computers, Vol. 2*. Academic Press, New York, 1961, pp. 379–421. CR-6342-3920.

Most of the areas of automata theory are included with the exception of switching theory and other engineering topics. A list of 119 references.

13. MINSKY, M. L. *Computation: Finite and Infinite Machines*. Prentice-Hall, Englewood Cliffs, N. J., 1967, 317 pp.

The concept of an "effective procedure" is developed. Also treats algorithms, Post productions, regular expressions, computability, infinite and finite-state models of digital computers, and computer languages.

14. MYHILL, J. Linear bounded automata. *WADD Tech. Note 60-165*. Wright-Patterson Air Force Base, Ohio, 1960.

The paper which first defined a new class of automata whose power lies between those of finite automata and Turing machines.

15. POST, E. L. Recursive unsolvability of a problem of Thue. *J. Symbol. Logic 11*, (1947), 1–11.

Contains results on one variant of the "word problem" for semigroups using Turing machine methods.

16. ROGERS, H., JR. *Theory of Recursive Functions and Effective Computability*. McGraw-Hill, New York, 1967, 482 pp.

A current and comprehensive account of recursive function theory. Proceeds in an intuitive semiformal manner, beginning with the recursively enumerable sets and ending with the analytical hierarchy.

17. SHANNON, C. E., AND MCCARTHY, J. (Eds.) *Automata Studies*. Princeton University Press, Princeton, N. J., 1956, 285 pp. CR-6565-8330.

A collection of many of the early papers on finite automata, Turing machines, and synthesis of automata which stimulated the development of automata theory. Philosophical papers, in addition to mathematical papers, are included since the aim of the collection is to help explain the workings of the human mind.

18. SHEPHERDSON, J. C., AND STURGIS, H. E. Computability of recursive functions. *J. ACM 10*, 2 (Apr. 1963), 217–255. CR-6451-5105.

A class of machines which is adequate to compute all partial recursive functions is obtained by relaxing the definition of a Turing machine. Such machines can be easily designed to carry out some specific intuitively effective procedure.

19. STEARNS, R. E., HARTMANIS, J., AND LEWIS, P. M. Hierarchies of memory limited computations. *1965 IEEE Conference Record on Switching Circuit Theory and Logic Design*, Special Publication 16 C 13, Institute of Electrical and Electronic Engineers, New York, Oct. 1965, pp. 179–190.

Turing computable functions are classified according to the relationship of the amount of storage required for a computation to the length of the input to the computation, i.e. the "Stearns-Hartmanis-Lewis hierarchy."

20. TRAKHTENBROT, B. A. *Algorithms and Automatic Computing Machines*, transl. by J. Kristian, J. D. McCawley, and S. A. Schmitt. D. C. Heath, Boston, 1963, 101 pp.

A translation and adaptation from the second Russian edition (1960) of the author's elementary booklet on solvability and Turing machines.

21. TURING, A. M. On computable numbers, with an application to the Entscheidungsproblem. *Proc. London Math. Soc., Ser. 2, 42*, (1936–1937), pp. 230–265.

The famous memoir on decision problems which initiated the theory of automata.

22. VON NEUMANN, J. *Theory of Self-Reproducing Automata*. (Edited and completed by A. W. Burks.) University of Illinois Press, Urbana, Illinois, 1966, 388 pp. CR-6700-0670.

Consists of all previously unpublished sections of Von Neumann's general theory of automata. Part I includes the kinematic model of self-reproduction. Part II, which is much longer, treats the logical design of a self-reproducing cellular automaton.

23. WANG, H. A variant to Turing's theory of computing machines. *J. ACM 4*, 1 (Jan. 1957), 61–92.

An abstract machine is defined which is capable of carrying out any computation and which uses only four basic types of instructions in its programs.

Course A8. Large-scale Information Processing Systems (3-0-3)

APPROACH

This course is intended to give the student some appreciation of how computers fit into information systems and how information systems fit into a "large organization framework." As this field is evolving rapidly, the most interesting and relevant material appears in articles; moreover, the field is so large that not all the relevant material can be covered. The course may be conducted as a lecture course, but assignment of individual readings in a seminar-type situation might be more suitable.

Many information processing systems are so large that they require a number of computer programs to be run on a continuing basis using large quantities of stored data. The process of establishing such a large system involves a number of steps: (1) the determination of the processing requirements; (2) the statement of those requirements in a complete and unambiguous form suitable for the next steps; (3) the design of the system, i.e. the specification of computer programs, hardware devices, and procedures which together can "best" accomplish the required processing; (4) the construction of the programs and procedures, and the acquisition of the hardware devices; and (5) the testing and operation of the assembled components in an integrated system. This course is designed to help prepare the student to participate in the development of such systems.

CONTENT

The numbers in square brackets after each topic listed below refer to the items listed in the bibliography which follows.

1. Examples of large-scale information systems. (10%) [12, 28, 30]

a. Computer centers. [20, 27, 34]
b. Information retrieval. [2]
c. Real-time and time-sharing. [15, 16, 33]
d. Business data processing. [14, 18, 19, 31, 32]

2. Data structures and file management systems. (20%) [1, 4, 5, 9, 10, 13, 17, 29, 38]
3. Systems design methodology. (40%) [22, 32]
   a. "Nonprocedural" languages. [8, 26, 38, 40]
   b. Systems design. [3, 11, 21, 23, 24, 25, 36, 37]
   c. Evaluation. [7]
4. Implementation problems. (10%) [6, 35]
5. Term project. (20%)

BIBLIOGRAPHY

1. Baum, C., and Gorsuch, L. (Eds.) Proceedings of the second symposium on computer-centered data base systems. TM-2624/100/00, System Development Corporation, Santa Monica, Calif., 1 Dec. 1965.
2. Berul, L. Information storage and retrieval, a state-of-the-art report. Report AD-630-089, Auerbach Corporation, Philadelphia, Pa., 14 Sept. 1964.
3. Briggs, R. A mathematical model for the design of information management systems. M.S. Thesis, U. of Pittsburgh, Pittsburgh, Pa., 1966.
4. Brooks, F. P., Jr., and Iverson, K. E. *Automatic Data Processing.* Wiley, New York, 1963, 494 pp.
5. Bryant, J. H., and Semple, P., Jr. GIS and file management. Proc. ACM 21st Nat. Conf., 1966, Thompson Book Co., Washington, D. C., pp. 97–107.
6. Buchholz, W. (Ed.) *Planning a Computer System.* McGraw-Hill, New York, 1962, 322 pp. CR-6346-4786.
7. Calingaert, P. System evaluation: survey and appraisal. *Comm. ACM 10,* 1 (Jan. 1967), 12–18. CR-6782-11,661.
8. Codasyl Development Committee, Language Structure Group. An information algebra, phase I report. *Comm. ACM 5,* 4 (Apr. 1962), 190–201. CR-6235-2621.
9. Connors, T. L. ADAM—generalized data management system. Proc. AFIPS 1966 Spring Joint Comput. Conf., Vol. 28, Spartan Books, New York, pp. 193–203. CR-6676-10,822.
10. Control Data Corporation. *3600/3800 INFOL Reference Manual.* Publ. No. 60170300, CDC, Palo Alto, Calif., July, 1966.
11. Day, R. H. On optimal extracting from a multiple file data storage system: an application of integer programming. *J. ORSA 13,* 3 (May–June, 1965), 482–494.
12. Desmonde, W. H. *Computers and Their Uses.* Prentice-Hall, Englewood Cliffs, N. J., 1964, 296 pp. CR-6561-6829.
13. Dobbs, G. H. State-of-the-art survey of data base systems. Proc. Second Symposium on Computer-Centered Data Base Systems, TM-2624/100/00, System Development Corporation, Santa Monica, Calif., 1 Dec. 1965, pp. 2-3 to 2-10.
14. Elliott, C. O., and Wasley, R. S. *Business Information Processing Systems.* Richard D. Irwin, Homewood, Ill., 1965, 554 pp.
15. Fife, D. W. An optimization model for time-sharing. Proc. AFIPS 1966 Spring Joint Comput. Conf., Vol. 28, Spartan Books, New York, pp. 97–104. CR-6676-10,869.
16. Franks, E. W. A data management system for time-shared file processing using a cross-index file and self-defining entries. Proc. AFIPS 1966 Spring Joint Comput. Conf., Vol. 28, Spartan Books, New York, pp. 79–86. CR-6676-10,754.
17. General Electric Company. *Integrated Data Store—A New Concept in Data Management.* Application Manual AS-CPB-483A, Revision of 7-67, GE Computer Division, Phoenix, Ariz., 1967.
18. Gotlieb, C. C. General purpose programming for business applications. In F. L. Alt (Ed.), *Advances in Computers, Vol. 1,* Academic Press, New York, 1960, pp. 1–42. CR-6016-0206.
19. Gregory, R. H., and Van Horn, R. L. *Automatic Data Processing Systems,* 2nd ed. Wadsworth Pub. Co., San Francisco, 1963, 816 pp. CR-6016-0301, of 1st ed.
20. Hutchinson, G. K. A computer center simulation project. *Comm. ACM 8,* 9 (Sept. 1965), 559–568. CR-6673-9617.
21. Katz, J. H. Simulation of a multiprocessor computer system. Proc. AFIPS 1966 Spring Joint Comput. Conf., Vol. 28, Spartan Books, New York, pp. 127–139. CR-6676-10,870.
22. Laden, H. N., and Gildersleeve, T. R. *System Design for Computer Application.* Wiley, New York, 1963, 330 pp.
23. Langefors, B. Some approaches to the theory of information systems. *BIT 3,* 4 (1963), 229–254. CR-6455-6399.
24. Langefors, B. Information system design computations using generalized matrix algebra. *BIT 5,* 2 (1965), 96–121.
25. Lombardi, L. Theory of files. Proc. 1960 Eastern Joint Comput. Conf., Vol. 18, Spartan Books, New York, pp. 137–141. CR-6236-3165.
26. Lombardi, L. A general business-oriented language based on decision expressions. *Comm. ACM 7,* 2 (Feb. 1964), 104–111. CR-6671-9013.
27. Lynch, W. C. Description of a high capacity, fast turnaround university computer center. *Comm. ACM 9,* 2 (Feb. 1966), 117–123. CR-6673-9546.
28. Maley, G. A., and Skiko, E. J. *Modern Digital Computers.* Prentice-Hall, Englewood Cliffs, N. J., 1964, 216 pp. CR-6561-7081.
29. McCabe, J. On serial files with relocatable records. *J. ORSA 13,* 4 (July–Aug. 1965), 609–618.
30. McCarthy, E. J., McCarthy, J., and Humes, D. *Integrated Data Processing Systems.* Wiley, New York, 1966, 565 pp.
31. McCracken, D. D., Weiss, H., and Lee, T.-H. *Programming Business Computers.* Wiley, New York, 1959, 510 pp. CR-6013-0076.
32. McGee, W. C. The formulation of data processing problems for computers. In F. L. Alt (Ed.) *Advances in Computers, Vol. 4,* Academic Press, New York, 1964, pp. 1–52.
33. Nielson, N. R. The simulation of time sharing systems. *Comm. ACM 10,* 7 (July 1967), 397–412.
34. Rosin, R. F. Determining a computer center environment. *Comm. ACM 8,* 7 (July 1965), 463–488.
35. Schultz, G. P., and Whister, T. L. (Eds.) *Management Organization and the Computer.* Free Press, Macmillan, New York, 1960, 310 pp.
36. Smith, J. L. An analysis of time-sharing computer systems using Markov models. Proc. AFIPS 1966 Spring Joint Comput. Conf., Vol. 28, Spartan Books, New York, pp. 87–95. CR-6676-10,835.
37. Turnburke, V. P., Jr. Sequential data processing design. *IBM Syst. J. 2,* (Mar. 1963), 37–48.
38. Ver Hoef, E. W. Design of a multilevel file management system. Proc. ACM 21st Nat. Conf., 1966, Thompson Book Co., Washington, D. C., pp. 75–86. CR-6781-11,185.
39. Young, J. W., Jr. Nonprocedural languages—a tutorial. Paper 7th Ann. Tech. Symposium, Mar. 23, 1965. South Calif. Chapters of ACM. Copies may be obtained from the author, Electronics Division, MS 50, National Cash Register, 2815 W. El Segundo Blvd., Hawthorne, Calif. 90750.
40. Young, J. W., Jr., and Kent, H. Abstract formulation of data processing problems. *J. Ind. Eng. 9,* 6 (Nov.-Dec. 1958), 471–479. (Also reprinted in *Ideas for Management, 1959.*)

Course A9. Artificial Intelligence and Heuristic Programming (3-0-3)

APPROACH

As this course is essentially descriptive, it might well be taught by surveying various cases of accomplishment in the areas under study. Each student should undertake some independent activity as part of his course work. This might take the form of a survey article on some aspect of the field: a program which simulates some of the rudimentary features of learning and forgetting; a program which plays some simple game like three-dimensional tic-tac-toe; or some other comparable activity. It would probably be best for the student to write any such programs in a list processing language.

CONTENT

The following outline is only a guide. Depending on the instructor's preferences and experience, variations will be introduced and new material will be added to the subject matter to be presented.

1. Definition of heuristic versus algorithmic methods using an example such as game playing. Description of cognitive processes taking place in deriving a new mathematical theorem. Outline of Polya's and Hadamard's approaches to mathematical invention. Discussion of the heuristic method as an exploratory and as an exclusive philosophy (cf. theorem proving à la Newell-Shaw-Simon, Robinson and Wang). Objectives, goals and purposes of work in areas under discussion. (3 lectures)

2. Game playing programs (chess, checkers, go, go-moku, bridge, poker, etc.). (3 lectures)

3. Theorem proving in logic and geometry. (3 lectures)

4. Formula manipulation on computers. (3 lectures)

5. Pattern recognition and picture processing. (3 lectures)

6. General problem solvers and advice takers. (4 lectures)

7. Question answering programs. (3 lectures)

8. Verbal and concept learning simulators. (3 lectures)

9. Decision making programs. (3 lectures)

10. Music composition by computers. (3 lectures)

11. Learning in random and structured nets. Neural networks. (3 lectures)

12. Adaptive systems. (3 lectures)

13. State-of-the-art in machine translation of languages and natural language processing. (4 lectures)

14. Questions of philosophical import: the mind-brain problem and the nature of intelligence, the relevance of operational definitions, and what is missing in present day "thinking machines." (2 lectures)

BIBLIOGRAPHY

The entries given below are grouped according to the items of the "Content" above to which they apply. This list serves only as a starting point and can be extended easily using the bibliographies listed below.

General reference

1. **Feigenbaum**, E. A., **and Feldman**, J. (Eds.) *Computers and Thought*. McGraw-Hill, New York, 1966, 535 pp. CR-6563-7473. Contains many of the articles listed below and a "Selected Descriptor-Indexed Bibliography" by Marvin Minsky.

Heuristic versus algorithmic methods [Item 1]

2. **Armer**, P. Attitudes toward intelligent machines. In *Computers and Thought*, pp. 389-405. CR-6125-0977 and CR-6236-2900.
3. **Findler**, N. V. Some further thoughts on the controversy of thinking machines. *Cybernetica 6*, (1963), 47-52.
4. **Hadamard**, J. *The psychology of invention in the mathematical field*. Dover Publications, New York, 1945, 145 pp. CR-6345-4614.
5. **Minsky**, M. Steps toward artificial intelligence. In *Computers and Thought*, pp. 406-450. CR-6232-1528.
6. **Nagel**, E. *The Structure of Science: Problems in the Logic of Scientific Explanation*. Harcourt, Brace & World, New York, 1961, 612 pp.
7. **Polya**, G. *Mathematics and Plausible Reasoning: Vol. I, Induction and Analogy in Mathematics; Vol. II, Patterns of Plausible Inference*. Princeton University Press, Princeton, N. J., 1954, 280 and 190 pp.

Game playing programs [Item 2]

8. **Berlekamp**, E. R. Program for double-dummy bridge problems—a new strategy for mechanical game playing. *J. ACM 10*, 3 (July 1963), 357-364. CR-6452-5297.
9. **Findler**, N. V. Computer models in the learning process. In *Proc. Internat. Symposium on Mathematical and Computational Methods in the Social and Life Sciences, Rome, 1966*.
10. **Newell**, A., **Shaw**, J. C., **and Simon**, H. A. Chess playing programs and the problem of complexity. In *Computers and Thought*, pp. 39-70. CR-6012-0048.
11. **Pervin**, I. A. On algorithms and programming for playing at dominoes, transl. from Russian. *Automation Express 1* (1959), 26-28. CR-6235-2328.
12. **Remus**, H. Simulation of a learning machine for playing Go. Proc. IFIP Congress, Munich, 1962, North-Holland Pub. Co., Amsterdam, pp. 192-194. CR-6341-3420.
13. **Samuel**, A. L. Some studies in machine learning using the game of checkers. In *Computers and Thought*, pp. 71-105.

Theorem proving in logic and geometry [Item 3]

14. **Davis**, M., **Logemann**, G., **and Loveland**, D. A machine program for theorem-proving. *Comm. ACM 5*, 7 (July 1962), 394-397.
15. **Gelernter**, H., **Hansen**, J. R., **and Loveland**, D. W. Empirical exploration of the geometry-theorem proving machine. In *Computers and Thought*, pp. 134-152. CR-6233-1928.
16. **Newell**, A., **Shaw**, J. C., **and Simon**, H. A. Empirical explorations with the logic theory machine: a case study in heuristics. In *Computers and Thought*, pp. 109-133.
17. **Robinson**, J. A. Theorem proving on the computer, *J. ACM 10*, 2 (Apr. 1963), 163-174. CR-6452-5460.
18. **Wang**, H. Proving theorems by pattern recognition. *Comm. ACM 3*, 4 (Apr. 1960), 220-234. CR-6016-0369.

Formula manipulation on computers [Item 4]

19. **Bond**, E., **Auslander**, M., **Grisoff**, S., **Kenney**, R., **Myszewski**, M., **Sammet**, J. E., **Tobey**, R. G., **and Zilles**, S. FORMAC—an experimental FORmula MAnipulation Compiler. Proc. ACM 19th Nat. Conf., 1964, Association for Computing Machinery, New York, pp. K2.1-1 to K2.1-19.
20. **Brown**, W. S. The ALPAK system for nonnumerical algebra on a digital computer, I and II. *Bell Syst. Tech. J. 42* (1963), 2081-2119, and *43* (1964), 785-804.
21. **Perlis**, A. J., **and Iturriaga**, R. An extension to ALGOL for manipulating formulae. *Comm. ACM 7*, 2 (Feb. 1964), 127-130.
22. **Sammet**, J. E. An annotated descriptor based bibliography on the use of computers for nonnumerical mathematics. *Com. Rev.* 7, 4 (Jul.-Aug. 1966), B-1 tc B-31.
23. **Slagle**, J. R. A heuristic program that solves symbolic integration problems in freshman calculus. In *Computers and Thought*, pp. 191-203. CR-6236-3068.

Pattern recognition and picture processing [Item 5]

24. **McCormick**, B. H., **Ray**, S. R., **Smith**, K. C., **and Yamada**, S. ILLIAC III: A processor of visual information. Proc. IFIP Congress, New York, 1965, Vol. 2, Spartan Books, New York, pp. 359-361.
25. **Tippett**, J. T., **Berkowitz**, D. A., **Clapp**, L. C., **Koester**, C. J., **and Vanderburgh**, A., **Jr.** (Eds.) *Optical and Electro-Optical Information Processing*, Proc. Symp. Optical and Electro-Optical Inf. Proc. Tech., Boston, Nov. 1964. M.I.T. Press, Cambridge, Mass., 1965, 780 pp. CR-6673-9829.
26. **Uhr**, L. (Ed.) *Pattern Recognition*. Wiley, New York, 1966, 393 pp. CR-6674-10,028.

General problem solver and advice taker [Item 6]

27. **McCarthy**, J. Programs with common sense. In D. V. Blake and A. M. Uttley (Eds.), *Proc. Symp. on Mechanisation of Thought Processes*, Two volumes, National Physical Laboratory, Teddington, England. H.M. Stationery Office, London, 1959, pp. 75-84.
28. **Newell**, A., **Shaw**, J. C., **and Simon**, H. A. A variety of intelligent learning in a general problem solver. In M. Yovits and S. Cameron (Eds.), *Self-Organizing Systems*, Pergamon Press, New York, 1960, pp. 153-159. CR-6236-2908.
29. **Newell**, A., **and Simon**, H. A. Computer simulation of human thinking. *Science 134*, 3495 (22 Dec. 1960), 2011-2017. CR-6234-2062.

Question answering programs [Item 7]

30. Bobrow, D. G. A question answering system for high school algebra word problems. Proc. AFIPS 1964 Fall Joint Comput. Conf., Vol. 26, Spartan Books, New York, pp. 591–614. CR-6562-7183.
31. Green, B. F., Wolf, A. K., Chomsky, C., and Laughery, K. Baseball: an automatic question answerer. In *Computers and Thought*, pp. 207–216. CR-6341-3417.
32. Lindsay, R. K. Inferential memory as the basis of machines which understand natural language. In *Computers and Thought*, pp. 217–233.
33. Raphael, B. A computer program which "understands." Proc. AFIPS 1964 Fall Joint Comput. Conf., Vol. 26, Spartan Books, New York, pp. 577–589. CR-6562-7207.
34. Simmons, R. F. Answering English questions by computer—a survey. *Comm. ACM 8*, 1 (Jan. 1965), 53–70. CR-6563-7643.

Verbal and concept learning [Item 8]

35. Feigenbaum, E. A. The simulation of verbal learning behavior. In *Computers and Thought*, pp. 297–309. CR-6234-2060.
36. Feigenbaum, E. A., and Simon, H. A. Forgetting in an associative memory. Preprints of papers presented at the 16th Nat. Meeting of the ACM, Los Angeles, Sept. 5–8, 1961, Association for Computing Machinery, New York. CR-6232-1667.
37. Hunt, E. B. *Concept Learning: An Information Processing Problem*. Wiley, New York, 1962, 286 pp. CR-6561-6872.
38. Miller, G. A., Galanter, E., and Pribram, K. *Plans and the Structure of Behavior*. Holt, Rinehart and Winston, New York, 1960.

Decision making programs [Item 9]

39. Clarkson, G. P. E. A model of the trust investment process. In *Computers and Thought*, pp. 347–371. CR-6563-7473.
40. Feldman, J. Simulation of behavior in the binary choice experiment. In *Computers and Thought*, pp. 329–346. CR-6342-3760.
41. Findler, N. V. Human decision making under uncertainty and risk: computer-based experiments and a heuristic simulation program. Proc. AFIPS 1965 Fall Joint Comput. Conf., Pt. I. Spartan Books, New York, pp. 737–752. CR-6673-9594.

Music composition [Item 10]

42. Computers in Music. Session 7, Tues. Nov. 8, at the AFIPS 1966 Fall Joint Computer Conf., San Francisco. (The papers for this session were not published in the conference proceedings.)
43. Gill, S. A technique for the composition of music in a computer. *Comput. J. 6*, 2 (July 1963), 129–133. CR-6451-4983.
44. Hiller, L. A., Jr., and Isaacson, L. M. *Experimental Music*. McGraw-Hill, New York, 1959, 197 pp. CR-6012-0047.
45. Mathews, M. V. The digital computer as a musical instrument. *Science 142*, 3592 (1 Nov. 1963), 553–557.
46. Reitman, W. R. *Cognition and Thought: An Information Processing Approach*. (Chap. 6). Wiley, New York, 1965, 312 pp.
47. Seay, A. The composer of music and the computer. *Comput. Autom. 13*, 8 (Aug. 1964), 16–18. CR-6563-7548.

Learning nets and neural networks [Item 11]

48. Arbib, M. *Brains, Machines and Mathematics*. McGraw-Hill, New York, 1964, 163 pp. CR-6455-6254.
49. Block, H. D. Adaptive neural networks as brain models. *Experimental Arithmetic, High Speed Computing and Mathematics*, Proc. of Symposia in Appl. Math. 15, American Mathematical Society, Providence, R. I., 1963, pp. 59–72. CR-6453-5608.
50. Lettvin, J. Y., Maturana, H., McCulloch, W. S., and Pitts, W. What the frog's eye tells the frog's brain. *Proc. IRE 47*, (1959), 1940–1951.
51. Rosenblatt, F. *Principles of Neurodynamics*. Cornell Aeronaut. Lab. Rep. 1196-G-8, Spartan Books, New York, 1962.
52. Young, J. Z. *A Model of the Brain*. Clarendon Press, Oxford, England, 1964, 384 pp.

Adaptive systems [Item 12]

53. Fogel, L. J., Owens, A. J., and Walsh, M. J. *Artificial Intelligence Through Simulated Evolution*. Wiley, New York, 1966, 170 pp.
54. Nilsson, N. J. *Learning Machines*. McGraw-Hill, New York, 1965, 137 pp. CR-6565-8177.
55. Tou, J. T., and Wilcox, R. H. (Eds.) *Computer and Information Sciences*. Proc. of Symposium at Northwestern University, 1963, Spartan Books, New York, 1964, 544 pp.
56. Von Foerster, H., and Zopf, G. W., Jr., (Eds.) *Principles of Self-Organization*. Pergamon Press, New York, 1962.
57. Yovits, M. C., Jacobi, G. T., and Goldstein, G. D. (Eds.) *Self-Organizing Systems, 1962*. Spartan Books, New York, 1962, 563 pp. CR-6456-6603.

Natural language processing [Item 13]

58. Bar-Hillel, Y. *Language and Information: Selected Essays on Their Theory and Application*. Addison-Wesley, Reading, Mass., 1964, 388 pp. CR-6562-7178.
59. Bobrow, D. G. Syntactic analysis of English by computer—a survey. Proc. AFIPS 1963 Fall Joint Comput. Conf., Vol. 24, Spartan Books, New York, pp. 365–387. CR-6671-8838.
60. Chomsky, N. *Aspects of the Theory of Syntax*. M.I.T. Press, Cambridge, Mass., 1965, 251 pp. CR-6676-10,735.
61. Garvin, P. L. (Ed.) *Natural Language and the Computer*. McGraw-Hill, New York, 1963, 398 pp. CR-6456-6569.
62. Hays, D. (Ed.) *Readings in Automatic Language Processing*. American Elsevier, New York, 1966, 202 pp.

Questions of philosophical import [Item 14]

63. MacKay, D. M. Mind-like behavior in artifacts. *Brit. J. Phil. Sci. 2*, (1951), 105–121.
64. Sayre, K. M., and Crosson, F. J. (Eds.) *The Modeling of Mind: Computers and Intelligence*. University of Notre Dame Press, Notre Dame, Ind., 1963, 275 pp. CR-6455-6205.
65. Simon, H. A. The architecture of complexity. *Proc. Am. Phil. Soc. 106*, (1962), 467–482.
66. Turing, A. M. Computing machinery and intelligence. In *Computers and Thought*, pp. 11–35.

Education E.I. Organick
Editor

A Computer Science Course Program for Small Colleges

Richard H. Austing
University of Maryland
and
Gerald L. Engel
The Pennsylvania State University

The ACM Subcommittee on Small College Programs of the Committee on Curriculum in Computer Science (C^3S) was appointed in 1969 to consider the unique problems of small colleges and universities, and to make recommendations regarding computer science programs at such schools. This report, authorized by both the subcommittee and C^3S, supplies a set of recommendations for courses and necessary resources.

Implementation problems are discussed, specifically within the constraints of limited faculty and for the purposes of satisfying a wide variety of objectives. Detailed descriptions of four courses are given; suggestions are made for more advanced work; and an extensive library list is included.

Key Words and Phrases: computer science education, course proposals, small colleges, programming course, social implications course, computer organization course, file organization course, bibliographies

CR Categories: 1.52

The work reported here was supported in part by National Science Foundation grant GJ-1177 to the Association for Computing Machinery. A preliminary version was presented for discussion at the second annual SIGCSE Symposium, St. Louis, Missouri in March 1972 and subsequently appeared in the IAG Journal under the title Computer Science Education in Small Colleges—A Report with Recommendations. Authors' addresses: Richard H. Austing, Computer Science Center, University of Maryland, College Park, MD. 20742; Gerald L. Engel, Computer Science Department, The Pennsylvania State University, University Park, PA. 16802; on leave from Hampden-Sydney College, Hampden-Sydney, VA 23368.

This report gives recommendations for the content, implementation, and operation of a program of computer science courses specifically directed to small colleges. In no way does this material represent a major program in computer science. It does describe a program for those schools with limited resources, but with an interest, enthusiasm, and desire for some course offerings in computer science. Those institutions interested in computer science and with the resources necessary for a major program in this field should refer to the existing reports of ACM's Committee on Curriculum in Computer Science (C^3S) [87a] and other curriculum studies. Institutions which desire to complement computer science course offerings with a set of courses in computational mathematics should consider the report of the Committee on the Undergraduate Program in Mathematics [86d].

The Program

Four courses are described and suggestions are made for additional study and courses for students interested in further work. No names have been given to the four courses, but they correspond roughly to the areas of algorithms and programming (Course 1), application of computers and their impact on society (Course 2), machine and systems organization (Course 3), and file and data organization (Course 4). Though these courses in a real sense represent a coherent program, they are structured so as to allow a student with limited objectives and limited time to pick and choose those parts most relevant to his needs.

Course 1 is the introduction, which in most cases gives a student his first experience in computer science. This is accomplished primarily by the presentation of a higher level programming language. Course 2 expands on Course 1 by giving the student further programming experience. In addition the student is introduced to a variety of applications of computers and the effects that these applications will have on the individual and on society. In Course 3, the student gains familiarity with various aspects of computer systems and how the parts of such systems interact. Finally, in Course 4 the concepts and applications of data representation and organization are considered.

Three of the courses (Courses 1, 3, and 4) correspond in basic content to courses in "Curriculum 68" [87a]. However, there is a good deal of difference in structure and emphasis in these courses from the way in which they are commonly taught. In order to allow as many students as possible to take the courses, the prerequisite structure is held to a minimum. Also, in order to provide a more general background, the courses (especially Courses 3 and 4) are more concerned with concepts of a particular system than with details or extensive programming exercises. For example, in Course 3 no particular assembler would be studied, but rather the general concept and vocabulary of computer systems would be presented. In this way a student, anticipating a career in business management, could equip himself with the tools to select a computer system without having to bury himself in the details of a particular system.

Course 2 does not have an equivalent in "Curriculum 68." This course in applications would, in most cases, be the natural sequel to the introductory programming course. It combines further experience in programming with a limited survey of application areas. Though programming would be an integral part of the course, something of the overall descriptive nature of the program would be involved. Where possible and appropriate, the students would be expected to use programs and data bases that are available. For example, if the class was studying simulation, it would be appropriate for the student to gain experience by using a computer-based traffic flow simulation to study the I/O problems involved, and possibly by studying some of the techniques involved in writing appropriate programs, but not necessarily by writing the program itself.

Implementation of this program would make instruction available to all students on campus at least at the level of being able to communicate intelligently with a computer. In addition advanced instruction would be readily accessible. For the student anticipating a career in computing or considering application for graduate work in computer science, several approaches are possible. Independent study courses can provide introductions to certain topics (courses in assembly language programming, programming languages, or even some large scale programming project would be appropriate). Also, since we are dealing with small schools, cooperation with other departments can be anticipated. Through this interdepartmental cooperation, certain courses can be modified to serve the student anticipating graduate work in computer science. Such a student should be advised to follow a mathematics curriculum, and could anticipate taking at least a computer oriented course offered by the mathematics department in probability and statistics, or a numerical analysis course, or a course in abstract algebra that would emphasize computer applications, or any of the computational mathematics courses recommended in the CUPM report [87b]. Finally, with the general introduction of computers in the undergraduate curricula as documented in the proceedings of the Conferences on Computers in the Undergraduate Curricula [86e], it seems reasonable to anticipate that an interested student can select several courses from various disciplines that make significant use of computers.

Implementation

One of the purposes of this program is to ensure its implementation with a minimal staff. Obviously, computing equipment must also be considered, and since most small schools are working under a small budget for computer services, the course structure reflects the fact that extensive computer power will probably not be available on campus. The courses recommended require that the students have access to a computer which has a higher level programming language for student use. Only one higher level language is required inasmuch as every computer installation satisfies that requirement. If additional languages are available, their use might be appropriate in one or more courses. Whether the computer is a small stand-alone or has one or more terminals makes little difference. The important requirement is that the students have easy access to the equipment and to student oriented software.

As important as the computer science course structure is, the most important area of computing at a small school is the service area. The cost of computing on campus, in terms of both equipment and personnel, can only be justified if computing services are used on a campus-wide basis. To achieve this, the development of a community of computer users on campus, as well as the excellent development of Course 1, is necessary and for schools that are not already involved in such programs, the first effort of the faculty member in charge of the development of computing must be made in these directions. The introduction of the additional course work should take place after these aspects of the program are completed.

The program requires one full-time instructor. In

most cases, Course 1 and Course 2 would be offered each semester, while Course 3 and Course 4 would be offered once each year. It is common practice in small schools to have the computer science faculty and computer center staff one and the same. It is clear that the demands of this program (at least nine hours per semester) plus the desirability of offering additional special courses at the more advanced level make this situation impossible. Thus the instructional staff and computer center staff should be separate. There should be, of course, a close relationship between the instructor and the center staff, but the instructor should have no administrative responsibilities in the center.

Another common practice in small schools is to take a faculty member from a department that is a computer user, and assign him the responsibility for computer science instruction. Such a practice often leads to the courses being not in computer science but rather in applications of computers. Whenever possible this should be avoided, but if it is necessary, the instructional material should be clearly separated from any other department of the school.

It is well to note that the present market situation places a small school in an excellent position to hire a computer scientist. Where possible this should be done, at least to the extent of bringing in the individual responsible for the implementation of the program. Where this cannot be done, a commitment should be made to allow an existing faculty member to develop himself in computer science education. Summer programs for this purpose are not plentiful, and doing such work in the normal environment of teaching and other responsibilities at the small school is close to impossible. Thus, where an existing faculty member is asked to be responsible for the program, it is strongly recommended that this faculty member be granted a year's leave of absence to work and gain experience in a computer science department. It is also recommended that universities with the facilities to do so develop programs that will help these faculty members to achieve their objective.

As with any program, the usual supporting facilities of the college are necessary. Though no great amount of specialized material is expected, it should be recognized that there will be a need for a rather large initial expenditure in the area of library materials, both books and periodicals. To provide a starting point for the development of a collection, a library list has been included.

Courses

There is much evidence that some exposure to computers should be an essential part of every college student's education. Many students will become users in their chosen occupations. Included in this group would be teachers, managers, researchers, and programmers who will need the computer as a tool. Other students will become directly involved in computer education and the computer industry. All students will be affected by the use of computers in our society.

As a minimum, students should acquire some understanding of the implications of the computer impact on individuals, organizations, and society. One way in which an academic institution can do this is to offer a survey type course in computers and society. However, there are some inherent difficulties with such an approach, particularly in schools which have no more than one or two faculty members in the computer science area. The breadth and amount of knowledge needed to give a worthwhile course of this type almost precludes its being offered by any one person. Developments and applications span such a wide range of areas that faculty from a variety of fields would need to be used. The course then might take on the flavor of a lecture series in which students would be presented a great deal of information but almost no feeling about what a computer is or how it should be used.

A better approach, as well as a more practical one in terms of faculty utilization, would consist of teaching fundamentals of computer science in a first course and allowing students the option of acquiring additional knowledge through their own reading, on-the-job training, or further course work in computer science or other disciplines. The first course described below follows this approach. It plays the role of a beginning course and the prerequisite course to each of the other three courses described. The latter three courses are designed not to be sequential. However, the most desirable path through them for students taking all of them would be in the order presented.

There is an intended overlap in the material of the four courses. Some ideas are worth repeating at different levels. Also, the same problem or concept can be enhanced by looking at it from different points of view or by bringing different material to bear on it.

Very few matters related to courses or curriculum are generally agreed upon among computer scientists. The question of what language to teach in a first course is no exception. Although there appears to be general agreement that a higher level language should be presented before an assembly language, there is a substantial difference of opinion regarding the specific language to use. APL, BASIC, FORTRAN, and PL/I, to name a few, each has a band of advocates. FORTRAN is still the most widely used general purpose language and is the most easily transferable from computer to computer. Despite its shortcomings, FORTRAN would seem to be the most useful for the greatest number of students and is the language recommended for the first course. PL/I, if it is available, could be chosen in place of FORTRAN, particularly because its capabilities for nonnumeric applications make it useful in Courses 2 and 4. If strong reasons compel a different choice of language, some modifications might be necessary in course topics or approach. The introduction of and programming in a second language (e.g. ALGOL, APL, SNOBOL) is not recommended; it greatly decreases the programming experience and competence the student acquires in the first course. However, if time permits, a short discussion of a different kind of language and a demonstration program could be added at the end of the course.

Course 1 (3 Credits)

Introduction. This is a first course which emphasizes good programming techniques in a higher level language. No programming background is assumed. Upon completion of this course, the student: (a) should have practical experience in programming, including segmentation of both a problem and a program for its solution, debugging, implementation of basic data structures such as lists, and use of "canned" programs; (b) should know basic characterization of computer organization; (c) should be able to distinguish among program assembly, loading, compilation and execution, including some of the kinds of programming errors that can occur at each stage; and (d) should know the details of the language and have a basic idea of the relation of its statements to machine code.

The topics listed for this course do not differ substantially from the topics included in the outline of course B1 in "Curriculum 68"; however, a shift in emphasis is recommended. Course B1 stressed the notion of algorithm, problem analysis, and the formulation of algorithms for problem solution. Learning a language, practice in its use, and concepts of computer organization were also emphasized, but mainly as the means to obtain the actual solution of the problem. Unfortunately, no texts have appeared which have achieved the goal of presenting the subject of problem solving in an effective way (several books by Polya might be considered exceptions to this statement but they are not of the algorithmic orientation specified in course B1). Judging from the great variety found in introductory computing courses, it would seem that few, if any, teachers have been able to achieve the goal. It is not an easy problem to solve, but it is worth working toward a solution.

On the other hand, it is possible to teach programming techniques with the aid of a language manual and, possibly, one of the existing texts. The textbook could be used as a source of problems, at least, and in some cases, to supplement discussions of appropriate programming techniques applied to specific classes of problems. By concentrating on programming, the instructor is better able to teach a language, put it in proper perspective with computer organizations and systems, develop good programming practices (including coding, debugging, and documentation), and motivate the need for algorithms in the solution process. Students should be required to use subprograms extensively (both their own and ones that are provided); this, in turn, would encourage at least one good problem solving technique—breaking up a problem into solvable parts.

An important benefit to the general approach suggested here is that the course is more easily defensible as a service course. Students could be urged to find problems in their own field of interest which they would program as course projects. Duplication of first courses for different groups of students could be minimized and, possibly, avoided entirely. For the first few semesters it might be difficult to obtain reasonable problems from a variety of areas, but as more faculty members become users, their fields of interest will become a source of good problems. In addition, a collection of (possibly large) data bases and subprograms can be accumulated and used as files to be referenced by student programs. The degree of success achieved by the computer center in developing a community of computer users has a significant influence here. As a result, some very interesting and nontrivial problems can be considered both in this course and in Course 2.

Though laboratory-like sessions for small groups of students may be desirable, they are not essential. If these sessions are used, an instructor may want to scatter them throughout the semester or bunch them at the beginning of the course and let the students program on a more individual basis toward the end of the course. Whether or not the laboratory sessions should be scheduled is a matter that is best decided by the instructor and/or the department.

Catalog Description. A first course in programming, using the FORTRAN language. Introductory concepts of computer organization and systems. Programming projects, including at least one from the student's field of interest.

Outline. Even though topics are listed sequentially, some topics (e.g. computer organization) should be distributed throughout the course with increasing degrees of detail. Problem analysis should be emphasized.

1. Overview of a computer. Basic computer modules, organization, and program execution. (5%)
2. Overview of problem solving process, beginning with the problem statement and ending with verification of the correct computer solution. (5%)
3. Introduction to the specific computer environment in which the student will work. Information needed by the student to interact with the computer in this course. (5%)
4. Language details. Components and types of assignment, control, and specification statements; data repre-

sentation and structures; storage allocation; I/O; subprograms; local and global variables; common and equivalence statements. (30%)
5. Programming techniques. Segmentation of problems and programs; comments and other documentation; debugging; library subroutines. (15%)
6. Simple data structures and list processing. Pointers; structures such as strings, stacks, linear and circular lists. (10%)
7. Limitations of FORTRAN. Nonnumeric programming; recursion. (5%)
8. Computer organization and systems. More detailed presentation of hardware and systems software, including registers, instruction codes, addressing, assembler, loader, compiler, and characteristics of components; peripheral units; past, present, and future developments. (20%)
9. Examinations. (5%)

Texts. A language manual, either the manufacturer's or one of the numerous manuals and primers that are available, should be used. Also, any local documentation concerning the installation's computer and/or systems should be readily available. No current book covers the material as presented in the outline, but parts of many books could be used as source material or student reference. For example, the following references are pertinent: 1, 3, 4, 11, 12, 15, 17, 22, 24, 28, 32, 34, 42, 59, 65, 66, 73, 77–80, 86a, 86d, and 88a–d.

Course 2

Introduction. This course emphasizes the use of computers in a variety of problem areas. It is an applications oriented course which should give the student concrete experience in solving representative problems of a practical nature. As in Course 1, large data bases can be established as experience in teaching the course is gained. Discussion of problems and problem areas should include algorithms, application techniques from Course 1, and social implications. New concepts and tools (e.g. complex data structures, tree search techniques, sorting methods) can be introduced as required in the context of specific problems, and the need for additional tools, including different kinds of languages, can be motivated. Occasionally, it might be feasible to invite a faculty member from another department or university or a local businessman to supplement material on a topic. Student assignments should vary, both in depth and in subject areas. In particular, a student who has completed Course 3 or 4 should be expected to use different techniques and solve larger or more difficult problems than a student who has completed only Course 1. Students should be encouraged to discover and solve problems in their own areas of interest.

Because students in this course have completed a programming course, no discussion should be necessary on such topics as what a computer is and how it works, number representation, flowcharts, and other elementary matters included in a computer appreciation-type course. However, a discussion of various systems (time-sharing, batch, etc.) should be included so that students are aware of the kinds of computer environments in which problems are solved.

The instructor should pose a suitably difficult problem in a real context, indicate possible approaches to its solution, break it up into smaller problems, discuss appropriate algorithms, introduce whatever new topics pertain to the problem, and let the student write a program to obtain the solution. If an entire problem is too difficult to solve in this way, one or more subproblems can be identified and handled as described. More advanced methods can be indicated when appropriate, and the student can be directed to appropriate references. Social and historical implications can be discussed at various stages of the solution process. As the course progresses, students should be expected to do more analysis and algorithm writing than specified above. The desired effects are that the student becomes acquainted with the computer's impact in a number of areas, is exposed to concepts and methods applicable to different kinds of problems, and gains practical experience in solving problems.

Catalog Description. Prerequisite, Course 1. Survey of computer applications in areas such as file management, gaming, CAI, process control, simulation, and modeling. Impact of computers on individuals and society. Problem solving using computers with emphasis on analysis. Formulation of algorithms, and programming. Projects chosen from various application areas including student's area of interest.

Outline. The selection and ordering of topics are highly dependent on the local situation. The topics are listed separately but should be combined as much as possible during discussion of problems. Problems and projects should have a practical flavor and should use a variety of computer oriented techniques and concepts. Attention should be given to the kind of technique that applies to a particular class of problems but not to other classes of problems. Each problem should be discussed in such a way that the student is aware of its relation to a real world context and sees the computer as a natural tool in the solution process.
1. Computer systems. Batch and interactive; real-time; information management; networks. Description of each system, how it differs from the others, and kinds of applications for which each system is best suited. (15%)
2. Large data bases. Establishment and use; data definition and structures. (10%)
3. Errors. Types; effects; handling. (5%)
4. Social implications. Human-machine interface, privacy; moral and legal issues. (15%)
5. Future social impact. Checkless society; CAI; national data bank. (10%)

6. **Languages**. Business oriented; list processing;simulation; string and symbol manipulation. Brief exposition of characteristics which make these languages appropriate for particular classes of problems. (10%)
7. Concepts and techniques used in solving problems from applications areas such as CAI, data management, gaming, information retrieval, and simulation. (25%)
8. Discussion of completed projects and/or examinations. (10%)

Texts. The italicized references cited below could serve as basic texts for this course. Many books and magazine articles could provide useful supplementary material either for class use or for student or teacher reference. Only a sampling of the available material is included in the Library List: 2, *3*, 8, 9, 14, 15, 16, 19, 34, *36*, 44, 56–59, 61, 63, 64, *68*, *70*, 72, 74, 76, 77, 85a, 85b, and 86a–e.

Course 3

Introduction. This course emphasizes the relationships between computer organization (hardware) and software. Each module's organization should be discussed, and its features should be related to the implementation of programming language features and assembly language instructions. Whenever possible, explanations should be included about why specific hardware features are better suited than others to certain types of problems or environments (e.g. real-time computing, interactive systems, data processing, scientific applications), and how this could affect selection of components. The effects of adding or changing modules should be viewed with respect to costs, capabilities, and software. Minicomputers should be discussed both as stand-alone computers and as components of larger systems.

Programming in assembly language should not be taught as such. However, students should be exposed to the use of macros and microprogramming. They should acquire a basic understanding of monitors, interrupts, addressing, program control, as well as implementation of arrays, stacks, and hash tables. In short, they should become familiar with assembly language concepts but in relation to their use in the total computer environment rather than through extensive programming. The need for assembly language programming experience is no longer great enough to argue that most students should have it. For those students who become interested in it, a special study course can be provided. With the background acquired in Course 3, a student should be able to gain programming experience without much additional guidance.

Catalog Description. Prerequisite, Course 1. Relationships among computer components, structures, and systems. Hardware features, costs, capabilities, and selection. Assembly language concepts and implementation.

Outline. Because this course is, at least to some extent, dependent on the specific computer available, the selection, ordering, and depth of coverage of topics will vary from institution to institution.
1. Processor. Arithmetic and control functions; relationships of features to language features; data handling; addressing. (20%)
2. Memory. Various types; cost, capabilities, and functions of each type; direct, random and sequential access; implementation of arrays, stacks, and hash tables. (20%)
3. I/O. Types, costs, and capabilities of units and media; control; channels; interrupts. (20%)
4. Communication among components. Effects of changing configurations; interactive and real-time systems. (5%)
5. Minicomputers. Capabilities as stand-alone computers; components of larger systems; costs. (10%)
6. Assembly language concepts. Instructions and their relations to components included above; macros, microprogramming. (20%)
7. Examinations. (5%)

Texts. No available text is suitable for this course. Material can be drawn from the following references and from manufacturers' manuals: 5, 6, 7, 13, 16, 26, 27, 29, 30, 31, 33, 35, 38–41, 43, 45–48, 53, 56, 60, 67, 69, 71, 74, 75, 81, 84, 86a, and 87b.

Course 4

Introduction. This is a course in file organization and manipulation. It stresses concepts, data structures, and algorithms used in the solution of non-numerical problems. Proper motivation for each should be given; an encyclopedia approach is not intended. Whenever several methods for achieving the same result are discussed (e.g. sorting or searching algorithms) comparative evaluations should be included. Differences between using core only and core plus auxiliary memory for various applications should be pointed out. If appropriate hardware is available, students should be assigned programming projects that require performing operations on large data bases and that require manipulating records on auxiliary memory devices. Immediate sources of problems are in the areas of mailing lists, registration, scheduling, student records, and library automation. If a suitable language for list processing applications is available, it could be taught and used in part of the course. Otherwise, characteristics of languages for this purpose should be given.

Catalog Description. Prerequisite, Course 1. Data structures, concepts and algorithms used in the solution of non-numerical problems. Applications to data management systems, file organization, information retrieval, list processing, and programming languages.

Outline. Neither mathematical applications nor mathematical properties of structures is included in this outline. They could become part of the course if students have sufficient background. Although some of the topics are discussed in Courses 1, 2 and 3, only the material in Course 1 is assumed.

1. Stacks, queues, arrays, lists. Structures; algorithms for manipulating, storage allocation and maintenance; applications. (25%)
2. Languages for list processing. Features of one or more languages (e.g. LISP, L^6, PL/I). (5%)
3. Trees. Binary; threaded; traversal schemes; storage representation; applications. (15%)
4. Hash coding. Addressing; collisions; applications of symbol tables; storage allocation. (15%)
5. Searching and sorting. Comparison and evaluation of methods; techniques for use with auxiliary memory devices; applications. (15%)
6. Complex structures. Hierarchical; indexed sequential; inverted list; multilinked; applications to large information systems including case studies with illustrations of why they might not work. (20%)
7. Examinations. (5%)

Texts. A text for this course could be chosen from the italicized items included in the following list. However, the text would have to be supplemented with material from other references. *10*, 20, 21, 24, 26, 28, 31, *37*, 41, 44, 47, *49*, 51, 54, *75*, and 81a.

Additional Recommended Courses

The four courses described above are designed to service a broad segment of the undergraduate student body with an extremely limited number of faculty members, possibly one. Students should also have the opportunity to take computer-oriented courses in their own departments. The number of possible courses in this category is too great to try to list. Instead, we will recommend additional courses for the student who is seriously interested in computer science whether or not that student intends to pursue a graduate degree program in the field.

Each of the following specific courses could be given for special study to one or a few students or as a regular course if the demand is great enough and an instructor is available. Other topics could be included but might not be possible to implement in a practical way unless access to a large computer were available.

Assembly Language Programming. This course would enable a student interested in software to apply the concepts learned in Course 3; it provides a means to become experienced in assembly language programming and an introduction to systems programming. Desirable goals for this course include proficiency in assembly language programming, particularly using the system on hand; knowledge of basic principles of systems programming; and implementation of specific segments of systems programs (e.g. I/O routines). Manufacturer's manuals would initially serve as texts. The COSINE Committee's report, "An Undergraduate Course on Operating Systems Principles" (June 1971) provides a number of ideas for possible topics and references after the student acquires some programming experience.

Structure of Programming Languages. This course would include an introduction to grammars, languages they generate, scanners, recognizers, and other topics as time allows. Reference material for this course might include portions of *Compiler Construction for Digital Computers* by David Gries, *Ten Mini-Languages* by H.F. Ledgard or *A Comparative Study of Programming Languages* by E. Higman. Also the features of languages such as ALGOL and SNOBOL4 could be studied.

Programming Languages. If any language other than those included in courses is available, a special-study programming course may be appropriate. As part of this course, a student might be required to design and implement a major software project of some benefit either to the center or to the user community. Such a course might carry only one credit and it might be best given as a month-long course in schools on 4-1-4 system.

Library List

The following list is not exhaustive. No attempt was made to compile a list of all books on any specific topic. Certain areas are omitted entirely; namely, programming language manuals, books directed toward specific computers, and books primarily oriented toward use in other disciplines (such as numerical methods, computers and music, and programming for the behavioral sciences).

1. Arden, B.W. *An Introduction to Digital Computing.* Addison-Wesley, Reading, Mass., 1963.
2. Baer, R.M. *The Digital Villain.* Addison-Wesley, Reading, Mass., 1972.
3. Barrodale, I., Roberts, F., and Ehle, B. *Elementary Computer Applications.* Wiley,,New York, 1971.
4. Barron, D.W. *Recursive Techniques in Programming.* American Elsevier, New York, 1968.
5. Barron, D.W., *Assemblers and Loaders.* American Elsevier, New York, 1969.
6. Beizer, B. *The Architecture and Engineering of Digital Computer Complexes.* Plenum Press, New York, 1971.
7. Bell, C.G., and Newell, A. *Computer Structures: Readings and Examples.* McGraw-Hill, New York, 1971.
8. Bemer, R.M. (Ed.) *Computers and Crisis.* ACM, New York, 1971.
9. Benice, D.D. (Ed.) *Computer Selections.* McGraw-Hill, New York, 1971.
10. Berztiss, A.T. *Data Structures: Theory and Practice.* Academic Press, New York, 1971.
11. Brooks, F., and Iverson, K. *Automatic Data Processing.* Wiley, New York, 1969.
12. Cole, R.W. *Introduction to Computing.* McGraw-Hill, New York, 1969.
13. Cuttle, G., and Robinson, P.B. (Eds.) *Executive Programs and Operating Systems.* American Elsevier, New York, 1970.
14. Davenport, W.P. *Modern Data Communications.* Hayden, New York, 1971.
15. Desmonde, W.H. *Computers and Their Uses.* Prentice-Hall, Englewood Cliffs, N.J., 1971.
16. Dippel, G., and House, W.C. *Information Systems.* Scott, Foresman, Chicago, 1969.

17. Dorf, R.C. *Introduction to Computers and Computer Science*. Boyd and Fraser, San Francisco, 1972.
18. Elson, M. *Concepts of Programming Languages*. Science Research Associates, New York. In press.
19. Feigenbaum, E.A., and Feldman, J. (Eds.) *Computers and Thought*. McGraw-Hill, New York, 1963.
20. Flores, I. *Sorting*. Prentice-Hall, Englewood Cliffs, N.J. 1969.
21. Flores, I. *Data Structures and Management*. Prentice-Hall, Englewood Cliffs, N.J., 1970.
22. Forsythe, A.I., Keenan, T.A., Organick, E.I., and Stenburg, W. *Computer Science: A First Course*. Wiley, New York, 1969.
23. Foster, J.M. *List Processing*. American Elsevier, New York, 1967.
24. Galler, B.A. *The Language of Computers*. McGraw-Hill, New York, 1962.
25. Galler, B.A., and Perlis, A.J. *A View of Programming Languages*. Addison-Wesley, Reading, Mass. 1970.
26. Gauthier, R., and Ponto, S. *Designing Systems Programs*. Prentice-Hall, Englewood-Cliffs, N.J., 1970.
27. Gear, C.W. *Computer Organization and Programming*. McGraw-Hill, New York, 1969.
28. Gear, C.W. *Introduction to Computer Science*. Science Research Associates, New York, In press.
29. Genuys, F. (Ed.) *Programming Languages*. Academic Press, New York, 1968.
30. Gordon, G. *System Simulation*. Prentice-Hall, Englewood-Cliffs, N.J. 1969.
31. Gries, D. *Compiler Construction for Digital Computers*. Wiley, New York, 1971.
32. Gruenberger, F. *Computing: An Introduction*. Harcourt Brace and Jovanovich, New York, 1969.
33. Gruenberger, F. *Computing: A Second Course*. Canfield Press, Cleveland, Ohio, 1971.
34. Gruenberger, F., and Jaffray, G. *Problems for Computer Solution*. Wiley, New York, 1965.
35. Gschwind, H.W. *Design of Digital Computers, An Introduction*. Springer-Verlag, New York, 1970.
36. Hamming, R. W. *Computers and Society*. McGraw-Hill, New York, 1972.
37. Harrison, M.C. *Data Structures and Programming*. Courant Institute of Mathematical Sciences, New York U., New York, 1970.
38. Hassitt, A. *Computer Programming and Computer Systems*. Academic Press, New York, 1967.
39. Hellerman, H. *Digital Computer System Principles*. McGraw-Hill, New York, 1967.
40. Higman, B. *A Comparative Study of Programming Languages*. American Elsevier, New York, 1967.
41. Hopgood, F.R.A. *Compiling Techniques*. American Elsevier, New York, 1969.
42. Hull, T.E., and Day, D.D.F. *Computers and Problem Solving*. Addison-Wesley, Don Mills, Ontario, Canada, 1970.
43. Husson, S. *Microprogramming: Principles and Practice*. Prentice-Hall, Englewood Cliffs, N.J., 1970.
44. IFIP. *File Organization*, selected papers from File 68—an I.A.G. Conference. Swets and Zeitinger N.V., Amsterdam, 1969.
45. Iliffe, J. K. *Basic Machine Principles*. American Elsevier, New York, 1968.
46. Iverson, K. *A Programming Language*. Wiley, New York, 1962.
47. Johnson, L.R. *System Structure in Data, Programs and Computers*. Prentice-Hall, Englewood Cliffs, N.J., 1970.
48. Katzan Jr., H. *Computer Organization and the System/370*. Van Nostrand Rheinhold, New York, 1971.
49. Knuth, D. *The Art of Computer Programming, Vol. 1, Fundamental Algorithms*. Addison-Wesley, Reading, Mass., 1969.
50. Knuth, D. *The Art of Computer Programming, Vol. 2, Seminumerical Algorithms*. Addison-Wesley, Reading, Mass. 1969.
51. Knuth, D. *The Art of Computer Programming, Vol. 3, Sorting and Searching*. Addison-Wesley, Reading, Mass., In press.
52. Korfhage, R. *Logic and Algorithms with Applications to the Computer and Information Sciences*. Wiley, New York, 1966.
53. Laurie, E. J. *Modern Computing Concepts—The IBM 360 Series*. Southwestern, Cincinnati, Ohio, 1970.
54. Lefkovitz, D. *File Structures for On-Line Systems*. Wiley, New York, 1967.
55. Martin, J. *Design of Real-Time Computer Systems*. Prentice-Hall, Englewood Cliffs, N.J., 1967.
56. Martin, J. *Telecommunications and the Computer*. Prentice-Hall, Englewood Cliffs, N.J., 1969.
57. Martin, J. *Introduction to Teleprocessing*. Prentice-Hall, Englewood Cliffs, N.J., 1972.
58. Martin, J., and Norman, A.R.D. *The Computerized Society*. Prentice-Hall, Englewood Cliffs, N.J., 1970.
59. Maurer, H.A., and Williams, M.R. *A Collection of Programming Problems and Techniques*. Prentice-Hall, Englewood Cliffs, N.J., 1972.
60. Maurer, W.D. *Programming: An Introduction to Computer Languages and Techniques*. Holden-Day, San Francisco, 1972.
61. Meadow, C. *The Analysis of Information Systems*. Wiley, New York, 1967.
62. Minsky, M. *Computation: Finite and Infinite Machines*. Prentice-Hall, Englewood Cliffs, N.J., 1967.
63. Oettinger, A.G., and Marks, S. *Run Computer Run*. Harvard U. Press, Boston, 1969.
64. Parkhill, D. *The Challenge of the Computer Utility*. Addison-Wesley, Reading, Mass., 1966.
65. Ralston, A. *Introduction to Programming and Computer Science*. McGraw-Hill, New York, 1971.
66. Rice, J. K., and Rice, J. R. *Introduction to Computer Science: Problems, Algorithms, Languages, Information and Computers*. Holt, Rinehart and Winston, New York, 1969.
67. Rosen, S. (Ed.) *Programming Languages and Systems*. McGraw-Hill, New York, 1967.
68. Rothman, S., and Mosmann, C. *Computers and Society*. Science Research Associates, New York, 1972.
69. Sammet, J. E. *Programming Languages: History and Fundamentals*. Prentice-Hall, Englewood Cliffs, N.J., 1969.
70. Sanders, D. *Computers in Society: An Introduction to Information Processing*. McGraw-Hill, New York, In press.
71. Sayers, A.P. (Ed.) *Operating Systems Survey*. Auerbach Corp., Princeton, N.J., 1971.
72. Sprague, R.E. *Information Utilities*. Prentice-Hall, Englewood Cliffs, N.J., 1970.
73. Sterling, T.D., and Pollack, S.V. *Computing and Computer Science*. Macmillan, New York, 1970.
74. Stimler, S. *Real-Time Data-Processing Systems*. McGraw-Hill, New York, 1969.
75. Stone, H.S. *Introduction to Computer Organization and Data Structures*. McGraw-Hill, New York, 1972.
76. Taviss, I. *The Computer Impact*. Prentice-Hall, Englewood Cliffs, N.J., 1970.
77. Teague, R. *Computing Problems for FORTRAN Solution*. Canfield Press, Cleveland, Ohio, 1972.
78. Trakhtenbrot, B. A. *Algorithms and Automatic Computing Machines*. D.C. Heath, Boston, 1963.
79. Walker, T. *Introduction to Computer Science: An Interdisciplinary Approach*. Allyn and Bacon, Boston, 1972.
80. Walker, T., and Cotterman, W.W. *An Introduction to Computer Science and Algorithmic Processes*. Allyn and Bacon, Boston, 1970.
81. Watson, R.W. *Timesharing System Design Concepts*. McGraw-Hill, New York, 1970.
82. Wegner, P. *Programming Languages, Information Structures and Machine Organization*. McGraw-Hill, New York, 1968.
83. Weingarten, F. *Translation of Computer Languages*. Holden-Day, San Francisco. In press.
84. Wilkes, M.V. *Time-Sharing Computer Systems*. American Elsevier, New York, 1968.
85. In addition to the above list, several collections of articles originally appearing in *Scientific American* have been published in book form by W.H. Freeman, San Francisco. Specifically, they are
   a. *Information*, 1966.
   b. *Computers and Computation*, 1971.
86. Various conference proceedings, journals, bulletins, and the like, should also be maintained in a library collection. The following are of special interest:
   a. *Communications of the ACM* (monthly); *Computing Reviews* (monthly); *Computing Surveys* (quarterly); Proceedings, ACM National Conference (yearly); *SIGCSE Bulletin* (ACM's Special Interest Group-Computer Science Education); *SIGCUE Bulletin* (ACM's Special Interest Group-Computer Uses in Education); *SIGUCC Bulletin* (ACM's Special Interest Group-University Computing Centers). (Information on these publications may be obtained from

ACM Headquarters Office, 1133 Avenue of the Americas, New York, NY 10036.)

b.) Proceedings, AFIPS Fall Joint Computer Conference (yearly); Proceedings, AFIPS Spring Joint Computer Conference (yearly). (Available from AFIPS Press, 210 Summit Avenue, Montvale, NJ 07645.)

c. Proceedings, IFIP Congress (every three years). (Available through North-Holland, P.O. Box 3489, Amsterdam.)

d. Proceedings, IFIP World Conference on Computer Education. (Distributed by Science Associates/International, New York.)

e. Proceedings, Conference on Computers in the Undergraduate Curriculum, 1970-1-2. (Available through Southern Regional Education Board, Atlanta, GA 30313.)

87. The following curriculum reports are relevant to computer science education:

a. Curriculum 68—Recommendations for academic programs in computer science. *Comm. ACM 11* (Mar. 1968), 151-197.

b. An undergraduate course on operating systems principles. COSINE Committee Report, June 1971. (Available from Commission on Education, National Academy of Engineering, 2101 Constitution Avenue, N.W., Washington, DC 20418.)

c. Curriculum recommendations for graduate programs in information systems. Report of the ACM Curriculum Committee on Computer Education for Management, *Comm. ACM 15* (May 1972), 363-398.

d. Recommendations for an undergraduate program in computational mathematics. Committee on the Undergraduate Program in Mathematics May 1971. (Available from CUPM, P.O. Box 1024, Berkeley, CA 94701.)

88. The following statistical reports provide information on the status of computing as obtained from recent surveys:

a. Hamblen, J.W. *Computers in Higher Education: Expenditures, Sources of Funds and Utilization for Research and Instruction: 1964-65 with Projections for 1968-69.* (1967) 325 pp. (Available through Southern Regional Education Board, Atlanta, GA 30313.)

b. Hamblen, J.W. *Inventory of Computers in U.S. Higher Education 1966-67: Utilization and Related Degree Programs.* (1970) 400 pp. (Available through Superintendent of Documents, U.S. Government Printing Office, Washington, D.C.)

c. Hamblen, J.W. *Inventory of Computers in U.S. Higher Education 1969-70: Utilization and Related Degree Programs.* (1972) 400 pp. (Available through Superintendent of Documents, U.S. Government Printing Office, Washington, D.C.)

d. Engel, G.L. Computer science instruction in small colleges —An initial report. *SIGCSE Bull. 3*, 2 (June 1971), 8-18.

CURRICULUM '78

Recommendations for the Undergraduate Program in Computer Science

A Report of the ACM Curriculum Committee on Computer Science

Editors: Richard H. Austing, University of Maryland
Bruce H. Barnes, National Science Foundation
Della T. Bonnette, University of Southwestern Louisiana
Gerald L. Engel, Old Dominion University
Gordon Stokes, Brigham Young University

Contained in this report are the recommendations for the undergraduate degree program in Computer Science of the Curriculum Committee on Computer Science (C^3S) of the Association for Computing Machinery (ACM).

The core curriculum common to all computer science undergraduate programs is presented in terms of elementary level topics and courses, and intermediate level courses. Elective courses, used to round out an undergraduate program, are then discussed, and the entire program including the computer science component and other material is presented. Issues related to undergraduate computer science education, such as service courses, supporting areas, continuing education, facilities, staff, and articulation are presented.

Key Words and Phrases: computer sciences courses, computer science curriculum, computer science education, computer science undergraduate degree programs, service courses, continuing education

CR Categories: 1.52

Contents

1. Introduction

Curriculum development work in computer science has been a continuing effort of the Curriculum Committee on Computer Science (C^3S) of the Association for Computing Machinery (ACM). The work leading to the material presented in this report was started under the chairmanship of C^3S of Preston Hammer, and continued when John Hamblen was appointed chairman in 1976.

In the time since the publication of "Curriculum '68" [1] by C^3S, many significant developments have occurred within computer science education, and many educational efforts have been undertaken by C^3S, other groups within ACM, and other professional organizations. As part of the background work in preparation of this report, an extensive survey of the literature of computer science education since "Curriculum '68" was prepared and published [2]. The efforts of C^3S since 1968 are summarized in this document.

The writing group, in its preparation of this set of recommendations, paid considerable attention to the developments as reported in the literature, and to informal comments received regarding "Curriculum '68." In addition to this, a variety of individuals, representing many different types of institutions, and many different interests within computer science, were brought into C^3S meetings and working sessions to present their ideas. A working draft of the report was prepared and published in the June 1977 *SIGCSE Bulletin* in order that the material receive as wide a distribution as possible, and to provide an opportunity for input from interested individuals. Prior to the publication of the working paper, draft reports on specific areas were widely circulated and numerous panel and discussion sessions were held both to inform interested parties of the thinking of the Committee and to allow for comments and suggestions on the work done to that point.

The wide circulation of the various drafts and working papers resulted in numerous suggestions and constructive criticisms, many of which have been incorporated into this final document. In addition to this input, a relationship of mutual benefit has developed by interaction with the parallel, but independent, development of the Model Curricula Subcommittee of the IEEE Computer Society leading to the publication of their curriculum guidelines in Computer Science and Engineering [3].

The writing group is most grateful to all those individuals who contributed to the effort. The Appendix contains the names and affiliations of those people who contributed by serving on C^3S, by supplying course outlines, by supplying comments on the draft report, and in other ways contributing to the final version presented here. The Committee, of course, assumes full responsibility for the substance of this material and the recommendations contained herein.

The report first presents the core curriculum common to all computer science undergraduate programs. This is presented in Section 2 in terms of elementary level material and courses, and intermediate level courses. Section 3 presents computer science electives that may be used to round out an undergraduate program. In Section 4, the full course of study is presented which includes the computer science component, and other material necessary in a program at the bachelor degree level. The important areas of service courses, including general service courses, supporting areas, and continuing education are discussed in Section 5. The report concludes by addressing the areas of facilities, staff, and articulation in Section 6.

In studying this report, it should be recognized that it is a set of guidelines, prepared by a group of individuals working in a committee mode. As such, the recommendations will not satisfy everyone, nor is it intended that they be appropriate to all institutions. It is the hope of the Committee that this report will further stimulate computer science educators to think about their programs and, as appropriate, to share their thinking with others. If this is done, the primary objective of the preparation of these guidelines will have been met.

2. Core Curriculum

2.1 Introduction

Within the present work, C^3S has considered the classification scheme of computer science as defined in "Curriculum '68" with a view to isolating those areas which should be common to all computer science undergraduate degree programs.

The core curriculum, described in this section, represents this refinement. The material is divided into a section on elementary material, including the specifications of topics at this level and the description of five sample courses, and the intermediate levels, including the description of three sample courses. This collection of eight courses represents one way to include the required core material in the computer science undergraduate major.

While the course material is detailed later on in the section, to gain perspective the eight courses (three semester hours each) are listed here:

CS 1. Computer Programming I
CS 2. Computer Programming II
CS 3. Introduction to Computer Systems
CS 4. Introduction to Computer Organization
CS 5. Introduction to File Processing
CS 6. Operating Systems and Computer Architecture I
CS 7. Data Structures and Algorithm Analysis
CS 8. Organization of Programming Languages

The structuring of the courses as to prerequisites is shown in Figure 1. The solid lines represent required prerequisites, while the dashed lines represent highly recommended prerequisites. This diagram includes courses representing only the computer science material considered to be essential to the program. The entire program, including relevant mathematics requirements, is illustrated in Figure 2 on page 160.

Fig. 1. Computer science core curriculum.

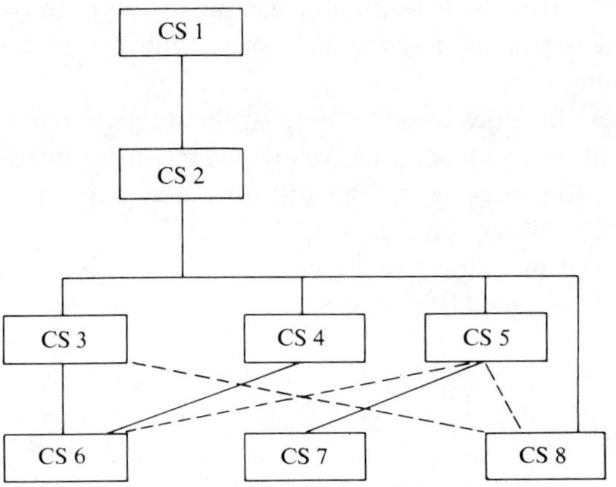

The discussion of the core course material in this section concentrates on the computer science components which are necessary for the undergraduate program. The relationship of this material to two-year programs (especially transfer programs) and the developing high school programs will be considered in Section 6.4.

The elementary core material represents subject matter necessary for all students in computer science in order to be able to achieve the objectives of the undergraduate major. The intermediate level core material follows naturally by providing the students who have been equipped with the basics of the field with the tools to be operational computer scientists.

2.2 Objectives

The core material is required as a prerequisite for advanced courses in the field and thus it is essential that the material be presented early in the program. In learning this material, the computer science student should be provided with the foundation for achieving at least the objectives of an undergraduate degree program that are listed below.

Computer science majors should:

1. be able to write programs in a reasonable amount of time that work correctly, are well documented, and are readable;
2. be able to determine whether or not they have written a reasonably efficient and well organized program;
3. know what general types of problems are amenable to computer solution, and the various tools necessary for solving such problems;
4. be able to assess the implications of work performed either as an individual or as a member of a team;
5. understand basic computer architectures;
6. be prepared to pursue in-depth training in one or more application areas or further education in computer science.

It should be recognized that these alone do not represent the total objectives of an undergraduate program, but only those directly related to the computer science component. Material addressing other requirements and electives is covered in Section 4.4.

2.3 Elementary Material

In order to facilitate the attainment of the objectives above, computer science majors must be given a thorough grounding in the study of the implementation of algorithms in programming languages which operate on data structures in the environment of hardware. Emphasis at the elementary level then should be placed on algorithms, programming, and data structures, but with a good understanding of the hardware capabilities involved in their implementation.

Specifically, the following topics are considered elementary. They should be common to all undergraduate programs in computer science.

Programming Topics

P1. Algorithms: includes the concept and properties of algorithms; the role of algorithms in the problem solving process; constructs and languages to facilitate the expression of algorithms.

P2. Programming Languages: includes basic syntax and semantics of a higher level (problem oriented) language; subprograms; I/O; recursion.

P3. Programming Style: includes the preparation of readable, understandable, modifiable, and more easily verifiable programs through the application of concepts and techniques of structured programming; program documentation; some practical aspects of proving programs correct. (Note: Programming style should pervade the entire curriculum rather than be considered as a separate topic.)

P4. Debugging and Verification: includes the use of debugging software, selection of test data; techniques for error detection; relation of good programming style to the use of error detection; and program verification.

P5. Applications: includes an introduction to uses of selected topics in areas such as information retrieval, file management, lexical analysis, string processing and numeric computation; need for and examples of different types of programming languages; social, philosophical, and ethical considerations.

Software Organization

S1. Computer Structure and Machine Language: includes organization of computers in terms of I/O, storage, control and processing units; register and storage structures, instruction format and execution; principal instruction types; machine arithmetic; program control; I/O operations; interrupts.

S2. Data Representation: includes bits, bytes, words and other information structures; number representation; representation of elementary data structures; data transmission, error detection and correction; fixed versus variable word lengths.

S3. Symbolic Coding and Assembly Systems: includes mnemonic operation codes; labels; symbolic addresses and address expressions; literals; extended machine operations and pseudo operations; error flags and messages; scanning of symbolic instructions and symbol table construction; overall design and operation of assemblers, compilers, and interpreters.

S4. Addressing Techniques: includes absolute, relative, base associative, indirect, and immediate addressing; indexing; memory mapping functions; storage allocation, paging and machine organization to facilitate modes of addressing.

S5. Macros: includes definition, call, expansion of macros; parameter handling; conditional assembly and assembly time computation.

S6. Program Segmentation and Linkage: includes subroutines, coroutines and functions; subprogram loading and linkage; common data linkage transfer vectors; parameter passing and binding; overlays; re-entrant subprograms; stacking techniques; linkage using page and segment tables.

S7. Linkers and Loaders: separate compilation of subroutines; incoming and outgoing symbols; relocation; resolving intersegment references by direct and indirect linking.

S8. Systems and Utility Programs: includes basic concepts of loaders, I/O systems, human interface with operating systems; program libraries.

Hardware Organization

H1. Computer Systems Organization: includes characteristics of, and relationships between I/O devices, processors, control units, main and auxiliary storage devices; organization of modules into a system; multiple processor configurations and computer networks; relationship between computer organization and software.

H2. Logic Design: includes basic digital circuits; AND, OR, and NOT elements; half-adder, adder, storage and delay elements; encoding-decoding logic; basic concepts of microprogramming; logical equivalence between hardware and software; elements of switching algebra; combinatorial and sequential networks.

H3. Data Representation and Transfer: includes codes, number representation; flipflops, registers, gates.

H4. Digital Arithmetic: includes serial versus parallel adders; subtraction and signed magnitude versus complemented arithmetic; multiply/divide algorithms; elementary speed-up techniques for arithmetic.

H5. Digital Storage and Accessing: includes memory control; data and address buses; addressing and accessing methods; memory segmentation; data flow in multimemory and hierarchical systems.

H6. Control and I/O: includes synchronous and asynchronous control; interrupts; modes of communication with processors.

H7. Reliability: includes error detection and correction, diagnostics.

Data Structures and File Processing

D1. Data Structures: includes arrays, strings, stacks, queues, linked lists; representation in memory; algorithms for manipulating data within these structures.

D2. Sorting and searching: includes algorithms for in-core sorting and searching methods; comparative efficiency of methods; table lookup techniques; hash coding.

D3. Trees: includes basic terminology and types; representation as binary trees; traversal schemes; representation in memory; breadth-first and depth-first search techniques; threading.

D4. File Terminology: includes record, file, blocking, database; overall idea of database management systems.

D5. Sequential Access: includes physical characteristics of appropriate storage media; sort/merge algorithms; file manipulation techniques for updating, deleting, and inserting records.

D6. Random Access: includes physical characteristics of appropriate storage media; physical representation of data structures on storage devices; algorithms and techniques for implementing inverted lists, multilists, indexed sequential, hierarchical structures.

D7. File I/O: includes file control systems (directory, allocation, file control table, file security); I/O specification statements for allocating space and cataloging files; file utility routines; data handling (format definition, block buffering, buffer pools, compaction).

2.4 Implementation Considerations

Throughout the presentation of the elementary level material, programming projects should be assigned; these projects should be designed to aid in the comprehension and use of language details, to exemplify the problem solving process, and/or to introduce more advanced areas of computer science.

Good programming style should be stressed in the teaching of all of this material. The discipline required to achieve style will promote the development of effective algorithms and should result in students writing correct, understandable programs. Thus emphasis in the programming exercises should be placed on efficient algorithms, structured programming techniques, and good documentation.

A specific course on structured programming, or on programming style, is not intended at the elementary level. The topics are of such importance that they should be considered a common thread throughout the entire curriculum and, as such, should be totally integrated into the curriculum. They provide a philosophy of discipline which pervades all of the course work.

Throughout the presentation of this elementary material, meaningful actual computer applications should be cited and reviewed. In the process of so doing, reference must be made to the social, philosophical, and ethical considerations involved in the applications. Like structured programming, these issues are of such importance to the development of the computer scientist that they must permeate the instruction at this level.

It would be desirable, though not necessary, for the

computer science major to be familiar with all of the elementary level topics before taking intermediate level courses. This, however, may not always be possible. Factors influencing how and when courses are offered which include the material are: the purpose and circumstances of a particular department within the context of its educational institution, the availability of computer resources, and whether an institution is on the quarter or semester system.

Most courses at this level should include laboratory sessions. These laboratories provide the student with the opportunity to gain practical experience by actually solving problems on the computer. Laboratory sessions should be implemented in such a way that the student can develop good programming techniques under close supervision. The instructor may or may not be the same as for the lecture portion of the course. The absence of a specific laboratory in a course description does not imply that programming should not be required.

2.5 Sample Elementary Level Courses

The following set of courses is provided merely as a sample to illustrate one of the ways in which core material at the elementary level might be presented. Other implementations are possible. No matter what implementation is attempted, however, all of the elementary material specified in Section 2.3 should be included so that students are equipped with adequate background for intermediate and advanced level material.

Each course described in the sample set is assumed to be offered on a semester basis. Suggested numbers of hours of credit are given in parentheses immediately after the course titles. For example, (2-2-3) indicates two hours of lectures and two hours of laboratory per week for a total of three semester hours of credit.

CS 1. Computer Programming I (2-2-3)

The objectives of this course are:

(a) to introduce problem solving methods and algorithm development;

(b) to teach a high level programming language that is widely used; and

(c) to teach how to design, code, debug, and document programs using techniques of good programming style.

COURSE OUTLINE

The material on a high level programming language and on algorithm development can be taught best as an integrated whole. Thus the topics should not be covered sequentially. The emphasis of the course is on the techniques of algorithm development and programming with style. Neither esoteric features of a programming language nor other aspects of computers should be allowed to interfere with that purpose.

TOPICS

A. *Computer Organization.* An overview identifying components and their functions, machine and assembly languages. (5%)

B. *Programming Language and Programming.* Representation of integers, reals, characters, instructions. Data types, constants, variables. Arithmetic expression. Assignment statement. Logical expression. Sequencing, alternation, and iteration. Arrays. Subprograms and parameters. Simple I/O. Programming projects utilizing concepts and emphasizing good programming style. (45%)

C. *Algorithm Development.* Techniques of problem solving. Flowcharting. Stepwise refinement. Simple numerical examples. Algorithms for searching (e.g. linear, binary), sorting (e.g. exchange, insertion), merging of ordered lists. Examples taken from such areas as business applications involving data manipulation, and simulations involving games. (45%)

D. *Examinations.* (5%)

CS 2. Computer Programming II (2-2-3)

Prerequisite: CS 1

The objectives of this course are:

(a) to continue the development of discipline in program design, in style and expression, in debugging and testing, especially for larger programs;

(b) to introduce algorithmic analysis; and

(c) to introduce basic aspects of string processing, recursion, internal search/sort methods and simple data structures.

COURSE OUTLINE

The topics in this outline should be introduced as needed in the context of one or more projects involving larger programs. The instructor may choose to begin with the statement of a sizeable project, then utilize structured programming techniques to develop a number of small projects each of which involves string processing, recursion, searching and sorting, or data structures. The emphasis on good programming style, expression, and documentation, begun in CS 1, should be continued. In order to do this effectively, it may be necessary to introduce a second language (especially if a language like Fortran is used in CS 1). In that case, details of the language should be included in the outline. Analysis of algorithms should be introduced, but at this level such analysis should be given by the instructor to the student.

Consideration should be given to the implementation of programming projects by organizing students into programming teams. This technique is essential in advanced level courses and should be attempted as early as possible in the curriculum. If large class size makes such an approach impractical, every effort should be made to have each student's programs read and critiqued by another student.

TOPICS

A. *Review.* Principles of good programming style, expression, and documentation. Details of a second language if appropriate. (15%)

B. *Structured Programming Concepts.* Control flow. Invariant relation of a loop. Stepwise refinement of both statements and data structures, or top-down programming. (40%)

C. *Debugging and Testing.* (10%)

D. *String Processing.* Concatenation. Substrings. Matching. (5%)

E. *Internal Searching and Sorting.* Methods such as binary, radix, Shell, quicksort, merge sort. Hash coding. (10%)

F. *Data Structures.* Linear allocation (e.g. stacks, queues, deques) and linked allocation (e.g. simple linked lists). (10%)

G. *Recursion.* (5%)

H. *Examinations.* (5%)

CS 3. Introduction to Computer Systems (2-2-3)
Prerequisite: CS 2

The objectives of this course are:

(a) to provide basic concepts of computer systems;
(b) to introduce computer architecture; and
(c) to teach an assembly language.

COURSE OUTLINE

The extent to which each topic is discussed and the ordering of topics depends on the facilities available and the nature and orientation of CS 4 described below. Enough assembly language details should be covered and projects assigned so that the student gains experience in programming a specific computer. However, concepts and techniques that apply to a broad range of computers should be emphasized. Programming methods that are developed in CS 1 and CS 2 should also be utilized in this course.

TOPICS

A. *Computer Structure and Machine Language.* Memory, control, processing and I/O units. Registers, principal machine instruction types and their formats. Character representation. Program control. Fetch-execute cycle. Timing. I/O operations. (15%)

B. *Assembly Language.* Mnemonic operations. Symbolic addresses. Assembler concepts and instruction format. Data-word definition. Literals. Location counter. Error flags and messages. Implementation of high level language constructs. (30%)

C. *Addressing Techniques.* Indexing. Indirect Addressing. Absolute and relative addressing. (5%)

D. *Macros.* Definition. Call. Parameters. Expansion. Nesting. Conditional assembly. (10%)

E. *File I/O.* Basic physical characteristics of I/O and auxiliary storage devices. File control system. I/O specification statements and device handlers. Data handling, including buffering and blocking. (5%)

F. *Program Segmentation and Linkage.* Subroutines. Coroutines. Recursive and re-entrant routines. (20%)

G. *Assembler Construction.* One-pass and two-pass assemblers. Relocation. Relocatable loaders. (5%)

H. *Interpretive Routines.* Simulators. Trace. (5%)

I. *Examinations.* (5%)

CS 4. Introduction to Computer Organization (3-0-3) or (2-2-3)
Prerequisite: CS 2

The objectives of this course are:

(a) to introduce the organization and structuring of the major hardware components of computers;
(b) to understand the mechanics of information transfer and control within a digital computer system; and
(c) to provide the fundamentals of logic design.

COURSE OUTLINE

The three main categories in the outline, namely computer architecture, arithmetic, and basic logic design, should be interwoven throughout the course rather than taught sequentially. The first two of these areas may be covered, at least in part, in CS 3 and the amount of material included in this course will depend on how the topics are divided between the two courses. The logic design part of the outline is specific and essential to this course. The functional, logic design level is emphasized rather than circuit details which are more appropriate in engineering curricula. The functional level provides the student with an understanding of the mechanics of information transfer and control within the computer system. Although much of the course material can and should be presented in a form that is independent of any particular technology, it is recommended that an actual, simple minicomputer or microcomputer system be studied. A supplemental laboratory is appropriate for that purpose.

TOPICS

A. *Basic Logic Design.* Representation of both data and control information by digital (binary) signals. Logic properties of elemental devices for processing (gates) and storing (flipflops) information. Description by truth tables, Boolean functions and timing diagrams. Analysis and synthesis of combinatorial networks of commonly used gate types. Parallel and serial registers. Analysis and synthesis of simple synchronous control mechanisms; data and address buses; addressing and accessing methods; memory segmentation. Practical methods of timing pulse generation. (25%)

B. *Coding.* Commonly used codes (e.g. BCD, ASCII). Parity generation and detection. Encoders, decoders, code converters. (5%)

C. *Number Representation and Arithmetic.* Binary number representation, unsigned addition and subtraction. One's and two's complement, signed magnitude and excess radix number representations and their pros and cons for implementing elementary arithmetic for BCD and excess-3 representations. (10%)

D. *Computer Architecture.* Functions of, and communication between, large-scale components of a computer system. Hardware implementation and sequencing of instruction fetch, address construction, and instruction execution. Data flow and control block diagrams of a simple processor. Concept of microprogram and analogy with software. Properties of simple I/O devices and their controllers, synchronous control, interrupts. Modes of communications with processors. (35%)

E. *Example.* Study of an actual, simple minicomputer or microcomputer system. (20%)
F. *Examinations.* (5%)

CS 5. Introduction to File Processing (3-0-3)
Prerequisite: CS 2

The objectives of this course are:

(a) to introduce concepts and techniques of structuring data on bulk storage devices;
(b) to provide experience in the use of bulk storage devices; and
(c) to provide the foundation for applications of data structures and file processing techniques.

COURSE OUTLINE

The emphasis given to topics in this outline will vary depending on the computer facilities available to students. Programming projects should be assigned to give students experience in file processing. Characteristics and utilization of a variety of storage devices should be covered even though some of the devices are not part of the computer system that is used. Algorithmic analysis and programming techniques developed in CS 2 should be utilized.

TOPICS

A. *File Processing Environment.* Definitions of record, file, blocking, compaction, database. Overview of database management system. (5%)
B. *Sequential Access.* Physical characteristics of sequential media (tape, cards, etc.). External sort/merge algorithms. File manipulation techniques for updating, deleting and inserting records in sequential files. (30%)
C. *Data Structures.* Algorithms for manipulating linked lists. Binary, B-trees, B*-trees, and AVL trees. Algorithms for traversing and balancing trees. Basic concepts of networks (plex structures). (20%)
D. *Random Access.* Physical characteristics of disk/drum and other bulk storage devices. Physical representation of data structure on storage devices. Algorithms and techniques for implementing inverted lists, multilist, indexed sequential, and hierarchical structures. (35%)
E. *File I/O.* File control systems and utility routines, I/O specification statements for allocating space and cataloging files. (5%)
F. *Examinations.* (5%)

2.6 Sample Intermediate Level Courses

Sample versions of three courses at the intermediate level are given to illustrate topics and material which should be required of all computer science majors. This material and the elementary level topics in Section 2.3 constitute the minimum requirements which should be common to all computer science undergraduate programs to achieve the basic objectives of those programs.

Courses which cover the intermediate level material contain a strong emphasis on fundamental concepts exemplified by various types of programming languages, architecture and operating systems, and data structures. Neither theoretical treatments nor case study approaches in and of themselves are adequate or appropriate at this level. Advanced level (elective) courses may be used for predominantly theoretical treatment of topics or for comprehensive case studies.

CS 6. Operating Systems and Computer Architecture I (2-2-3)
Prerequisite: CS 3 and CS 4
(CS 5 recommended)

The objectives of this course are:

(a) to develop an understanding of the organization and architecture of computer systems at the register-transfer and programming levels of system description;
(b) to introduce the major concept areas of operating systems principles;
(c) to teach the inter-relationships between the operating system and the architecture of computer systems.

COURSE OUTLINE

This course should emphasize concepts rather than case studies. Subtleties do exist, however, in operating systems that do not readily follow from concepts alone. It is recommended that a laboratory requiring hands on experience be included with this course.

The laboratory for the course would ideally use a small computer where students could actually implement sections of operating systems and have them fail without serious consequences to other users. This system should have, at a minimum, a CPU, memory, disk or tape, and some terminal device such as a teletype or CRT. The second best choice for the laboratory experience would be a simulated system running on a larger machine.

The course material should be liberally sprinkled with examples of operating system segments implemented on particular computer system architectures. The interdependence of operating systems and architecture should be clearly delineated. Integrating these subjects at an early stage in the curriculum is particularly important because the effects of computer architecture on systems software has long been recognized. Also, modern systems combine the design of operating systems and the architecture.

TOPICS

A. *Review.* Instruction sets. I/O and interrupt structure. Addressing schemes. Microprogramming. (10%)
B. *Dynamic Procedure Activation.* Procedure activation and deactivation on a stack, including dynamic storage allocation, passing value and reference parameters, establishing new local environments, addressing mechanisms for accessing parameters (e.g. displays,

relative addressing in the stack). Implementing non-local references. Re-entrant programs. Implementation on register machines. (15%)

C. *System Structure.* Design methodologies such as level, abstract data types, monitors, kernels, nuclei, networks of operating system modules. Proving correctness. (10%)

D. *Evaluation.* Elementary queueing, network models of systems, bottlenecks, program behavior, and statistical analysis. (15%)

E. *Memory Management.* Characteristics of the hierarchy of storage media, virtual memory, paging, segmentation. Policies and mechanisms for efficiency of mapping operations and storage utilization. Memory protection. Multiprogramming. Problems of auxiliary memory. (20%)

F. *Process Management.* Asynchronous processes. Using interrupt hardware to trigger software procedure calls. Process stateword and automatic SWITCH instructions. Semaphores. Ready lists. Implementing a simple scheduler. Examples of process control problems such as deadlock, producer/consumers, readers/writers. (20%)

G. *Recovery Procedures.* Techniques of automatic and manual recovery in the event of system failures. (5%)

H. *Examinations.* (5%)

CS 7. Data Structures and Algorithm Analysis (3-0-3)

Prerequisite: CS 5

The objectives of this course are:

(a) to apply analysis and design techniques to nonnumeric algorithms which act on data structures;

(b) to utilize algorithmic analysis and design criteria in the selection of methods for data manipulation in the environment of a database management system.

COURSE OU.LINE

The materia: in this outline could be covered sequentially in a course. It is designed to build on the foundation established in the elementary material, particularly on that material which involves algorithm development (P1, P3) and data structures and file processing (D1, D7). The practical approach in the earlier material should be made more rigorous in this course through the use of techniques for the analysis and design of efficient algorithms. The results of this more formal study should then be incorporated into data management system design decisions. This involves differentiating between theoretical or experimental results for individual methods and the results which might actually be achieved in systems which integrate a variety of methods and data structures. Thus, database management systems provide the applications environment for topics discussed in the course.

Projects and assignments should involve implementation of theoretical results. This suggests an alternative way of covering the material in the course, namely to treat concepts, algorithms, and analysis in class and deal with their impact on system design in assignments. Of course, some in-class discussions of this impact would occur, but at various times throughout the course rather than concentrated at the end.

TOPICS

A. *Review.* Basic data structures such as stacks, queues, lists, trees. Algorithms for their implementation. (10%)

B. *Graphs.* Definition, terminology, and property (e.g. connectivity). Algorithms for finding paths and spanning trees. (15%)

C. *Algorithms Design and Analysis.* Basic techniques of design and analysis of efficient algorithms for internal and external sorting/merging/searching. Intuitive notions of complexity (e.g. NP-hard problems). (30%)

D. *Memory Management.* Hashing. Algorithms for dynamic storage allocation (e.g. buddy system, boundary-tag), garbage collection and compaction. (15%)

E. *System Design.* Integration of data structures, sort/merge/search methods (internal and external) and memory media into a simple database management system. Accessing methods. Effects on run time, costs, efficiency. (25%)

F. *Examinations.* (5%)

CS 8. Organization of Programming Languages (3-0-3)

Prerequisite: CS 2 (CS 3 and CS 5 highly recommended)

The objectives of this course are:

(a) to develop an understanding of the organization of programming languages, especially the run-time behavior of programs;

(b) to introduce the formal study of programming language specification and analysis;

(c) to continue the development of problem solution and programming skills introduced in the elementary level material.

COURSE OUTLINE

This is an applied course in programming language constructs emphasizing the run-time behavior of programs. It should provide appropriate background for advanced level courses involving formal and theoretical aspects of programming languages and/or the compilation process.

The material in this outline is not intended to be covered sequentially. Instead, programming languages could be specified and analyzed one at a time in terms of their features and limitations based on their run-time environments. Alternatively, desirable specification of programming languages could be discussed and then exemplified by citing their implementations in various languages. In either case, programming exercises in each language should be assigned to emphasize the implementations of language features.

Topics

A. *Language Definition Structure.* Formal language concepts including syntax and basic characteristics of grammars, especially finite state, context-free, and ambiguous. Backus-Naur Form. A language such as Algol as an example. (15%)

B. *Data Types and Structures.* Review of basic data types, including lists and trees. Constructs for specifying and manipulating data types. Language features affecting static and dynamic data storage management. (10%)

C. *Control Structures and Data Flow.* Programming language constructs for specifying program control and data transfer, including DO . . . FOR, DO . . . WHILE, REPEAT . . . UNTIL, BREAK, subroutines, procedures, block structures, and interrupts. Decision tables, recursion. Relationship with good programming style should be emphasized. (15%)

D. *Run-time Consideration.* The effects of the run-time environment and binding time on various features of programming languages. (25%)

E. *Interpretative Languages.* Compilation vs. interpretation. String processing with language features such as those available in SNOBOL 4. Vector processing with language features such as those available in APL. (20%)

F. *Lexical Analysis and Parsing.* An introduction to lexical analysis including scanning, finite state acceptors and symbol tables. An introduction to parsing and compilers including push-down acceptors, top-down and bottom-up parsing. (10%)

G. *Examinations.* (5%)

3. Computer Science Electives

3.1 Introduction

In this section a variety of computer science electives will be considered which are appropriate at the elementary and advanced levels. Elective courses at the elementary level, while enhancing the program of a student, normally should not be used to meet the requirements of the major program. Elective courses at the advanced level should be selected to meet major requirements as well as to allow the student to explore particular areas of computer science in more detail.

3.2 Elementary Level

At the elementary level it would be highly desirable to provide a mechanism for offering courses in specific programming languages such as APL, Cobol, LISP, or PL/I which could be taken as electives by computer science majors or majors in other disciplines. The extent of the course, the number of credits offered and the prerequisites would depend on the language offered and the purpose for offering it. One convenient way to achieve this goal would be to include in the curriculum a Programming Language Laboratory for variable credit (i.e. one to three semester hours). The prerequisite could be designated in general as "consent of instructor" or more specifically as CS 1 or CS 2 and the laboratory could be taken for repeated credit provided that different languages were taught. In addition to its function as an elective, the laboratory could be offered in conjunction with an intermediate or advanced course, thus enabling an instructor to require students to learn a specific language at the same time they take a course (e.g. LISP in the laboratory along with CS 7—Data Structures and Algorithm Analysis).

3.3 Advanced Level

Ten advanced level elective courses are specified. Computer Science departments should offer as many as possible of these courses on a regular basis, but few departments are expected to have sufficient resources to offer all, or even a large majority, of them. Possible additional courses which could be offered as special topics are listed in Section 3.4.

CS 9. Computers and Society (3-0-3)

Prerequisite: elementary core material

The objectives of this course are:

(a) to present concepts of social value and valuations;

(b) to introduce models which describe the impact of computers on society;

(c) to provide a framework for professional activity that involves explicit consideration of and decisions concerning social impact;

(d) to present tools and techniques which are applicable to problems posed by the social impact of computers.

Much debate surrounds the role of this course in the curriculum. While few will disagree that professional computer scientists should be instructed to evaluate social issues regarding that which they do, it has been argued that such a course is not a computer science course, but rather should be in the area of the social sciences. Another argument is presented which states that this material is so important that it should not merely be covered in a single course, but instead should be integrated throughout the curriculum. Although this latter argument has validity, it is difficult to insure sufficient coverage of topics when they are scattered throughout a number of courses. As a result it is recommended that this course be considered at least as a strongly recommended elective. If, in fact, the material to meet the above objectives is not covered in the other intermediate and advanced level courses in this program, then this course should be required.

A computer science major taking an advanced level computers and society course would be expected to be familiar with the elementary material described in the previous section. All of that material, however, is not necessarily prerequisite for such a course. The prerequisite should, in fact, be chosen in such a manner that nonmajors would also be able to take the course. A mixture of majors in such a course would provide broadening interchange and would benefit both the computer science students and the other majors. The course should be taught by the computer science faculty, but team-teaching with faculty from other disciplines should be encouraged. The course could be general and treat a number of computer impact topics, or specific, and treat in depth one of the topics (such as legal issues in computing). This recommendation is conditioned on the assumption that instructors who present material on societal impact, whether as an entire course or as part of other courses, will try to include both sides of or approaches to issues without instilling their own philosophical leanings on complex societal issues. For example, certain topics contain political overtones which should be discussed, but which, if not done carefully, can give the material a political science flavor it does not deserve.

A strict outline is not given. The number of topics and extent of coverage as well as the instructional techniques used can vary considerably and still meet the objectives of the course. A term project involving computer applications that are manifested in the local community is strongly recommended. Possible topics, but certainly not an exhaustive list, that could be included in such a course are as follows:

A. History of computing and technology
B. The place of the computer in modern society
C. The computer and the individual
D. Survey of computer applications
E. Legal issues
F. Computers in decision-making processes
G. The computer scientist as a professional
H. Futurists' views of computing
I. Public perception of computers and computer scientists

CS 10. Operating Systems and Computer Architecture II (2-2-3)

Prerequisite: CS 6; Corequisite: a course in statistics

COURSE OUTLINE

This course continues the development of the material in CS 6. Emphasis should be on intrasystem communication.

TOPICS

A. *Review.* I/O and interrupt structure. Addressing schemes. Memory management. (10%)

B. *Concurrent Processes.* Concepts of processes in parallel. Problems associated with determinancy, freedom from deadlock, mutual exclusion, and synchronization. (15%)

C. *Name Management.* Limitations of linear address space. Implementation of tree-structured space of objects for the support of modular programming. (15%)

D. *Resource Allocation.* Queueing and network control policies. Concepts of system balancing and thrashing. Job activation/deactivation. Process scheduling. Multiprogramming systems. (25%)

E. *Protection.* Contraints for accessing objects. Mechanism to specify and enforce access rules. Implementation in existing systems. (15%)

F. *Advanced Architecture and Operating Systems Implementations.* Pipelining and parallelism. User interface considerations. Introduction to telecommunications, networks (including minicomputers) and distributed systems. (15%)

G. *Examinations.* (5%)

CS 11. Database Management Systems Design (3-0-3)

Prerequisites: CS 6 and CS 7

COURSE OUTLINE

This course should emphasize the concepts and structures necessary to design and implement a database management system. The student should become acquainted with current literature on the subject and should be given an opportunity to use a database management system if possible.

During the course the student should gain an understanding of various physical file organization and data organization techniques. The concept of data models should be covered and the network, relational, and hierarchical data models should be explored. Examples of specific database management systems should be examined and related to the data models discussed. The student should become familiar with normalized forms of data relations including canonical schema representations. Techniques of systems design and implementation should be discussed and practiced. Data integrity and file security techniques should be explored. The major experience of the course should be the design and implementation of a simple database management system that would include file security and some form of query into the system.

TOPICS

A. *Introduction to Database Concepts.* Goals of DBMS including data independence, relationships, logical and physical organizations, schema and subschema. (5%)

B. *Data Models.* Hierarchical, network, and relational models with a description of the logical and data structure representation of the database system. Examples of implementations of the various models. (15%)

C. *Data Normalization.* First, second, and third normal forms of data relations. Canonical schema. Data independence. (5%)

D. *Data Description Languages.* Forms, applications, examples, design strategies. (10%)

E. *Query Facilities.* Relational algebra, relational calculus, data structures for establishing relations. Query functions. Design and translation strategies. (15%)

F. *File Organization.* Storage hierarchies, data structures, multiple key systems, indexed files, hashing. Physical characteristics. (25%)
G. *Index Organization.* Relation to files. Inverted file systems. Design strategies. (5%)
H. *File Security.* Authentication, authorization, transformation, encryptions. Hardware and software techniques. Design strategies. (10%)
I. *Data Integrity and Reliability.* Redundancy, recovery, locking, and monitoring. (5%)
J. *Examinations.* (5%)

CS 12. Artificial Intelligence (3-0-3)
Prerequisite: CS 7

COURSE OUTLINE

This course introduces students to basic concepts and techniques of artificial intelligence, or intelligent systems, and gives insights into active research areas and applications. Emphasis is placed on representation as a central and necessary concept for work in intelligent systems. Strategies for choosing representations as well as notational systems and structures should be discussed. Students should understand, for example, that the selection of a programming language is really a basic representational choice and that an important component of that choice is whether the programming language is really the basic representational mode or whether it is a translator/interpreter of an intermediate representational mode such as the predicate calculus or other notational system (e.g. modal or fuzzy logics).

Other issues of importance in this course are natural language, vision systems, search strategies, and control. The extent and type of coverage will vary. The use of natural language and vision systems in applications of intelligent systems research to other disciplines should be emphasized. Search strategies should be seen as being implicit in representation and control. General issues related to control should be discussed and illustrated by examples of existing systems. A variety of applications could be mentioned at the beginning of the course as motivation for studying intelligent systems. These applications could then be elaborated on at appropriate times throughout the course or at the end.

Students could profit from a background in LISP because of its widespread use in artificial intelligence work. A Programming Language Laboratory as described in Section 3.2 could be used to provide this background either concurrently or with CS 7. If neither alternative is possible, then an introduction to LISP could be included in the course during the discussion of representation, but there would not be enough time for an in-depth treatment of the language.

TOPICS

A. *Representation.* Constraints and capabilities of notational systems such as logics and programming languages. Notational structures such as trees, networks, statistical representations, and frames. Strategies for choosing representations (e.g. exploiting natural constraints in data, representation of similar patterns as in analogies). Introduction to LISP. (40%)
B. *Search Strategies.* Tree and graph searches (e.g. depth and breadth first, minimax, alpha-beta). Heuristics. (15%)
C. *Control.* General characteristics of production and procedurally oriented systems. Parallel vs. serial processing. Existing systems to illustrate issues (e.g. HEARSAY II, DENDRAL, MYCIN). (20%)
D. *Communication and Perception.* Introduction to concepts related to current research in natural language and in vision systems. Use of tactility in intelligent systems. (10%)
E. *Applications.* Sampling of current work in such areas as psychology, medicine, science, architecture, and such machines as industrial robots. (10%)
F. *Examinations.* (5%)

CS 13. Algorithms (3-0-3)
Prerequisites: CS 7 and CS 8

COURSE OUTLINE

This course should develop students' abilities as writers and critics of programs by exposing students to problems and their algorithmic solution. As programming is both art and science, student programmers can benefit considerably from analysis of case studies in a wide variety of areas. All options for presenting algorithms in a very high level language should be considered, without regard for whether a processor exists for that language. Translation of each algorithm to a more machine-readable form can be given separately, if necessary. Careful choice of the level of abstraction appropriate to a given problem should be made as a means of adjusting students' load in the course.

Domain independent techniques should emerge during the course as algorithm-rich topics are presented from various areas. One convenient classification of topics into areas to ensure breadth of coverage is: combinatorics, numerical analysis, systems programming, and artificial intelligence. Algorithms from a majority of these areas should be analyzed, although not necessarily in the order indicated in the outline. The percentage ranges are intended to give instructors flexibility in choosing areas and topics.

TOPICS

A. *Combinatorics.* Algorithms for unordered and ordered sets, graphs, matrices (within the semi-ring paradigm), bit vectors. (10-25%)
B. *Numerical Analysis.* Algorithms for integer arithmetic (fast multiplication, prime testing, sieves, factoring, greatest common denominator, linear Diophantine equations), real arithmetic (Taylor series, how various calculators work), polynomial arithmetic, random numbers, matrix operations (inversion, determinants). (10-25%)

C. *Systems Programming.* Algorithms in text processors (pattern matching) language processors (parsing, storage management), operating systems (scheduling, synchronization), database management (sorting, searching). (10-25%)

D. *Artificial Intelligence.* Algorithms in natural language processing (concordances, context-free parsers), robotics (vision, manipulator operation), theorem proving and problem solving (decision methods, search heuristics). (10-25%)

E. *Domain Independent Techniques.* Divide-and-conquer. Solution of recurrence equations. Dynamic programming. (15%)

F. *Examinations.* (5%)

CS 14. Software Design and Development (3-0-3) or (2-2-3)

Prerequisites: CS 7 and CS 8

COURSE OUTLINE

This course presents a formal approach to state-of-the-art techniques in software design and development and provides a means for students to apply the techniques. An integral part of the course is the involvement of students working in teams in the organization, management, and development of a large software project. The team project aspect can be facilitated either by scheduling separate laboratories or by using some of the lecture periods to discuss practical aspects of the team projects.

TOPICS

A. *Design Techniques.* Formal models of structured programming. Demonstrations of code reading and correctness. Stepwise refinement and reorganization. Segmentation. Top-down design and development. Information hiding. Iterative enhancement. Structured design. Strength and coupling measures. (50%)

B. *Organization and Management.* Milestones and estimating. Chief programmer teams. Program libraries. Walk-throughs. Documentation. (15%)

C. *Team Project.* Organization, management, and development of a large scale software project by students working in teams. (30%)

D. *Examinations.* (5%)

CS 15. Theory of Programming Languages (3-0-3)

Prerequisite: CS 8

COURSE OUTLINE

This is a course in the formal treatment of programming language translation and compiler design concepts. Course material builds on the background established in CS 8, specifically on the introduction to lexical analysis, parsing, and compilers. Emphasis should be on the theoretical aspects of parsing context-free languages, translation specifications, and machine-independent code improvement. Programming projects to demonstrate various concepts are desirable, but extensive projects to write compilers, or major components of compilers, should be deferred to a special topics course on compiler writing.

TOPICS

A. *Review.* Grammars, languages, and their syntax and semantics. Concepts of parsing and ambiguity. BNF description of Algol. (15%)

B. *Scanners.* Finite state grammars and recognizers. Lexical scanners. Implementation of symbol tables. (20%)

C. *Parsers.* Theory and examples of context-free languages and push-down automata (PDA). Context-free parsing techniques such as recursive descent, LL(k), precedence, LR(k), SLR(k). (40%)

D. *Translation.* Techniques of machine-independent code generation and improvement. Inherited and synthesized attributes. Syntax directed translation schema. (20%)

E. *Examinations.* (5%)

CS 16. Automata, Computability, and Formal Languages (3-0-3)

Prerequisites: CS 8 and MA 4 (see Sect. 4.1)

COURSE OUTLINE

This course offers a diverse sampling of the areas of theoretical computer science and their hierarchical interconnections. Basic results relating to formal models of computation should be introduced. Stress should be given to developing students' skills in understanding rigorous definitions in computing environments and in determining their logical consequences. In this regard strong emphasis should be placed on problem assignments and their evaluations.

Material need not be presented in the order specified, but it is important to give nearly equal emphasis among the major areas. Topics within each area can be covered in greater depth in appropriate special topics courses.

TOPICS

A. *Finite State Concepts.* Acceptors (including nondeterminism). Regular expressions. Closure properties. Sequential machines and finite state transducers. State minimization. (30%)

B. *Formal Grammars.* Chomsky hierarchy grammars, pushdown acceptors and linear bounded automata. Closure properties and algorithms on grammars. (35%)

C. *Computability and Turing Machines.* Turing machine as acceptor and transducer. Universal machine. Computable and noncomputable functions. Halting problem. (30%)

D. *Examinations.* (5%)

CS 17. Numerical Mathematics: Analysis (3-0-3)

Prerequisites: CS 1 and MA 5

COURSE OUTLINE

This course with CS 18 forms a one-year introduction to numerical analysis. The courses are intended to be independent of each other. Students should be expected not only to learn the basic algorithms of numerical computation, but also to understand the theoretical foundations of the algorithms and various problems related to the practical implementations of the algorithms. Thus each topic implies a discussion of the algorithm, the related theory, and the benefits, disadvantages, and pitfalls associated with the method. Programming assignments should be given to illustrate solutions of realistic problems rather than just the coding of various algorithms. Topics such as convergence and error analysis for specific algorithms should be treated in a theoretical manner. Floating point arithmetic and use of mathematical subroutine packages are included in both courses because they should be discussed throughout the courses as they relate to specific problems. All other topics in each course should be covered sequentially. The depth to which topics are treated may vary, but most, if not all, topics should be discussed.

TOPICS

A. *Floating Point Arithmetic.* Basic concepts of floating point number systems. Implications of finite precision. Illustrations of errors due to roundoff. (15%)
B. *Use of Mathematical Subroutine Packages.* (5%)
C. *Interpolation.* Finite difference calculus. Polynomial interpolation. Inverse interpolation. Spline interpolation. (15%)
D. *Approximation.* Uniform approximation. Discrete least-squares. Polynomial approximation. Fourier approximation. Chebyshev economization. (10%)
E. *Numerical Integration and Differentiation.* Interpolatory numerical integration. Euler-McLauren sum formula. Gaussian quadrature. Adaptive integration. Fast Fourier transform. Richardson extrapolation and numerical differentiation. (15%)
F. *Solution of Nonlinear Equations.* Bisection. Fixed point iteration. Newton's method. Secant method. Muller's method. Aitken's process. Rates of convergence. Efficient evaluation of polynomials. Bairstow's method. (15%)
G. *Solution of Ordinary Differential Equations.* Taylor series methods. Euler's method, with local and global error analysis. Runge-Kutta methods. Predictor-corrector methods. Automatic error monitoring–change of step size and order. Stability. (20%)
H. *Examinations.* (5%)

CS 18. Numerical Mathematics: Linear Algebra (3-0-3)

Prerequisites: CS 1 and MA 5

COURSE OUTLINE

The same remarks apply to this course as to CS 17.

TOPICS

A. *Floating Point Arithmetic.* Basic concepts of floating point number systems. Implications of finite precision. Illustrations of errors due to roundoff. (15%)
B. *Use of Mathematical Subroutine Packages.* (5%)
C. *Direct Methods for Linear Systems of Equations.* Gaussian elimination. Operational counts. Implementation, including pivoting and scaling. Direct factorization methods. (20%)
D. *Error Analysis and Norms.* Vector norms and matrix norms. Condition numbers and error estimates. Iterative improvement. (15%)
E. *Iterative Methods.* Jacobi's method. Gauss-Seidel method. Acceleration of iterative methods. Overrelaxation. (15%)
F. *Computation of Eigenvalues and Eigenvectors.* Basic theorems. Error estimates. The power method. Jacobi's method. Householder's method. (15%)
G. *Related Topics.* Numerical solution of boundary value problems for ordinary differential equations. Solution of nonlinear systems of algebraic equations. Least-squares solution of overdetermined systems. (10%)
H. *Examinations.* (5%)

3.4 Special Topics

The special topics courses should be offered whenever departmental resources are sufficient to do so. Thus content and prerequisites may vary each time they are offered because the available material is changing rapidly and different faculty members may have widely differing opinions of what should be included in a course. Most importantly, the material should be current and topical. In time, some of the material should be integrated into courses previously specified or may replace entire courses in the curriculum. Monitoring of this phase of the program should be a continuing activity of individual departments and C^3S.

Examples of special topics courses include:

A. Microcomputer Laboratory
B. Minicomputer Laboratory
C. Performance Evaluation
D. Telecommunications/Networks/Distributed Systems
E. Systems Simulation
F. Advanced Systems Programming
G. Graphics
H. Compiler Writing Laboratory
I. Structured Programming
J. Topics in Automata Theory
K. Topics in Computability
L. Topics in Formal Language Theory
M. Simulation and Modeling

4. The Undergraduate Program

4.1 Introduction

Outlines of eighteen computer science courses are included in previous sections. Eight of the courses indicate one of the ways in which the core material might be presented. Ten courses along with thirteen topics courses

Fig. 2. Recommended computer science and mathematics courses.

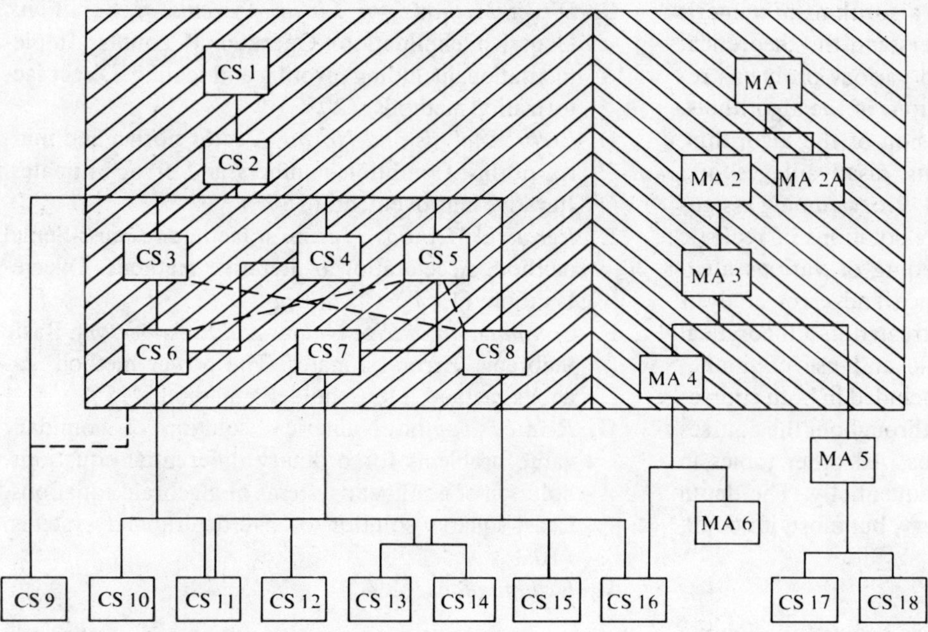

illustrate the kind of elective material to be offered at an advanced level.

The eighteen computer science courses are as follows:

CS 1. Computer Programming I
CS 2. Computer Programming II
CS 3. Introduction to Computer Systems
CS 4. Introduction to Computer Organization
CS 5. Introduction to File Processing
CS 6. Operating Systems and Computer Architecture I
CS 7. Data Structures and Algorithm Analysis
CS 8. Organization of Programming Languages
CS 9. Computers and Society
CS 10. Operating Systems and Computer Architecture II
CS 11. Database Management Systems Design
CS 12. Artificial Intelligence
CS 13. Algorithms
CS 14. Software Design and Development
CS 15. Theory of Programming Languages
CS 16. Automata, Computability, and Formal Languages
CS 17. Numerical Mathematics: Analysis
CS 18. Numerical Mathematics: Linear Algebra

The structure of these courses is given in Figure 2. The following set of mathematics courses is included in the structure for completeness and because of its relevance to an undergraduate program in computer science:

MA 1. Introductory Calculus
MA 2. Mathematical Analysis I
MA 2A. Probability
MA 3. Linear Algebra
MA 4. Discrete Structures
MA 5. Mathematical Analysis II
MA 6. Probability and Statistics

Their role and the extent to which they conform to the needs of a computer science major are discussed in Section 4.3.

Solid and dashed lines represent, respectively, absolute and recommended prerequisites. The shaded area depicts the core curriculum in computer science and required mathematics courses.

4.2 Computer Science Requirements and Electives

The computer science major will consist of the eight courses of the core material plus four additional courses selected from the recommended computer science advanced electives with no more than two in any one specific subfield of the disciplines. Within the requirements for the four elective courses, the special topics courses specified in Section 3.4 should also be considered as possible electives for the major.

It should be noted that as students proceed through the computer science portion of the program, they begin at a very practical level and as they progress the work becomes more conceptual and theoretical. At the junior level the program is strongly conceptual while in the senior year the program may be fully theoretical, or involve a significant amount of theory supplemented with laboratory activities.

4.3 Mathematics Requirements

An understanding of and the capability to use a number of mathematical concepts and techniques are vitally important for a computer scientist. Analytical and algebraic techniques, logic, finite mathematics, aspects of linear algebra, combinatorics, graph theory, optimization methods, probability, and statistics are, in various ways, intimately associated with the development of computer science concepts and techniques. For example, probability and statistics develop the required tools for measurement and evaluation of programs and systems, two important aspects of computer science. Analysis, as commonly contained in calculus courses, gives the mathematical bases for important concepts such as sets, relations, functions, limits, and convergence. Discrete structures provides the bases for semigroups, groups, trees, graphs, and combinatorics, all of which have applications in algorithms analysis and testing, as well as in data structure design. Thus mathematics requirements are integral to a computer science curriculum even though specific courses are not cited as prerequisites for most computer science courses. Unfortunately, the kind and amount of material needed from these areas for computer science usually can only be obtained, if at all, from the regular courses offered by departments of mathematics for their own majors.

Ideally, computer science and mathematics departments should cooperate in developing courses concentrating on discrete mathematics which are appropriate to the needs of computer scientists. Such courses, however, if offered by mathematics departments, would substantially increase their service course load and would constitute a heavy additional commitment of their resources. On the other hand, these course offerings could constitute an applied mathematics component which, in turn, might provide attractive alternatives for some mathematics departments. Suitable computer oriented mathematics course offerings constitute an important topic which should be explored more thoroughly both on local (i.e. individual institutions) and national levels. Specific course recommendations, however, are outside the domain of this report.

Until such time as suitable courses become readily available, it will be necessary to rely on the most commonly offered mathematics courses for the mathematical background needed by computer science majors. One set of such courses was recommended in 1965 by the Committee on Undergraduate Programs in Mathematics (CUPM) of the Mathematical Association of America. Courses MA 1, 2, 2A, 3, 5, and 6 in the structure included in Section 4.1 are intended to be CUPM recommended courses. Details on course contents can be found in the CUPM report [5].

MA 4 represents a more advanced course in discrete structures than that given in "Curriculum '68". The course will build on concepts developed by the study of calculus and linear algebra and will emphasize applications of discrete mathematics to computer science. In particular, if techniques in probability are not included in an earlier course, some emphasis should be given to them in this course. A number of examples of suitable outlines for this course have appeared in the literature, primarily in the *SIGCSE Bulletin* [6, 7, 8, 9, 10].

If courses of the type cited above are the only kind of mathematics courses available, then MA 1, MA 2, MA 2A, MA 3, and MA 4 should be required of all computer science majors. In addition, MA 5 or MA 6 may be required depending on which advanced level computer science electives are selected. If more appropriate courses are provided as a result of interaction between computer science and mathematics departments, then the specification of required mathematics courses and the prerequisite structure should be reconsidered.

4.4 Other Requirements and Electives

As specified in this report, the minimum requirements are 36 semester hours in computer science and 15 semester hours in mathematics. This is certainly less than half of the required hours of a typical undergraduate degree program.

Additional requirements and electives will vary with the requirements of the individual institutions and hence only the most general of recommendations can be given.

It is certainly recognized that writing and communication skills must be emphasized throughout the program. This must be accomplished by requiring appropriate courses in the humanities, and also by emphasis on these skills in the courses within the computer science program itself. Surveys of employers stress the need for these skills as a requirement for employment.

Science and engineering departments represent fruitful areas for support of a computer science program. For those institutions with access to an engineering program, courses such as switching circuits and digital logic should be utilized. Within the science departments, a number of options are available to meet general university requirements. In addition to courses in fields such as physics, it should be noted that the increasing emphasis on computing in the biological and environmental sciences offers additional options for students.

A large portion of the job market involves work in business oriented computer fields. As a result, in those cases where there is a business school or related department, it would be most appropriate to take courses in which one could learn the technology and techniques appropriate to this field. For those students choosing this path, business courses develop the background necessary to function in the business environment.

The general university requirements in the social sciences, with careful advising, will generally be adequate, although it should be recognized that increasing use of computers in these fields may make it appropriate for some students to devise a minor in such an area if that is within their interests.

In consideration of this entire area of general requirements and electives, it must be recognized that a person who is going into the computer job market at the bachelor's level will, in all likelihood, initially be a systems, scientific, engineering, or business programmer. As a result, the student is well advised to work out a program with an advisor that will provide a meaningful and thorough background in the area of the student's interest. The general liberal arts requirements of the institution will give the necessary breadth to the program. A well developed concentration in an area other than computer science will put the student in a position to develop and grow in that area as well as in computer science.

5. Service Courses

5.1 Introduction

There is a great need and demand for computer science material by students who do not intend to major in computer science. Faculty of computer science departments must be willing to offer different courses for those students than for majors when that is appropriate. Service courses should be offered by computer science faculty rather than by faculty in other departments. This, of course, implies that the courses must be made appealing by providing appropriate computer science content in a manner that is attuned to the needs, levels, and backgrounds of the students taking such courses.

There is some possibility that certain courses can be team-taught by faculty from computer science and from one or more other disciplines, but it must be recognized that this approach is difficult. Heads of departments must make difficult decisions regarding how much of the department's teaching resources is to be used for majors and how much is to be used for students in other disciplines. In making these decisions, it is essential that the department and institution properly acknowledge and reward faculty who are working in this area, if the courses are to maintain a high level of excellence.

A variety of service courses must be considered to satisfy the diverse needs of groups of students. Among the categories of undergraduate level courses are the following: (a) liberal arts or general university requirements; (b) supporting work for majors in other disciplines; and (c) continuing education.

5.2 General Service Courses

Students taking a course to satisfy a requirement such as a general university requirement may come from any discipline other than computer science. Some of the science, engineering, or mathematics oriented students may profit most by taking the same first course recommended for computer science students (CS 1). This has an immediate advantage for students who become interested enough in computing to want additional computer science courses. They will have the prerequisite for the second (and subsequent) courses for the computer science major. Those students who stop after one or two of these courses at least have excellent basic programming techniques to apply to computer oriented work in their discipline.

Other students will require more specialized study than that listed in CS 1. For many of these students the courses listed in the section on elementary computer science electives may be more appropriate.

It must still be recognized that a different course (or courses) must be provided for majors in the fields mentioned above as well as for majors in business oriented fields, social sciences, education, and humanities. Service courses for these students normally should include a combination of computer appreciation, programming, applications, and societal impact. Different mixes of these broad areas should be considered for different groups, and the amount of each is best determined by each institution. Topics within each area should be as pertinent to the group served as possible, especially in the language chosen to illustrate programming. To meet this goal, feedback from students is important and communication between computer science and other departments, including periodic review of the courses, is essential. The course should have no prerequisites and it should be made clear to the students that the course is not intended for those who want additional work in computer science. If local conditions warrant, the material could be presented in two semesters rather than one.

Though as indicated, full specification of such courses is impossible, an example can be given to illustrate the kind of course under consideration:

CSS 1. Computer Applications and Impact (3-0-3)

COURSE OUTLINE

A survey of computer applications in areas such as file management, gaming, CAI, process control, simulation, and modeling. Impact of computers on individuals and society. Problem solving using computers with emphasis on analysis, formulation of algorithms, and programming. Projects chosen from various application areas of student interest.

TOPICS (percentages dependent on local situations)

A. *Computer Systems:* Batch and interactive, real time, information management, networks. Description of each system, how it differs from the others, and kinds of applications for which each system is best suited.
B. *Databases:* Establishment and use. Data definition and structures.
C. *Errors:* Types, effects, handling.
D. *Social Implications:* Human-machine interface. Privacy. Moral and legal issues.
E. *Future Social Impact:* Checkless society. CAI. National data banks.
F. *Languages:* As appropriate, introduction to a business oriented language, a symbol manipulation language, and/or a procedure oriented language. Brief exposition of characteristics which make these languages appropriate for particular classes of problems.
G. *Concepts and Techniques Used in Solving Problems:* Selected from appropriate application areas such as CAI, data management, gaming, information retrieval, and simulation.
H. *Projects and Examinations.*

5.3 Supporting Areas

A number of students will choose computer science as a supporting (or minor) area. Various possibilities for sets of courses should be available. One of the ways to achieve this by using the same courses as taken by a computer science major is to require courses CS 1 and CS 2; at least two of the courses CS 3, CS 4, CS 5; and at least two of the courses CS 6, CS 7, CS 8. Additional courses could then be taken as student interest and program requirements would allow. Computer science faculty should communicate with faculty from other departments to determine the needs of the other departments and to indicate how certain courses or course combinations might satisfy the needs.

In those cases where existing courses are not appropriate as supporting work for other majors, new courses should be created, probably to be offered as upper division level courses. Two alternatives for establishing sets of courses for use as supporting work are as follows: (a) CS 1 and CS 2, one course combining material from CS 5 and CS 7, and one course combining material from CS 3, CS 4, and CS 6; and (b) CS 1 and CS 2, one course combining material from CS 3 and CS 5, and one course combining material from CS 4, CS 6, and CS 7. Alternative (a) attempts to combine similar topics from different levels while alternative (b) attempts to combine different topics from similar levels. It should be recognized that students who complete either of the latter two alternatives may not be well enough prepared to take a more advanced computer science course for which any of the courses CS 6, CS 7, or CS 8 are prerequisite.

5.4 Continuing Education

Continuing education is an area which has grown so rapidly and includes such a large variety of interests that it is virtually impossible to specify course possibilities. Nevertheless, computer science departments must address the needs appropriate to their local situations. Some of the possibilities which should be considered are: (a) adult education courses, probably versions of the courses suggested to meet general university requirements; (b) professional development seminars, usually consisting of one day to several weeks devoted to a specific topical area (e.g. minicomputers, database management systems); and (c) courses offered in the evenings or on weekends (on or off campus), possibly regular course offerings or modifications of them primarily for employed persons who need to acquire or enhance their computer science background. The latter possibility would include full-scale baccalaureate or master's degree programs.

6. Other Considerations

6.1 Introduction

Implementation of the computer science curriculum recommendations given in this report implies more than the development of a coherent program of courses. Articulation with other educational institutions and with employers of graduates of such programs must be given serious attention, and a commitment must be made to provide and maintain these resources. In most cases, such commitments go well beyond the boundaries of computer science departments.

Specific requirements involving such areas as staff, equipment, and articulation will vary among institutions depending on such things as size, location, capability, and mission of the school and program. As a result, specific recommendation in these areas cannot be given. However, in this section, general guidelines for implementation in these areas are discussed.

6.2 Facilities

In order to implement the full set of recommendations contained in this report, a wide range of computing facilities will be required. Equipment such as data entry devices, microcomputers, minicomputers, and medium or large-scale computer systems all play separate and important roles in the development of the computer scientist.

Data entry devices such as card punches, teletypewriters, and display terminals should be provided for program preparation and communication between student and computer. Such equipment should be conveniently located and in a large enough area for both easy and convenient student access and use. This equipment may be provided and maintained by the central computing facility at the institution for general student and faculty use, or, if enrollments in the computer science program and demands for service warrant, the equipment may be located and maintained by the department with some restriction on the use by other departments. To implement successfully an adequate program that insures easy and ready access to such facilities, close cooperation and planning is necessary that will involve the computer science department, the computer center, and, perhaps, other departments which use these computer facilities.

Microcomputers are quite desirable in teaching details of computer architecture previously only attainable by extensive programming of "hypothetical computers," simulators, or textbook discussions. They have provided a relatively inexpensive and highly versatile resource which can be used in a variety of ways including combining several such units into reasonably sophisticated and powerful computer systems. Their use is becoming so widespread that in addition to using microcomputers in a systems course, under some circumstances, consideration may be given to offering a laboratory course in which each student, or a group of students in the course, would purchase a suitable kit and construct a computer.

The availability of one or more minicomputers in a department allows the students to obtain "hands-on" experience as well as the opportunity to utilize interactive systems and programming languages which may not be available, or practical, on a medium or large-scale computer system. This kind of equipment also allows the student to work on software development projects, and other projects that might not be possible due to restrictions on the use of the central facility. It is desirable that the department maintain and schedule such minicomputer facilities in such a way that student usage and software development can proceed in an orderly fashion through laboratory course work and individual projects.

A medium or large-scale computer, normally operated and maintained as a central facility at the institution for use by all departments, should provide appropriate hardware and software support for the major program. Auxiliary memory is required in order to store files so that access methods specified in the core courses can be implemented and tested. Suitable input/output devices and system facilities are needed so that rapid turnaround of student jobs is possible, interactive computing is available, and programming languages used in the curriculum are supported.

Regardless of what specific items of computer equipment are available to support a curriculum in computer science, effective teaching and research in the field require laboratory facilities. Computer science is in part an empirical science which involves implementing procedures as well as studying theoretically based processes. Because systems, algorithms, languages, and data structures are created, studied, and measured via combinations of hardware and software, it is essential that appropriate laboratory facilities be made available that are comparable to those necessary in the physical and biological sciences and engineering disciplines. This implies that appropriate laboratory facilities are available for student and faculty use, and may imply that additional laboratory space is required by certain faculty and students for special purposes. The initial budgetary support for establishing these laboratories may be substantial, and continuing regular budgetary support is essential for successful implementation of a program.

While we have thus far stressed the hardware facilities necessary for the recommended curriculum, equal attention must also be given to software. In order for the student to master the material in the core and elective courses, sufficient higher level languages must be available. Additionally, special purpose systems such as statistical systems, database management systems, information storage and retrieval systems, and simulation systems should be available for student use. It must be recognized in planning that many of these systems require a significant initial and continuing investment on the part of the institution. Where possible, fast turnaround or interactive systems should be considered in order to provide as much access as possible for the student.

In addition to the computer related facilities required for the recommended curriculum, there is also a requirement for those resources of a university that are normally associated with any discipline. Adequate library facilities, including significant holdings of periodicals are absolutely necessary, and the implementor of this report is referred to the basic library list [4] for a basis of establishing a library collection to support the instructional program.

While traditional library support is essential to the computer science program, it must be recognized that the field requires some additional resources that may not be necessary in other disciplines. Specifically, the student of computer science must have available, in some form, language, programming, and systems manuals as well as documentation for programs and other materials directly related to the development and use of systems. This material must be easily and conveniently available to the student at all times.

6.3 Staff

Insofar as it is possible, the vast majority of faculty members in departments offering the curriculum that has been recommended in this report should have their primary academic training in computer science. At the same time, it remains the case that demand exceeds supply for these individuals and it is often necessary, and in some cases desirable, to acquire faculty with degrees in other disciplines, but who have experience in computing through teaching or employment in government, business, or industry.

The size of the department will depend on available resources, required teaching loads, commitments to offering service courses, and commitments to continuing education programs. Approximately six full-time equivalent faculty members are necessary to offer a minimal program that would include the core courses as well as a selection of elective and service courses. Most of these faculty members should be capable of offering all of the core courses in addition to elective courses in their areas of specialization. Additional continuing instructional support may be available from the computer center, and from other departments such as mathematics which may offer numerical analysis or other applied mathematics courses that could be cross-listed by both departments. In addition, adjunct faculty from local government, business, or industry are valuable additions in many cases. Such individuals are often able to bring a different perspective to the program; however, care must be taken to insure that the program does not become overly dependent on individuals who may be unable to perform continuing service.

Because of the rapid growth of this field, consideration must be given to providing ongoing opportunities for faculty development, such as a sabbatical leave program, opportunities to attend professional development seminars, and interchange programs with industry.

A department which operates its own laboratory facilities should consider obtaining a full-time staff member to maintain such systems, be responsible for necessary documentation and languages, and coordinate other activities connected with the laboratory. Such a staff member would provide continuity in the development of the laboratory resource.

The field is still developing rapidly, and as was indicated earlier, is at least in part empirical in nature. As a result faculty will be required to devote a great deal of time to course development, software development, development of laboratory resources, and development of service offerings. To provide for continuing excellence in these areas, it must be recognized that they are essential contributions to the program and profession, and as such should be considered within the context of the reward structure of the institution.

6.4 Articulation

It is imperative that departments offering computer science programs keep in close contact with secondary schools, community and junior colleges, graduate schools, and prospective employers of their graduates. This requires a continuing, time consuming effort. Primary responsibility for this effort could be placed with one faculty member, whose teaching load should then be reduced. Experience has shown that person-to-person contact on a continuing basis is necessary for successful articulation.

Usually, a central office in a four-year institution has direct contact with secondary schools. With computing becoming more prevalent at that level, however, it is highly useful and appropriate for a departmental representative to maintain contact with those local secondary schools which offer, or desire to offer, courses in computing.

Articulation agreements exist in many areas between four-year institutions and community and junior colleges. These agreements need to be updated frequently as programs or courses change, and personal contact between departments is necessary to keep abreast of these changes. Transfer programs in community and junior colleges are often geared to programs at four-year institutions. As a result, proposed changes in the four-year program which influence transfer programs should be promulgated as soon as possible so that the community and junior colleges can incorporate such changes, thereby reducing the lag between programs to the benefit of transfer students.

Some of the graduates of the recommended program will continue academic work in computer science in graduate school, but most will seek employment upon graduation. Departments must be aware of the graduate school requirements so that their programs prepare students adequately for advanced work in the field, but they must also maintain communication with employers in order to know what job requirements exist so that the faculty can advise students more effectively. Feedback from recent graduates of the program is quite useful in this regard and should be encouraged as much as possible. In order to most effectively implement this aspect of the program, faculty members should have available to them graduate school brochures, Civil Service Commission documents, and whatever else can come from personal contacts with employees in government and industry, as well as from the professional societies.

References

1. Curriculum Committee on Computer Science (C³S). Curriculum '68, recommendations for academic programs in computer science. *Comm. ACM 11,* 3 (March 1968), 151-197.
2. Austing, R.H., Barnes, B.H., and Engel, G.L. A survey of the literature in computer science education since Curriculum '68. *Comm. ACM 20,* 1 (Jan. 1977), 13-21.
3. Education Committee (Model Curriculum Subcommittee) of the IEEE Computer Society. A curriculum in computer science and engineering. Committee Report, IEEE Pub. EH0119-8, January 1977.
4. Joint Committee of the ACM and the IEEE Computer Society. A library list on undergraduate computer science–computer engineering and information systems. Committee Report, IEEE Pub. EH0131-3, 1978.
5. Committee on the Undergraduate Program in Mathematics. A general curriculum in mathematics for colleges. Rep. to Math. Assoc. of America, CUPM, Berkeley, Calif., 1965.
6. Special Interest Group on Computer Science Education. SIGCSE Bulletin, (ACM) *5,* 1 (Feb. 1973).
7. Special Interest Group on Computer Science Education. SIGCSE Bulletin, (ACM) *6,* 1 (Feb. 1974).
8. Special Interest Group on Computer Science Education. SIGCSE Bulletin, (ACM) *7,* 1 (Feb. 1975).
9. Special Interest Group on Computer Science Education. SIGCSE Bulletin, (ACM) *8,* 1 (Feb. 1976).
10. Special Interest Group on Computer Science Education. SIGCSE Bulletin, (ACM) *8,* 3 (Aug. 1976).

Appendix

Contributors to the C³S Report

Robert M. Aiken, University of Tennessee
Michael A. Arbib, University of Massachusetts
Julius A. Archibald, SUNY at Plattsburgh
William Atchison, University of Maryland
Richard Austing, University of Maryland
Bruce Barnes, National Science Foundation
Victor R. Basili, University of Maryland
Barry Bateman, Southern Illinois University
Della T. Bonnette, University of Southwestern Louisiana
W.P. Buckley, Aluminum Company of America
Frank Cable, Pennsylvania State University
Gary Carlson, Brigham Young University
B.F. Caviness, Rensselaer Polytechnic Institute
Donald Chand, Georgia State University
Sam Conte, Purdue University
William Cotterman, Georgia State University
Daniel Couger, University of Colorado
John F. Dalphin, Indiana University–Purdue University at Fort Wayne
Gene Davenport, John Wiley and Sons
Charles Davidson, University of Wisconsin
Peter Denning, Purdue University
Ed Desautels, University of Wisconsin
Benjamin Diamant, IBM
Karen A. Duncan, MITRE Corporation
Gerald Engel, Old Dominion University
Michael Faiman, University of Illinois
Patrick Fischer, Pennsylvania State University
Arthur Fleck, University of Iowa
John Gannon, University of Maryland
Norman Gibbs, College of William and Mary
Malcolm Gotterer, Florida International University
David Gries, Cornell University

(Appendix continued on next page)

(Appendix continued from preceding page)

H.C. Gyllstrom, Univac
Douglas H. Haden, New Mexico State University
John W. Hamblen, University of Missouri-Rolla
Preston Hammer, Grand Valley State Colleges
Richard Hamming, Naval Postgraduate School
Thomas R. Harbron, Anderson College
Stephen Hedetniemi, University of Oregon
Alex Hoffman, Texas Christian University
Charles Hughes, University of Tennessee
Lawrence John, University of Dayton
Karl Karlstrom, Prentice-Hall
Thomas Keenan, National Science Foundation
Sister M.K. Keller, Clarke College
Douglas S. Kerr, The Ohio State University
Rob Kling, University of California, Irvine
Joyce C. Little, Community College of Baltimore
Donald Loveland, Duke University
Robert Mathis, Old Dominion University
Daniel McCracken, President, ACM
Robert McNaughton, Rensselaer Polytechnic Institute
M.A. Melkanoff, University of California, Los Angeles
John Metzner, University of Missouri-Rolla
Jack Minker, University of Maryland
Howard Morgan, University of Pennsylvania
Abbe Mowshowitz, University of British Columbia
Michael Mulder, Bonneville Power Administration
Anne E. Nieberding, Michigan State University
James Ortega, North Carolina State University
F.G. Pagan, Memorial University of Newfoundland
John L. Pfaltz, University of Virginia
James Powell, North Carolina State University
Vaughn Pratt, Massachusetts Institute of Technology
Anthony Ralston, SUNY at Buffalo
Jon Rickman, Northwest Missouri State College
David Rine, Western Illinois University
Jean Sammet, IBM
John F. Schrage, Indiana University–Purdue University at Fort Wayne
Earl Schweppe, University of Kansas
Sally Y. Sedelow, University of Kansas
Gary B. Shelly, Anaheim Publishing
James Snyder, University of Illinois
Theodor Sterling, Simon Fraser University
Gordon Stokes, Brigham Young University
Alan Tucker, SUNY at Stony Brook
Ronald C. Turner, American Sign and Indicator Corporation
Brian W. Unger, The University of Calgary
James Vandergraft, University of Maryland
Peter Wegner, Brown University
Patrick Winston, Massachusetts Institute of Technology
Peter Worland, Gustavus Adolphus College
Marshall Yovits, The Ohio State University
Marvin Zelkowitz, University of Maryland

Report

Recommendations for Master's Level Programs in Computer Science

A Report of the ACM Curriculum Committee on Computer Science

Editors: Kenneth I. Magel, University of Missouri-Rolla
Richard H. Austing, University of Maryland
Alfs Berztiss, University of Pittsburgh
Gerald L. Engel, Christopher Newport College
John W. Hamblen, University of Missouri-Rolla
A.A.J. Hoffmann, Texas Christian University
Robert Mathis, Old Dominion University

The ACM Committee on Curriculum in Computer Science has spent two years investigating master's degree programs in Computer Science. This report contains the conclusions of that effort. Recommendations are made concerning the form, entrance requirements, possible courses, staffing levels, intent, library resources, and computing resources required for an academic, professional, or specialized master's degree. These recommendations specify minimum requirements which should be met by any master's programs. The Committee believes that the details of a particular master's program should be determined and continually updated by the faculty involved. A single or a small number of model programs are not as appropriate at the graduate level as at the bachelor's level.

Key Words and Phrases: computer science courses, computer science curriculum, computer science education, computer science graduate programs, master's programs.

CR Categories: 1.52

Contents

1.0 Introduction

The Committee on Curriculum in Computer Science (C^3S)* of the Association for Computing Machinery has within its charter the obligation to address computer science education at the baccalaureate level and above. The Committee intends that this document establish a basis for master's degree programs of substance while at the same time permitting sufficient flexibility to allow for adaptation to the objectives and resources of individual colleges and universities. A second objective of the report is to provide guidance to those institutions which have begun or are about to begin a master's program without specifying a rigid blueprint for the establishment of such programs. Finally, and perhaps most importantly, the Committee hopes this report will foster meaningful interchange among computer science educators regarding instructional programs at the master's level.

Graduate programs in computer science preceded the introduction of undergraduate programs, the earliest programs appearing in the early 1960s. "Curriculum '68" [5] concentrated on the definition and specification of undergraduate programs but did consider master's programs also. Specifically the following recommendation was given:

> The master's degree program in computer science should consist of at least nine courses. Normally at least two courses—each in a different subject area—should be taken from each of the following subject divisions of computer science:
>
> I. Information Structures and Processes
> II. Information Processing Systems
> III. Methodologies
>
> Sufficient other courses in computer science or related areas should be taken to bring the student to the forefront of some area of computer science [5, p. 163].

The section on the master's curriculum concludes with the statement:

> This proposed program embodies sufficient flexibility to fulfill the requirements of either an "academic" degree obtained in preparation for further graduate study or a terminal "professional" degree. Until clearer standards both for computer science research and the computing profession have emerged, it seems unwise to attempt to distinguish more definitely between these two aspects of master's degree programs [5, p. 164].

The Committee believes that the discipline has matured enough that we can now see this distinction between academic and professional programs beginning to appear. We reject, however, the concept of an utterly terminal program. In our view all programs should provide the possibility of additional study in the field. This report tries to establish the common aspects of master's programs in computer science and indicates possible differences and distinctions.

Some attention was given to master's level programs by C^3S following the publication of "Curriculum '68." The results of this work were presented by Melkanoff [8] in 1973. Further work in this area was deferred, however, while work progressed on the new C^3S recommendations at the undergraduate level. The new undergraduate recommendations were published as "Curriculum '78" in the March 1979 *Communications of the ACM* [2].

In an independent effort, the ACM Curriculum Committee on Computer Education for Management (C^3EM) (now the Subcommittee on Curriculum in Information Systems) developed guidelines for a master's program in Information Systems [1, 9]. They clearly define a related professional degree program. The scope and extent of existing graduate programs in computer science have been recently surveyed [4, 7].

2.0 The Need for Master's Programs

The classical objective of academic master's programs is the preparation for study at the doctoral level, and this remains an important aspect of such programs. Different goals exist for professional programs, but we believe that all programs should prepare the student for study beyond the master's level.

Among the objectives for students in master's programs is entry into the computer field at a relatively high level of responsibility and expertise. Computer Science is such a new and rapidly expanding field that individuals entering with a master's degree in this field will almost immediately move to positions with great responsibility. This, in turn, implies the requirement for an advanced level of prior training in both technical and related areas (e.g., communication skills).

Many people already in the field desire additional training in computer science. These individuals may have undergraduate degrees in computer science and desire to advance; or they may have had considerable experience in computing, but little formal education in the field. While this latter group should be declining in number as more undergraduate computer science majors enter the job market, the demand does exist and will continue to do so in the foreseeable future. In addition, there will be a continuing need for individuals with a bachelor's degree in computer science to update their training.

In all of these cases, the master's degree provides both motivation for the student and a standard for reward by the employer.

The two-year colleges are offering a large number of courses in data processing and related topics. For most faculty positions in such institutions, a master's degree is a minimum requirement and a master's in computer science is an appropriate preparation.

Increasingly, precollege instruction in computer science is being offered. Consequently, there is a need for a master's program to prepare individuals to teach computer science at the precollege level. Further exploration of such a master's program should be done jointly by

* The Curriculum Committee on Computer Science (C^3S) became a subcommittee of the Curriculum Committee on Computer Education in 1978.

this Committee and the ACM Subcommittee on Elementary and Secondary Education.

Graduate enrollments in computer science, information systems, and other related programs have grown steadily since their inception in the early 1960s. Even though growth rates are substantial, estimates of demand for personnel with graduate degrees in such programs far exceed the supply. During the 80s, the need for master's graduates is estimated to be approximately 34,000 annually. During this same period, annual production will only increase from about 3,000 to 4,000 [6].

3.0 Goals

3.1 Basic Intent

The basic intention of a master's program in computer science is to develop the student's critical professional thinking and intuition. The curriculum must be structured to provide a balanced mixture of learning experiences to make the graduate capable of sound professional decisions. As a result the graduate should be able to assume responsible positions in business, government, and education at the research, development, and planning levels. The program should also provide an excellent foundation for further formal training.

The primary emphasis of the program should be on the concepts, theory, and practice of computer science. Students should have a broad understanding of the field. Techniques and methodologies of computer science should be discussed and used. Intensive education in specific areas of computer science and/or training in an application area is desirable. An academically oriented program will encourage students to develop and use abstract models. A professionally oriented program will encourage students to apply abstract models and computer science concepts in practical situations.

Academically oriented programs will tend to attract full-time students, and these students are generally oriented toward further education and research. Students in professional programs are generally oriented toward careers in industry or government, and such programs are frequently designed to accommodate part-time students.

3.2 Communication Skills

Computer scientists require special communication skills. They must be able to communicate with the rest of their organizations in understandable terms, both orally and in writing. They must be able to communicate with their co-workers, users of their computer systems, and other professionals who require computer expertise. They must be able to produce documentation for a complex computing system which is clear, concise, unambiguous, and accurate. They must be able to produce well organized reports which clearly delineate objectives, method of solution, results, and conclusions for a complex task.

3.3 Current Literature Level

Graduates should be cognizant of the pertinent literature in their field of choice and be able to read, interpret, and use this material. They should find it a normal procedure to review current journals to keep abreast of new trends and ideas. They should be able to recognize and use techniques relevant to their present endeavors.

3.4 Professionalism

Since graduates could assume responsible positions in some organizations they should be able to function effectively as members of teams. They should possess qualities of leadership along with technical skills so as to effectively lead a group to the successful completion of a task.

Master's students should take an active part in the activities of any local professional computer science organization which may exist. They should be aware of the societal impact of computing as incorporated in the ACM Code of Ethics [12].

4.0 Entrance Requirements

4.1 Admission Requirements

The Graduate Record Examinations (GRE) Advanced Computer Science Test has been available since October 1976. Its purpose is to help graduate committees assess the qualifications of applicants with a bachelor's degree in Computer Science for advanced study in computer science. The Advanced Test in Computer Science is one of a number of measures that might be used to evaluate a candidate for admission to the M.S. degree program. The verbal part of the GRE may help measure the communication skill level of applicants and the quantitative part is a good general indicator of numeric manipulation capabilities.

A "B" average for the undergraduate degree is a common requirement for admission to graduate study. Some schools provide a "special" status for those who do not meet entrance requirements with subsequent reevaluation for admission to full status.

4.2 Prerequisites

The student entering a master's program ideally should have a B.S. in Computer Science or at least the material included in CS 1 through CS 8 of "Curriculum '78" [2] or SE-1 through SE-4 and CO-1 through CO-4 of the IEEE Computer Society Model Curriculum [11], and mathematics through calculus, linear algebra, and one course in statistics. Course titles for CS 1 through CS 8 are given in Appendix B. Discrete structures, maturity in both abstract reasoning and the use of models, and one or more years of practical experience in computer science are desirable. Of course, the applicant must satisfy the general entrance requirements of the institution's graduate school or department.

Some schools may admit students who do not meet the entrance requirements listed above. These students will have to remove deficiencies early in their graduate studies.

Removal of academic deficiencies might be through any or all of the following approaches:

a. Require students to take specific existing undergraduate courses for no credit toward the master's degree;
b. Establish special "immigration" courses that rapidly cover the material in the areas of deficiency; or
c. Provide the students with self-study outlines in conjunction with appropriate proficiency examinations.

Any courses taken to remove deficiencies must be in addition to the program required for the master's degree.

5.0 Program Organization

5.1 Course Work

Formal course work is provided to give the students a mixture of practical and theoretical work. Such courses will typically begin at a level in which the courses may be taken by advanced undergraduate students or graduate students.

The specific graduate courses which are offered reflect the expertise and judgment of the faculty involved. Graduate programs reflect their specific environments far more than do undergraduate programs. It is possible to envision several independent axes, e.g., software/hardware, theory/practice, and numeric/nonnumeric computation. Each department should determine where on each axis its program should be, consistent with available resources and expertise. These emphases should be re-evaluated at least every three years.

Nevertheless, the Committee believes all master's programs should have some aspects in common. Accordingly, a list of possible courses is given below. Departments planning master's programs should start with this list. In preparing these course descriptions, the Committee drew on material from well-established master's degree programs at

Georgia Institute of Technology
University of Illinois
University of Maryland
University of Missouri-Rolla
Northwestern University
University of North Carolina at Chapel Hill
Ohio State University
Purdue University
Rutgers: The State University of New Jersey
Stanford Unversity
The University of Texas at Austin [13].

Computer Science is a rapidly changing field. The courses listed here reflect the present state of the field and will require periodic updating. Descriptions of these courses are given in Appendix B. They provide a starting point for developing or updating a master's degree program.

Typical courses which should be offered, under the topical areas within which they fall, might be as follows. Courses CS 9 through CS 18 are described in [2]. Courses CS 19 through CS 38 are described in Appendix B.

A. *Programming Languages*

CS 14 Software Design and Development
CS 15 Theory of Programming Languages
CS 19 Compiler Construction
CS 20 Formal Methods in Programming Languages
CS 21 Architecture of Assemblers
CS 25 High Level Language Computer Architecture

B. *Operating Systems and Computer Architecture*

CS 10 Operating Systems and Computer Architecture II
CS 22 Performance Evaluation
CS 23 Analytical Models for Operating Systems
CS 24 Computer Communication Networks and Distributed Processing
CS 26 Large Computer Architecture
CS 27 Real-Time Systems
CS 28 Microcomputer Systems and Local Networks

C. *Theoretical Computer Science*

CS 13 Algorithms
CS 16 Automata, Computability, and Formal Languages
CS 29 Applied Combinatorics and Graph Theory
CS 30 Theory of Computation

D. *Data and File Structures*

CS 11 Database Management Systems Design
CS 31 Information Systems Design
CS 32 Information Storage and Access
CS 33 Distributed Database Systems

E. *Other Topics*

CS 9 Computers and Society
CS 12 Artificial Intelligence
CS 34 Pattern Recognition
CS 35 Computer Graphics
CS 36 Modeling and Simulation
CS 17 Numerical Mathematics: Analysis
CS 18 Numerical Mathematics: Linear Algebra
CS 37 Legal and Economic Issues in Computing
CS 38 Introduction to Symbolic and Algebraic Manipulation

These courses are representative of those being offered today in established master's programs. Some overlap considerably with others, e.g., CS 19 and CS 21 or CS 22 and CS 23. These pairs are included to provide alternative examples. The Committee does not propose that both members of a pair be offered. Further, the Committee expects the appropriate courses to change frequently as the field matures. Additional courses may be offered to reflect the interests of the faculty.

In considering the courses that should be taken in the master's program it should be recognized that one of the purposes of such a program is to supply the opportunity for additional course work over that possible in an undergraduate program. Some of the courses, appropriately, are available for the graduate student and advanced undergraduates, although the reasons for selection may be different.

The master's program should provide both breadth in several areas, and depth in a few. In addition, it should allow a degree of flexibility to address individual needs. The typical program will consist of 30 to 36 semester hours.

The program should include at least two courses from A, two courses from B, and one course from each of C, D, and E. The student who has not been exposed to numerical analysis as an undergraduate should take CS 17. Students with strong undergraduate backgrounds in computer science may have already satisfied some of these requirements and may thus proceed to more advanced courses. Their degrees probably will be more specialized than those of students with weaker backgrounds.

The entire program should contain at least four computer science courses which are for graduate students only.

5.2 Culminating/Unifying Activity

Beyond the course work, each student should be required to participate in some summarizing activity.

A thesis, project, seminar, or comprehensive examination exemplifies a kind of culminating activity for the program. They provide a format for a student to combine concepts and knowledge from a number of different courses. They also provide a method of judging a student's performance outside the narrow confines of a single course. They may also be useful in insuring a uniform standard in a program that may cover many years and use many different instructors.

These culminating activities can be very time-consuming for both students and faculty. Faculty loads must allow the necessary time for the preparation, supervision, and evaluation of these activities

5.3 Seminar

A seminar in which the students make presentations can be useful for providing experience and improving the communication skills of students. The seminar provides an opportunity for the student to explore the literature and make formal presentations. The seminar is also useful in developing and encouraging the habit of reading and discussing the current literature in computer science.

5.4 Thesis or Project

A thesis or project usually taking more than one semester should be done by each student. This is suggested to extend the student's experience in analysis and design and the evaluation and application of new research findings or technological advances. Relating projects to work environments can strengthen a professional program.

The thesis or project provides the primary means by which the student gains practical experience in applying computing techniques and methodologies. It also provides a basis for developing written and oral communication skills and documentation experience. Finally, it provides the opportunity for exploring recent concepts in the literature and demonstrating an understanding of those concepts.

A project is much more difficult to evaluate than course work or a thesis. However, because of the importance of the project within the program its careful evaluation is vitally important. Successful completion means:

a. The product produced performs as prescribed.
b. The project has been properly documented both in terms of nontechnical descriptions and in terms of technical diagrams and formal documentation.
c. A formal public oral presentation has been given. This is seen as a mechanism for encouraging both a high level of presentation and a high technical standard for the project.

Through a seminar and a project the student can gain practical experience in the evaluation, selection, and decision making process.

5.5 Comprehensive Examination

An alternative to the thesis may be a comprehensive examination. This examination serves a purpose similar to the thesis or project discussed previously. It summarizes the entire program. The examination should consist of:

a. review and analysis of articles from current literature; and/or
b. questions that integrate material from more than one course.

The period of time over which degree requirements are satisfied will be considerably longer for part-time students than for full-time students. The former, therefore, should be supplied with reading guides prior to the comprehensive examination. Indeed, in order to encourage a reading habit in all students some examination questions should be related to required readings rather than to course work.

6.0 Resource Requirements

6.1 Faculty

Most faculty are qualified to teach in more than one area of specialization. Although in the past most computer science faculty received degrees in other disciplines, it is recommended that master's programs not be implemented without experienced computer science faculty or faculty formally trained in computer science. A minimum of five computer science faculty members is required to provide adequate breadth for a stand-alone master's program. If the department offers a bachelor's program as well, then at least eight faculty members would be required for both programs. Limited use of qualified adjunct faculty is appropriate in some special circumstances, but at least three quarters of the courses must be offered by regular full-time faculty.

6.2 Computing Equipment

Every computer science master's program must have access to adequate computer systems. The amount of computing power which must be available depends on how many students will be in the program at one time and their specializations.

An area of specialization such as computer graphics or design automation requires very special and possibly dedicated computing facilities, both hardware and software. Programs specializing in information systems place heavy demands on a large computer system with appropriate software.

For the study of computer systems and languages a variety of languages and operating systems must be available. A dedicated system under departmental control is optimal for hands-on experience. Programs and experiments dealing with the security of systems usually require a dedicated system.

Proper arrangements must be made for maintenance of the computing facility and laboratory equipment. Plans and provisions also need to be made for growth and periodic modernization of equipment resources.

6.3 Library

The list of books and magazines for undergraduate programs prepared by a joint committee of ACM and IEEE is the only available list of reference material [10]. It is a good starting point, but suffers from being for undergraduates rather than graduate students and being current only to 1977. Additional materials, particularly selected applied and theoretical journals, are required for a master's program. Besides faculty and computing equipment, substantial library resources are essential for an adequate master's program in computer science. Sizable current expenditure funds are needed to maintain collections, but at most universities such funds will be insufficient by themselves. An additional special allocation of tens of thousands of dollars will be needed to establish a basic holding in the first place.

7.0 Specializations

A specialization program in the context of "master's level programs in computer science" is defined as a professional program which, in general, would be administered by a Computer Science department, but which differs from traditional and/or academic programs in several important aspects. Here the emphasis is on the "specialist." A number of schools have already developed such programs. Almost always the title of the program is the key to the area of specialization and alerts the potential student to the nontraditional (in the computer science sense) nature of the offering. Examples of such programs include health computing (also called medical information science), library information science, and software design and development. In each case the professional practitioner produced by these specialist programs is expected to draw upon a broadly based knowledge of the technical foundations of computer science and be able to apply these concepts in the context of a particular application area, e.g., medicine or software development. These specialists are expected to be the professional level link between computer science and another specific technical area. Justification for suggesting that these programs be administered by computer science rests with the degree to which computer science dominates the course load imposed on the student.

There are intrinsic benefits from Computer Science departments having specialist programs. Nevertheless, it is not feasible for a particular department to have a specialist program unless it has a nucleus of faculty with appropriate similar interests and expertise. Emphasis and content will vary widely.

On the other hand, the Committee wants to discourage a somewhat frivolous proliferation of programs with specialist names. A specialist program should build on a more general Computer Science master's program rather than be a relatively inexpensive shortcut to a master's level program. Therefore, the following guidelines are presented:

a. There must be a clear and continuing need for individuals with a particular training both locally and nationally. This need must be expected to last for several years.

b. There must be a distinct body of knowledge which these individuals need and which is not provided by a generalist degree of the type presented earlier in this report.

c. There must be at least three full-time faculty members available with expertise in this body of knowledge.

d. Any needed resources (e.g., special hardware, databases) must be available in sufficient quantity locally. Provision must be made for periodic updating and improvement of these resources to keep pace with the state of the art.

8.0 Conclusions

This report is the product of compromise. More than 200 Computer Science educators were consulted in its preparation. The Committee started out to produce a model curriculum for Computer Science master's degree programs similar to the model curriculum for bachelor's degree programs described in [2]. We quickly determined that even a small group of computer scientists could not agree on a model curriculum. We tried to develop separate model curricula for academic, professional, and specialization programs, but could not reach a consensus on any of those. Next we tried to develop a list of core concepts which every master's graduate should know. Lists of anywhere from five to thirty concepts were generated and rejected. What one person felt should be in the core another felt was relatively unimportant.

Computer Science is a volatile field. The Committee tried to determine in which directions the field was moving. We wanted to produce a forward looking report. Again, we could not reach a consensus. Each expert disagreed with the others.

This report makes some recommendations for what a master's degree in Computer Science should be and what it should not be. The report does not provide a blueprint for a master's program because the Committee believes the field is too new to have just one or even a small number of blueprints. The Computer Science faculty at an institution must be the ultimate determiners of what should and what should not be in the program. This report provides some recommendations for minimums which should be in every program. Beyond that we must defer to the mature, reasoned judgments of the local faculty.

* * * *

Appendix A

Contributors

The following people have made substantial contributions to this report:

Robert M. Aiken, University of Tennessee
* Richard H. Austing, University of Maryland
* Bruce Barnes, National Science Foundation
* Alfs T. Berztiss, University of Pittsburgh
* Della T. Bonnette, University of Southwestern Louisiana
Stephen E. Cline, Prentice-Hall, Inc.
* John F. Dalphin, Indiana-Purdue University at Fort Wayne
* Gerald L. Engel, Christopher Newport College
Richad E. Fairley, Colorado State University
** John W. Hamblen, University of Missouri-Rolla
* Alex A. J. Hoffman, Texas Christian University
Lawrence A. Jehn, University of Dayton
* William J. Kubitz, University of Illinois
Joyce Currie Little, Community College of Baltimore
* Kenneth I. Magel, University of Missouri-Rolla
* Robert F. Mathis, Old Dominion University
* John R. Metzner, University of Missouri-Rolla
David Moursund, University of Oregon
* James D. Powell, Burroughs-Wellcome Co.
David Rine, Western Illinois University
Kenneth Williams, Western Michigan University
Anthony S. Wojcik, Illinois Institute of Technology
Marshall C. Yovits, Indiana-Purdue University at Indianapolis

* Committee members   ** Committee chairman

Appendix B

Course Descriptions

The descriptions are very brief to allow faculty to adjust these courses to their own environments. The Committee recognizes the need to develop an objective list of acceptable textbooks. For some of these courses, no textbook yet exists. Articles from the recent literature must be used. The Committee anticipates the availability of a textbook list in the SIGCSE Bulletin within the next two years.

Courses CS 1 through CS 18 are described in [2]. Courses CS 1, through CS 8 are prerequisite to a master's program.

CS 1	**Computer Programming I**
CS 2	**Computer Programming II**
CS 3	**Introduction to Computer Systems**
CS 4	**Introduction to Computer Organization**
CS 5	**Introduction to File Processing**
CS 6	**Operating Systems and Computer Architecture I**
CS 7	**Data Structures and Algorithm Analysis**
CS 8	**Organization of Programming Languages**
CS 9	**Computers and Society**
CS 10	**Operating Systems and Computer Architecture II**
CS 11	**Database Management Systems Design**
CS 12	**Artificial Intelligence**
CS 13	**Algorithms**
CS 14	**Software Design and Development**
CS 15	**Theory of Programming Languages**
CS 16	**Automata, Computability, and Formal Languages**
CS 17	**Numerical Mathematics: Analysis**
CS 18	**Numerical Mathematics: Linear Algebra**

The three numbers in parentheses following the course names below are: classroom hours per week, laboratory hours, and total course credit.

CS 19 Compiler Construction (3-0-3)
Prerequisite: CS 8

An introduction to the major methods used in compiler implementation. The parsing methods of LL(k) and LR(k) are covered as well as finite state methods for lexical analysis, symbol table construction, internal forms for a program, run time storage management for block structured languages, and an introduction to code optimization.

CS 20 Formal Methods in Programming Languages (3-0-3)
Prerequisite: CS 8

Data and control abstractions are considered. Advanced control constructs including backtracking and nondeterminism are covered. The effects of formal methods for program description are explained. The major methods for proving programs correct are described.

CS 21 Architecture of Assemblers (3-0-3)
Prerequisite: CS 6

Anatomy of an assembler: source program analysis, relocatable code generation, and related topics. Organization and machine language of two or three architecturally different machines; survey and comparison of these machines in various programming environments.

CS 22 Performance Evaluation (3-0-3)
Prerequisite: CS 6

A survey of techniques of modeling concurrent processes and the resources they share. Includes levels and types of system simulation, performance prediction, benchmarking and synthetic loading, hardware and software monitors.

CS 23 Analytical Models for Operating Systems (3-0-3)
Prerequisite: CS 6

An examination of the major models that have been used to study operating sysems and the computer systems which they manage. Petri nets, dataflow diagrams, and other models of parallel behavior will be studied. An introduction to the fundamentals of queueing theory is included.

CS 24 Computer Communication Networks and Distributed Processing (3-0-3)
Prerequiste: CS 6

A study of networks of interacting computers. The problems, rationales, and possible solutions for both distributed processing and distributed databases will be examined. Major national and international protocols including SNA, X.21, and X.25 will be presented.

CS 25 High Level Language Computer Architecture (3-0-3)
Prerequiste: CS 6

An introduction of architectures of computer systems which have been developed to make processing of programs in high level languages easier. Example systems will include SYMBOL and the Burroughs B1700.

CS 26 Large Computer Architecture (3-0-3)
Prerequisite: CS 6

A study of large computer systems which have been developed to make special types of processing more efficient or reliable. Examples include pipelined machines and array processing. Tightly coupled multiprocessors will be covered.

CS 27 Real-Time Systems (3-0-3)
Prerequisite: CS 6

An introduction to the problems, concepts, and techniques involved in computer systems which must interface with external devices. These include process control systems, computer systems embedded within aircraft or automobiles, and graphics systems. The course concentrates on operating system software for these systems.

CS 28 Microcomputer Systems and Local Networks (2-2-3)
Prerequisite: CS 6

A consideration of the uses and organization of microcomputers. Typical eight or sixteen bit microprocessors will be described. Microcomputer software will be discussed and contrasted with that available for larger computers. Each student will gain hands-on experience with a microcomputer.

CS 29 Applied Combinatorics and Graph Theory (3-0-3)
Prerequisites: CS 7, 13

A study of combinatorial and graphical techniques for complexity analysis including generating functions, recurrence relations, Polya's theory of counting, planar directed and undirected graphs, and NP complete problems. Applications of the techniques to analysis of algorithms in graph theory and sorting and searching.

CS 30 Theory of Computation (3-0-3)
Prerequisites: CS 7, 16

A survey of formal models for computation. Includes Turing Machines, partial recursive functions, recursive and recursively enumerable sets, the recursive theorem, abstract complexity theory, program schemes, and concrete complexity.

CS 31 Information System Design (3-0-3)
Prerequisites: CS 6, 11

A practical guide to Information System Programming and Design. Theories relating to module design, module coupling, and module strength are discussed. Techniques for reducing a system's complexity are emphasized. The topics are oriented toward the experienced programmer or systems analyst.

CS 32 Information Storage and Access (3-0-3)
Prerequisites: CS 6, 11

Advanced data structures, file structures, databases, and processing systems for access and maintenance. For explicitly structured data, interactions among these structures, accessing patterns, and design of processing/access systems. Data administration, processing system life cycle, system security.

CS 33 Distributed Database Systems (3-0-3)
Prerequisites: CS 11, 24

A consideration of the problems and opportunities inherent in distributed databases on a network computer system. Includes file allocation, directory systems, deadlock detection and prevention, synchronization, query optimization, and fault tolerance.

CS 34 Pattern Recognition (3-0-3)
Prerequisites: CS 6, 7

An introduction to the problems, potential, and methods of pattern recognition through a comparative presentation of different methodologies and practical examples. Covers feature extraction methods, similarity measures, statistical classification, minimax procedures, maximum likelihood decisions, and the structure of data to ease recognition. Applications are presented in image and character recognition, chemical analysis, speech recognition, and automated medical diagnosis.

CS 35 Computer Graphics (3-0-3)
Prerequisites: CS 6, 7

An overview of the hardware, software, and techniques used in computer graphics. The three types of graphics hardware: refresh, storage, and raster scan are covered as well as two-dimensional transformations, clipping, windowing, display files, and input devices. If a raster scan device is available, solid area display, painting and shading are also covered. If time allows, three-dimensional graphics can be included.

CS 36 Modeling and Simulation (3-0-3)
Prerequisites: CS 6, 7

A study of the construction of models which simulate real systems. The methodology of solution should include probability and distribution theory, statistical estimation and inference, the use of random variates, and validation procedures. A simulation language should be used for the solution of typical problems.

CS 37 Legal and Economic Issues in Computing (3-0-3)
Prerequisites: CS 9, 12

A presentation of the interactions between users of computers and the law and a consideration of the economic impacts of computers. Includes discussion of whether or not software is patentable, as well as discussion of computer crime, privacy, electronic fund transfer, and automation.

CS 38 Introduction to Symbolic and Algebraic Manipulation (3-0-3)
Prerequisite: CS 7

A survey of techniques for using the computer to do algebraic manipulation. Includes techniques for symbolic differentiation and integration, extended precision arithmetic, polynomial manipulation, and an introduction to one or more symbolic manipulation systems. Automatic theorem provers are considered.

References

1. Ashenhurst, R. L. (Ed.) Curriculum recommendations for graduate professional programs in information systems, a report of the ACM Curriculum Committee on Computer Education for Management. *Comm. ACM 15*, 5 (May 1972), 363–398.

2. Austing, R.H., Barnes, B.H., Bonnette, D.T., Engel, L., and Stokes, G. (Eds.) Curriculum '78: Recommendations for the undergraduate program in computer science, a report of the ACM Curriculum Committee on Computer Science. *Comm. ACM 22*, 3 (March, 1979), 147–166.

3. Austing, R.H., Barnes, B.H., and Engel, G.L. A survey of the literature in computer science education since curriculum '68. *Comm. ACM 20*, 1 (Jan. 1977), 13–21.

4. Berztiss, A.T. The M.S. program in computer science. SIGCSE Bulletin (ACM) *11*, 1 (Feb. 1979), 61–69.

5. Curriculum Committee on Computer Science (C^3S). Curriculum '68: Recommendations for academic programs in computer science, a report of the ACM Curriculum Committee on Computer Science. *Comm. ACM 11*, 3 (March 1968), 151–197.

6. Hamblen, J.W. *Computer Manpower—Supply and Demand—by States.* Information Systems Consultants, R.R. 1, Box 256A, St. James, Mo., 1973, 1975, and 1979.

7. Hamblen, J.W., and Baird, T.B. *Fourth Inventory of Computers in U.S. Higher Education, 1976–77.* EDUCOM, Princeton, N.J., 1979.

8. Melkanoff, M.A. An M.S. program in computer science. SIGCSE Bulletin (ACM) *5*, 1 (Feb. 1973), 77–82.

9. Teichroew, D. (Ed). Education related to the use of computers in organizations, position paper by the ACM Curriculum Committee on Computer Education for Management. *Comm. ACM 14*, 9 (Sept. 1971), 575–588.

10. Joint Committee of ACM and IEEE-CS. *A Library List on Undergraduate Computer Science, Computer Engineering, and Information Systems.* ACM, New York, 1978.

11. IEEE Computer Society. A curriculum in computer science and engineering. EH 0119-8, Los Alamitos, Calif., Nov. 1976.

12. Association for Computing Machinery. *Professional Code of Ethics.* ACM, New York.

13. Association for Computing Machinery. *Administrative Directory.* ACM, New York, 1980.

REPORTS

LETTERS TO THE EDITOR

FORUM

Letter to the Editor
Vol. 11, No. 9, September 1968, p. 594

On Computer Appreciation in the Undergraduate Curriculum

Key Words and Phrases: computer appreciation courses, undergraduate curriculum
CR Categories: 1.52, 1.59, 2.12

EDITOR:

The article on computer appreciation courses in the undergraduate curriculum edited by Dr. Elliot Organick, "Panel Discussion on Computer Appreciation" [*Comm. ACM 11*, 4 (Apr. 1968), 263], presented the problem of acquainting the educated public with computer technology.

The need to communicate the capabilities of the computer seems to be best satisfied at the college level. However, to insist that appreciation courses be created to show the applications of computer technology to areas of scientific endeavor is to insist that mathematics appreciation courses be established. Obviously the sciences aren't taught without extensive references to mathematics. What is needed is the introduction of computer applications to the content of courses in the science and liberal arts areas. This would not presuppose any knowledge of computers or programming languages, but would provide a real and meaningful application of computers to noncomputer science people.

This doesn't mean that one should not undertake the creation of computer appreciation courses, but is intended only to point out that computers must be shown in a real application, not an artificially constructed one. The curriculum which offers an introduction to computers, but not reinforcement of computer concepts and applications in the scientific as well as the liberal arts curriculum, does little to acquaint the managers, industrialists, scientists, and government officials with computer capabilities.

The artificially constructed problems found in many appreciation courses consist of sorting, finding zeros of polynomials, prime number generators, and searching techniques. These problems to the engineer or architect, historian or sociologist, are not indicative of the significance of computer capabilities, but are only special cases of the field of computer science—a field which may be interesting, but may not be meaningfully connected to any other. The difficulty is not in the selection of problems that will generalize in a natural way to other important problems; it is in the recognition by noncomputer science instructors that the computer has come of age in the noncomputer science field, thereby providing a natural entrance to the computer science field. When the impetus is on "applications," the student can go from the general to the specific. The applications point the way to the study and appreciation of computers.

It is at this point that the computer appreciation course should be introduced. It should not consist of languages and elementary problems but of the ideas in computer techniques which should be independent of hardware and software. The awkward grammar of FORTRAN or the tedious coding of machine language programs has no place here. Ideas must be taught, not the memorization of standard procedures.

Only when computer applications are taught as part of the subject material in noncomputer science courses can the capabilities of computer technology be understood in a computer appreciation course. The computer will then take on its proper role as a tool, an instrument of scientific investigation.

JEFFREY P. KRISCHER
Department of Defense
13821 Briarwood Drive
Laurel, MD. 20810

Letter to the Editor
Vol. 11, No. 10, October 1968, p. 658

Comment on Curriculum 68

Key Words and Phrases: computer science curriculum, computer case studies, system case studies
CR Categories: 1.52

EDITOR:

May I point out a deficiency in Curriculum 68 [*Comm. ACM 11*, 3(Mar. 1968) 151–197]: its lack of orientation to the practitioners of computer systems analysis.

A good education should not be solely directed toward academicians whose only economic justification is to teach in order to turn out recursively new generations of academicians. Such has been the problem in the teaching of economics since it was defined as a subject without institutional content. University economic departments (notably not in the schools of business) have turned out trained economic theoreticians who have found little relationship between their academic knowledge and the existing practices which guide business firms and government. A balanced education in economics must properly emphasize the descriptions of existing economic institutions as well as the inadequate theories of economics.

Thus, in the education of the undergraduate computer scientist (?), emphasis must be given to a description of what a practitioner of computer science does as well as to the teaching of the inadequate theories of the science (?).

If this is not done, practical men will place the required "institutional" courses in other departments of the university. This would be comparable to the current practice of taking business "institutional" courses in the school of business and not in the economics department.

Concretely, I find it difficult to accept an undergraduate curriculum in this field which would not include six academic hours in the study of existing computer systems, i.e. case studies. The college graduate trained in computer science will work most likely in the environment of such systems. Why not, therefore, give the apprentice scientist a frame of reference for the application of theories that are being taught.

In a way, the report attempts to circumvent this criticism by stating:

> It is also likely that the majority of application programmers in such areas as business data processing, scientific research and engineering analysis will continue to be specialists educated in the related subject matter areas, although such students can undoubtedly profit by taking a number of computer courses.

The implication is that computer science can be isolated from a system of application. However, upon close examination the recommended course work is highly slanted towards the needs of physical scientists and engineers. Very much neglected are the knowledge requirements of business systems designers and information technologists.

RAYMOND P. WISHNER
American University
Center for Technology
Washington, D. C.

Letter to the Editor
Vol. 11, No. 12, December 1968, p. 801

On Master's Level Curricula Survey

Key Words and Phrases: surveys, education, computer science curricula
CR Categories: 1.52

EDITOR:

After reading R. W. Elliott's article, "Master's Level Computer Science Curricula" [*Comm. ACM 11*, July 1968], I begin to wonder about the "marketability" of students with a master's degree in Computer Science and exactly where they fit into the computer and information processing community. The article conveys the impression that current M.S. students are weak and inadequately trained in the areas where industry requires the most help.

I make this statement as chairman of a two-year associate degree program in Computer Technology. Our graduates (1) are thoroughly familiar with the programming languages of FORTRAN, COBOL, RPG, ALGOL, and PL/I, as well as a machine and assembly language on a third generation computer; (2) have been exposed to courses in data processing management, system design, and commercial or scientific applications; (3) have had at least one course in numerical analysis and computer mathematics; (4) have taken computer application courses in statistics, linear programming, PERT, CPM, and simulation; and (5) have been trained using the "hands on" approach to operate computers and other peripheral devices and to debug their programs.

Obviously, the M.S. student, in view of his academic experience, should be superior to the A.A.S. student. However, the A.A.S. student is at least "marketable" and has a place in the real and practical world of computing.

From my contacts in industry it has been disappointing to observe some recent M.S. students who have been trained in the theoretical aspects of computer science but who were not able to apply their training to the solution of the practical problems facing industry. I strongly feel that more effort should be exerted in tying in the various A.A.S. degree programs with the existing B.S., M.S., and Ph.D. programs in areas of Computer Science, since all these programs are part of a continuum called computing and information processing.

JOHN MANIOTES
Computer Technology
Purdue University Calumet Campus
Hammond, IN 46323

Letter from the ACM Vice-President
Vol. 20, No. 10, October 1977, p. 683

Trends in Graduate Computer Science Education (Will They All Find Work?)

This generation of computer science graduate students enjoys the prospect of a strong demand for its services, but a "Ph.D. glut" some years down the road is a worrisome possibility. Computer science education must adapt to changing educational and employment patterns if it is to remain effective.

These are among the conclusions I come to after leading a discussion by senior computer science educators, industrial employers, and ACM leadership, at an informal meeting held before the National Computer Conference earlier this year in Dallas. This letter is a summary of that discussion; I won't call it a consensus because the process of reviewing an earlier draft of this letter made it clear that on some crucial issues educational leaders are at variance on how they see the future.

Here, then, is my view of the future of graduate computer science education, guided by the insights of some two dozen people at a face-to-face meeting, by the Conte-Taulbee reports on computer science Ph.D.'s. (*Comm. ACM,* June 1976, June 1977), by my travels and discussions at colleges and universities, and by reviewers. For three other views in what I hope will be a continuing dialog, see the ACM Forum in this issue for letters by Professors Denning, Nunamaker, and Sibley.

1. For a number of years some of us have worried that computer science might develop an oversupply of Ph.D.'s, as has happened in a number of other fields. I have tried to track this matter on the thought that if we could get early warning signals, it might be possible to find some way to soften the crunch.

That problem will probably have to be faced someday, but, it appears, not right away. This year's graduates have had their pick of jobs, academic or industrial as their interests dictate, at high salaries. Schools trying to hire new faculty are, in some cases, in desperate straits. There are some indications of a new industrial demand for Ph.D.'s, although it may be that this demand is confined to a rather few industrial research organizations. Industry is becoming increasingly attractive to both Ph.D. and Master's students, because of substantial salary differentials between industrial and academic jobs and because academic tenure has become difficult to obtain.

In short, graduate students now in school have rosy employment prospects.

Mind you, I am not saying that the function of education is to maximize students' starting salary offers. Education is different from vocational training. Still, however much we prize the aspects of a true education that go beyond the merely vocational, we do seek to prepare our students to play a useful role in society. The ability to get a job is—perhaps unfortunately—the most obvious measure of social usefulness. If large numbers of graduates, however well educated, could not find work, we would surely feel that somehow things were out of kilter.

And that will probably happen at some point. The very success of today's graduate programs is a strong incentive to expansion; once the new faculty members are in place and an enlarged pipeline of students is full, it is painful to cut back. Today's euphoria about employment must not blind us to the fact that nothing can grow forever, and that there really is *some* limit to the number of computer science Ph.D.'s that the world needs. The top graduates will never have a problem, but in an oversupply situation, some of those below the top are going to be in trouble.

2. One of the most rapidly-growing areas of computer education is that of Master's degree programs, especially those in information systems management. Often these are relatively new ventures in the Business School. Others have existed for some time within departments of computer science or electrical engineering. These are terminal Master's programs, usually two years, directed toward students who will be working in applications and possibly later in their careers moving into management.

A computer science graduate whose academic work has focused on individual research in some useful but narrowly-defined specialty is rather poorly equipped to step into such a teaching environment. People running information systems management programs say that they can find almost no qualified new graduates for teaching positions. It is necessary either to recruit from industry or to engage in on-the-job training.

It is becoming less and less true that the typical Ph.D. in computer science goes into teaching in a department similar to the one from which he or she graduates. More are going into industry, apparently, and those who go into teaching are increasingly in Master's and undergraduate programs, where a research-oriented Ph.D. may be a rather poor preparation.

The implications of these shifts in the employment of Ph.D.'s may not be clear in detail, but it is fairly obvious that some overhaul of curriculum and methods may be required.

3. As measured by employment opportunities, society has a place for both Ph.D.'s and Master's graduates who know about computers—but the two are quite different and should not be confused. Just as a chipmunk is not a squirrel that didn't grow up, a Master's graduate is not just a Ph.D. candidate who ran out of money or failed the qualifying exam. Of course we need Ph.D.'s. But we also need the rather different preparation of the applications-oriented Master's. For many industrial jobs, a person with a Master's is *at least* as attractive as one with a Ph.D.—in some cases more so. A Master's degree is a decided plus over the Bachelor's, if the preparation is right, but, except for some research environments, a Ph.D. does not necessarily add to a prospective employee's qualifications.

4. The features of a computer science education attractive to employers can be identified as follows:

First, multidisciplinary preparation is valuable. The person who knows computers *and* accounting, or computers *and* hospital administration, or computers and whatever, will usually have a decided advantage over the narrowly-trained person. The combination of a Bachelor's in computer science and a Master's in some application area, or vice versa, is especially attractive.

Second, the graduate needs to have *some* area of specialization, some area in which he or she comes to grips with an intellectual discipline, masters a portion of it, and learns how to approach the learning of a body of new material—which will be a life-long process.

Third, college experience in working in teams is highly desirable. Most work in business involves team operations, whether formalized under such names as chief programmer team or not, and the educational experience should reflect this fact. Various programs exist, ranging from simple procedures in which students in programming classes have to modify each other's programs, to extensive group projects working with local industry. It is widely agreed that such experience is a very large advantage for any graduate. Setting up programs to provide such experience can require significant time, effort, and expense, but the payoff is large.

Unfortunately, the educational system is largely geared to an individualistic approach to measurement and rewards. There are shining exceptions to be sure, but the faculty generally doesn't know how to give grades for joint projects, and students are conditioned against putting the control of their evaluation in the hands of other students. This is a difficult problem, but one that must be tackled if education is to adapt to the needs of society.

Fourth, it is agreed that almost all technical graduates are deficient in communication skills, and that most know little about how to motivate others. No one seems to be able to offer much guidance on what to do about this essentially universal complaint, except to note that experience working in teams helps to uncover latent communication and leadership skills in those students who have them.

* * * * *

Computer science education thrives. The people involved seem to be enjoying themselves, the graduates currently find work, the needs of society are being addressed (if not always met). But the winds of change blow here as elsewhere, and constant evolutionary adaptation is required. The law of survival is still "Adapt or die."

The ACM will play its part as it has in the past. The curriculum reports on computer science education (*Comm. ACM,* March 1968) and computer education for management (*Comm. ACM,* May 1972, December 1973) have had a profound impact on education. It is to be expected that the reports on undergraduate computer science education and on community college programs, now in draft form in the SIGCSE Bulletin (June 1977), will have a similar impact. Coordination among various efforts is improving. The ACM—and computer science education—may develop hardening of the arteries someday, but there is very little sign of it so far.

—Daniel D. McCracken

Acknowledgments and Attendees. The meeting mentioned at the beginning of the letter originated in earlier conversations with Robert M. Graham, of the University of Massachusetts, and Walter J. Karplus, of the University of California at Los Angeles.

The attendees were: William F. Atchison, University of Maryland and chairman of the ACM Education Board; Richard Austing, University of Maryland and chairman of the ACM Special Interest Group on Computer Science Education; Cyril H.P. Brookes, University of New South Wales; David S. Burris, University of Southern Mississippi; Sam D. Conte, Purdue University and chairman of the Computer Science Board; William Cotterman, Georgia State University and the ACM Council; Joel Cyprus, Texas Instruments; Gordon B. Davis, University of Minnesota; George Dodd, General Motors Research and ACM secretary; Gerald Engel, Virginia Institute of Marine Science and vice-chairman, ACM Education Board; Herbert R.J. Grosch, consultant and ACM president; John Hamblen, University of Missouri at Rolla and chairman of the ACM Committee on Curriculum in Computer Sciences; Fred Harris, University of Chicago and ACM director of the Institute for Certification of Computer Professionals (ICCP); Thomas E. Murray, Del Monte Corporation and chairman, ACM Special Interest Group on Business Data Processing; Jay F. Nunamaker, University of Arizona and chairman of the ACM Committee on Curriculum on Computer Education for Management; Oliver R. Smoot, CBEMA and ACM director of ICCP; Orrin E. Taulbee, University of Pittsburgh and chairman of the ACM Committee on Computer Science Conferences; Judy Townley, Harvard University; Marshall Yovits, Ohio State University and ACM Council.

ACM Forum
Vol. 20, No. 10, October 1977, p. 774

Comments on Vice-President's Letter on Graduate Education In This Issue

□ The Vice-President has made some interesting observations (see pages 683-684) about Computer Science (CS) education. Herewith are some relevant further observations.

1. *Philosophy of Education.* In the past decade or so, the philosophy of American education has shifted noticeably, away from the traditional concept of "scholarship" toward a new concept of "vocationalism." The reasons for this originate in Big Education run by Big Government, with its mission of "educating" as many students as possible and preparing them for "useful roles" in society. In this view a Ph.D. is merely an admission certificate to glutted academic ranks, and it "overqualifies" for most jobs. Many students believe that employers will hire no one whose education "exceeds" the minimum required for the job. Educators must deal with the attitude that the student who chooses a broad education does so at the expense of job training and utility to society.
2. *"Ph.D. Glut."* We presently experience no oversupply of Ph.D. holders in CS. This is because jobs are plentiful; attractive offers are made to holders of Bachelor's and Master's degrees. Few students feel inclined to work for the highest degree, when similar pay and more job security are available immediately. But a Ph.D. glut is likely to develop, for the job market will eventually tighten.
3. *"Tapping the Pipeline."* Many an employer hires topnotch students in the early stages of their Ph.D. studies, offering a good salary at a Master's level—much to the satisfaction of both employer and student. This phenomenon may have a curious side effect; if the very best students are plucked from the pipeline, the second best are left to complete Ph.D. studies. The result could be a decline in the quality of Ph.D. holders. Put that in your pipe.
4. *EE vs. CS Tensions.* Tensions between Electrical Engineering (EE) and CS are resurfacing. Symbolized by Texas Instruments' trademarked "solid state software," many people find plausible the argument that all important software will be hard-burned into cheap chips for plugging into a calculator or personal computer. Some EE departments have taken the position that, being now so close to hardware, software research belongs in the EE department—even if the CS department has been offering software engineering and programming methodology courses for years. Such conflict serves no one. Our profession is unique, including in its purview both purely scientific and purely engineering subjects. Possibly ACM (and IEEE?) education committees should study this, seeking a mitigating position.

These issues are probably less troublesome at private universities, which still can afford high admission standards and lighter teaching loads. But the majority who receive degrees in computer science and engineering do so courtesy of the State, in whose universities these issues are real.

PETER J. DENNING
Computer Science Department
Purdue University
W. Lafayette, IN 47907

□ I agree with Dan McCracken's remark that "Computer Science education must adapt to changing educational and employment patterns if it is to remain effective." However, before we change or adapt, we must decide how the proposed changes relate to the existing structure of Computer Science programs. In the spirit of McCracken's letter, I have a number of comments related to graduate computer education, not just graduate computer science education.

In the context of my comments, the Information Systems discipline is defined as being concerned with the use of computers for the management and operation of organizations. Information Systems programs must stress two components: (1) functional areas in business and management, and (2) technical topics in computing related to analyzing, designing, and building information systems.

The ACM Curriculum Committee on Computer Education for Management (C^3EM) has been discussing the issues raised in McCracken's letter since 1970. In May 1972, the ACM C^3EM Committee published in *Communications* an extensive report dealing with curriculum in Information Systems. The task of the current C^3EM Committee is to update the 1972 report with findings on how well the 1972 recommendations have been implemented. Preliminary results of our study are as follows:

Most common name in use in university programs for undergraduate and graduate programs in "Information Systems Area:"

Number	Name of Program
27	Management Information Systems
18	Information Systems
5	Business Information Systems
•	•
•	•
•	•
2	Information Systems Management
142	

There are 37 distinct names or permutations of words to label Information Systems programs.

	Location of Information Systems Programs	
	Business or Management College	Computer Science Department
Bachelor	64	8
Master	35	12
Ph.D.	18	5

The ACM C^3EM survey indicates that Business and Management

Schools are very active in the development of Information Systems programs.

A second point concerns McCracken's implications that Information Systems programs should be implemented by Computer Science departments. The implication being made is that Computer Science departments must stress applications in order to survive. While this may be in part true, it is fallacious to state that all Computer Science departments must develop Information Systems programs as a major area of concentration. There are many potential facets to a Computer Science department; the large number of areas of specialization assure that a department can develop expertise in, at most, only a few of them. Information Systems programs should exist somewhere within the university structure, but it is not clear that the Information Systems program should necessarily be in a Computer Science department. The important consideration is that a successful Information Systems program must have the cooperation and support of the Computer Science department. The Computer Science and the Information Systems groups *must* be willing to work together.

Indeed, the Computer Science department of the future will have to be able to cooperate with an even larger community of applications-oriented faculty in other areas of the university. Graduate computer education has always been, and should continue to be, a cooperative venture between people of various disciplines. Cooperation between areas and resulting multi-disciplinary programs assure precisely the type of integrated training McCracken desires.

Finally, I disagree with the statement that the training of a research-oriented Ph.D. may be a rather poor preparation for a faculty position in Information Systems education. Now more than ever, qualified researchers are needed in the Information Systems area. The question is not whether there should be research, but what type of research should be done. Research-oriented Ph.D.'s are sorely needed in Information Systems to assure that all organizations using such systems are capable of utilizing rationally our constantly changing technology. This background is especially needed for faculty teaching in either undergraduate or Master's programs. The very nature of the university environment demands that Information Systems faculty members also be competent researchers. The Information Systems programs at many universities are also producing many of the Ph.D's to teach the Information Systems programs that are currently being developed at the undergraduate and graduate level.

I think it is important for McCracken to recognize the need for programs in Information Systems, but it is clearly misleading to label the changes that are occurring with respect to Information Systems as trends in graduate computer science education. It would be more appropriate to label McCracken's remarks as trends in graduate computer education.

J.F. NUNAMAKER JR.
Chairman, ACM C³EM
Professor of Management
Information Systems and
Computer Science
The University of Arizona
Tucson, AZ 85721

□ I read with interest a prepublication version of Dan McCracken's Vice-President's Letter and would like to express two allied if slightly differing points of view.

1. Why does everyone seem to think the Ph.D. (and lower degree) job market is about to dry up? Maybe we are just producing the wrong products at the University.

2. What are the educational units of interest? Maybe Computer Science and Business are not enough (or at least they have ill defined boundaries).

First, the question of growth and the job market for highly educated "information and computer scientists." A recent study of the Department of Commerce states that the "information sector" in 1967 accounted for 46 percent of the U.S. Gross National Product. Now even if we remove the entertainment, purely electrical engineering, and line communication industry from this, we are left with a large and probably growing percentage, composed of hardware, software, and "systemeering" personnel, possibly in the ratios of 1 to 4 to 2.

For such a potentially large industrial and governmental need, there must be a large body of educators—after all, engineering colleges at major universities have several hundred faculty members, and though the vicissitudes of fortune effect their distribution, the overall number now appears to have stabilized. The whole area of "informationeering" (to coin a new word) could well support university faculties of the size of a hundred or so in the future; the other question is, however, "Should it be in one department or several?"

I thus reach my second question, and approach it with an analogy: that of science and engineering. We have Physics departments which deal with the structure and properties of matter, and we have Electrical Engineering departments which deal with a particular branch of applied Physics. No physicist expects to go into industry as a designer or builder of electric generators, while hardly any engineer expects to do research on the basic properties of materials (there are exceptions, of course).

There is one basic science which we can call Computer Science–and provide it with a mathematical and theoretical existence. It includes automata theory, numerical analysis, switching theory, some concepts of digital circuitry (though this might overlap Electrical Engineering), linguistics, the more abstract parts of artificial intelligence, theory and some applications of statistics and probability (e.g. queueing theory) in computing systems, aspects of networking (though again this impinges on Electrical and Systems Engineering), and the more basic theory of programming languages and systems design.

Juxtaposed to this, we have another area which could be called Computer and Information Engineering, or Information Systems Management, which deals with the practice and building of automated information systems. Maybe Information Systems Management is really a group of departments with some basic "software engineering" generality in much the same way as a university engineering college. Thus we might have hospital information systems, and social information systems departments, etc., though I think that the level of our knowledge is not yet sufficient to fractionate ourselves to this extent.

The basic syllabus of Information Systems Management is presumably a grounding in Computer Science, particularly the more practical aspects, and a knowledge of information systems with respect to potential interfaces, the user and human factor aspects, and the problems of building large scale systems. This latter includes information systems analysis and design, management aspects of large scale systems, operation research and statistics applications in large scale systems, and understanding of the important building blocks (like operating systems and data base management systems), governmental aspects (such as privacy and the law as it applies to computing), social problems (such as crime, discrimination, and monopolies as they apply to the information systems field), and the general organizational theory as it applies to management of change and the introduction of large scale information systems into an enterprise. The important point here, however, is the fact that the syllabus transcends business and encompasses most of the "soft" sciences (e.g. Sociology and Urban Studies).

I feel that it is not necessary to belabor the parts of these two different curricula; there are several good examples of the efficiency and effectiveness of having such a split. On the other hand, attempts to put both computer scientists and information engineers into the same department have led to problems. Apparently the body of knowledge and the methodology of research are too different. It is difficult to see how some of the faculty will ever get tenure and promotion when members of the other part consider them either too theoretical to be of use or beneath academic contempt. Apparently, we are talking about two different "breed of cat" that cannot be judged by the same criteria.

One of my Swedish colleagues has a joint appointment with the business school, partly because he feels that the biggest problem in practice is management and not technology; another friend thinks that the business school only turns out second rate students who are not worth considering. But maybe our biggest problem in industry and in the acceptance of the "computer scientist" in industry is that we are trying to train and sell physicists to do engineering jobs.

EDGAR H. SIBLEY
Department of Information
System Management
University of Maryland
College Park, MD 20742

A Report by the ACM Accreditation Committee
Vol. 20, No. 11, November 1977, p. 891

A Report by the ACM Accreditation Committee

Accreditation Guidelines for Bachelor's Degree Programs in Computer Science

Introduction

The Accreditation Committee of the Association for Computing Machinery (ACM) was formed in 1967 to provide information and guidance to various educational endeavors relating to the use and development of computing systems. The efforts of the committee were directed toward establishing a set of standards for specified programs that could be used in determining whether a program was worthy of accreditation.

The Association for Computing Machinery determined that ACM would not become an accrediting agency and arrangements were made to work with existing accrediting bodies. ACM would provide information to be used by these groups in their accreditation studies in whatever way the agency deemed appropriate. This information is also expected to be used by guidance counselors and prospective students to aid in the assessment of programs covered by the guidelines. Copies of the guidelines will be made available for these purposes.

The first report of the committee in May 1969 dealt with guidelines for data processing schools. This report is one of a series that will be issued on guidelines for computer education and computer facilities in institutions of higher education. These reports are intended for use in the institutional self study portion of the regional accrediting activities of the Federation of Regional Accrediting Commissions of Higher Education.

The rapid increase in Computer Science or computer oriented departments at the college or university level in the last few years has led to some concern over the educational product. It has been recognized that some guidance is necessary to maintain an identifiable area of training. The following guidelines are the recommendations of the Association for Computing Machinery, approved by the Education Board in January 1977, and the Executive Committee in June 1977. These are considered to be minimum requirements for an acceptable degree program in computer science. The guidelines cover curriculum, faculty, course offerings and facilities.

1.0 Curriculum

The following topics are a minimum set of concepts to be provided in the curriculum.

1.1 Programming Topics

1.11 Algorithms. The concept and properties of algorithms. The role of algorithms in the problem solving process. Flowcharts and languages to facilitate the expression of algorithms.

1.12 Languages. Basic syntax of a higher level (problem oriented) language. Subprograms. I/O. Recursion.

1.13 Programming Style. The need for discipline and style. Concepts and techniques of structured programming. Documentation.

1.14 Debugging and Verification. Selection of test data, techniques for error detection. Relation of programming style to use of error detection and program verification.

1.2 Software Organization

1.21 Computer Structure and Machine Language. Organization of computers in terms of input-output, storage, control and processing units. Register and storage structures, instruction format and execution, principle instruction types, and machine language programming. Machine arithmetic, program control, input-output operations and interrupts.

1.22 Digital Representation of Data. Bits, bytes, words, codes, and other information structures. Radices and radix conversion, representation of integers, floating-point, and multiple-precision numbers, roundoff errors.

1.23 Symbolic Coding and Assembly Systems. Mnemonic operation codes, labels, symbolic addresses and address expressions. Literals, extended machine operations and pseudo operations. Error flags and messages. Scanning of symbolic instructions and symbolic table construction. Concepts of design and operation of assemblers.

1.24 Addressing Techniques. Absolute addressing, indexing, indirect addressing, relative addressing, and base addressing. Memory mapping functions, storage allocation, associative addressing, concepts of paging, and machine organization to facilitate modes of addressing.

1.25 Program Segmentation and Linkage. Subroutines, co-routines, and functions. Subprogram loading and linkage, common data linkage, transfer vectors, overlay subprograms, and stacking techniques.

1.3 Hardware Organization

1.31 Computers. Basic characteristics and organization including memory, processors, control and input-output. How programs are executed. Representation of information.

1.32 Computer Systems Organization. Characteristics and use of tapes, disks, drums, cores, and other large volume devices in storage hierarchies. Processing unit organization. Characteristics of input-output channels and devices, peripheral and satellite processes, multiple processor configurations, computer networks, and remote access terminals.

1.33 Data Communications. Protocol, full and half duplex, packet switching.

1.4 Data Structures and File Processing

1.41 Data Structures. Arrays, strings, stacks, queues, linked lists. Representation in memory. Algorithms for manipulating data within the structures.

1.42 Trees. Basic terminology and types. Representation as binary trees. Traversal schemes. Representation in memory. Breadth-first and depth-first search techniques. Threading.

1.43 File Terminology. Record, file, blocking, and database.

1.44 Sequential Access. Physical characteristics of tapes. Sort/merge algorithms. File manipulation techniques for updating, deleting, and inserting records.

1.45 Direct Access. Physical characteristics of disk/drums and other storage devices. Physical representation of data storage devices. Physical representation of data structures on storage devices. Algorithms and techniques for implementing inverted lists, multilists, indexing, and sequential and hierarchical structure.

1.5 Systems Programming

1.51 Job Control Languages. Consideration for command language interpreter, macro facilities in control languages, user interface considerations.

1.52 Operating Systems. Concepts of processors in parallel. Problems of resolving deadlock, exclusion and synchronization. Processor scheduling, queueing and network control, concepts of system balancing. Memory management.

1.53 Compilers. Syntax and semantics of languages, lexical analysis, parsing, information structures, code generation.

2.0 Faculty

2.1 Number of Faculty Members

A minimum of 4 full-time equivalent faculty members will be needed to staff a department covering the recommended course offerings and provide adequate individual professional development time for the faculty members.

2.2 Qualifications

All the faculty will be formally educated in computer science or have equivalent work or informal educational experience in the computer science field. Continued formal and informal professional development experiences will be provided to keep faculty abreast of recent developments in computer science.

2.3 Teaching Load

The faculty teaching load must not exceed 12 hours per faculty member per semester. In terms of student load, a faculty member who is teaching full-time must not have more than 360 student semester/quarter credit hours to teach each semester or quarter without significant help in terms of student assistants or lab assistants in the courses involved. The teaching load should be reduced appropriately for any faculty member who has extensive research, laboratory supervision, or university committee responsibilities.

3.0 Course Offerings

A minimum of 10 different computer science courses should be offered leading to the Bachelor's degree. These courses must cover the topics contained in the section on curriculum. The courses must be a graduated set of courses with early courses preparing students for the courses that follow with a more advanced treatment of a topic.

4.0 Computer Facilities

There will be a hands on facility available for student use sometime during the students' course work in the department. Laboratory experiences will be provided for some of the upper division courses on a dedicated computer or via simulation on a shared system. The students must have access to a time-shared or batch oriented computer system with several high level languages, such as Fortran, Cobol, PL/I, Snobol, Algol, LISP, APL, GPSS, GASP IV, etc., available.

This system must have sufficient speed and capacity to provide a normal turnaround of submitted student programs of at least three times a day.

PREPARED BY:

ACM Accreditation Committee

Gordon E. Stokes, Chairman

Brigham Young University

Committee Members:

Anita Cochran

Bell Telephone Labs

Sam Conte

Purdue University

John Gorgone

Purdue University

John Hamblen

University of Missouri-Rolla

Joyce Currie Little

Community College of Baltimore

Ottis Rechard

University of Denver

Marshall Yovits

Ohio State University

ACM Forum
Vol. 21, No. 2, February 1978, p. 184

The University User Service

□ At the same time that guidelines for degree programs in computer science are being presented ("Accreditation Guidelines for Bachelor's Degree Programs in Computer Science," CACM, November 1977) and a call for continued and strengthened cooperation between disciplines is heard (J.F. Nunamaker Jr., ACM Forum, October 1977), it seems appropriate to consider tapping the university computer center's user service as an educational resource.

User services offer a unique opportunity for on-the-job training in an environment that includes individuals drawn from the computer science and engineering areas as well as from the humanities and social sciences. Typical user services' projects range from the installation of a general usage tool such as a language compiler to the extension of some software technique to a particular faculty or graduate research problem.

There are obstacles to be overcome, however, before a cooperative program could be implemented. First, there is no guarantee that user services represent a good mix of academic interests. Too often a single academic group dominates—commonly a technically oriented area. Study options within user services should not duplicate courses offered by computer science or engineering departments.

Another difficulty is that the computer center, as administrator of a computer installation, lacks academic status and is thus unable to give academic credit. This is partially overcome at some centers where user services personnel hold faculty appointments. But this tends to bias the emphasis toward the credit-granting department, thereby losing the advantage of neutrality.

Faculty members who are given temporary financial assistance by the computer center for release time for computer-related research tend to do little to encourage interdisciplinary student involvement. Their sympathies lie with the department from which they expect to return upon termination of computer services' funding.

Granting academic credit is a necessity to insure the viability of any academic program. A committee with faculty membership drawn from various academic departments could de velop, oversee, and accredit multidisciplinary work-study programs within user services. Committees with the appropriate membership mix are already in existence at many universities, serving in an advisory capacity concerning the computer center's policies and budget. It would be a natural extension of their duties to develop and maintain academic programs.

I would be interested to hear if something like this has ever been tried.

Hilda Standley
2745 Rathbun Dr.
Toledo, OH 43606

ACM Forum
Vol. 21, No. 4, April 1978, p. 329

A Core of Computer Knowledge

In my computer-related employment, I have become increasingly aware of the need for defining a "core" of basic knowledge (information, topics, subjects) that everyone claiming computer-related expertise should be conversant with and interested in. As a member of Council, I find the need for a definition of such a core of basic knowledge to be a consideration in many important activities of ACM. In the remainder of this letter, I will use the word "core" in place of the expression "a core of basic knowledge."

A schematic diagram below illustrates my view of the relation between the core and four of the more important ACM activities. Consider each of these activities and their relation to the core, proceeding clockwise beginning with the Journal for all Members (JAM).

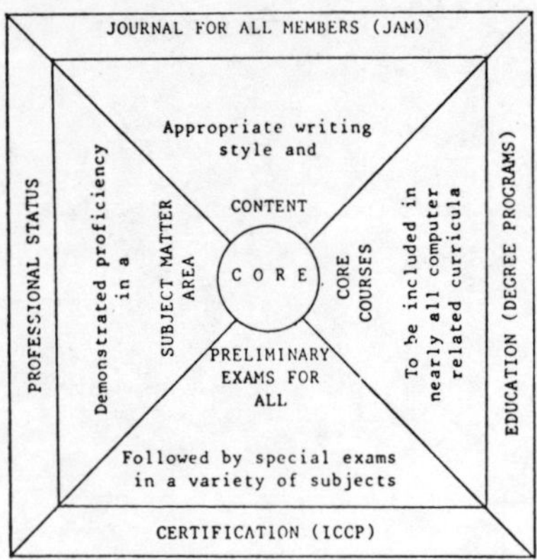

There has been much discussion of a JAM. The style and content of *Communications* has been criticized and some have attempted to define an appropriate style and content for a JAM. It seems to me that we will be unable to prescribe the appropriate content for a JAM until we define the core. (We may also be unable to prescribe the appropriate style but that is beyond the scope of this letter.)

Computer science is still a newly emerging discipline. Academicians have defined its content implicitly in terms of the curricula associated with computer science degrees. But this definition varies depending on whether we are talking about computer science or information science or data processing or a computer specialty in electrical engineering. Surely, we should be able to prepare specifications for a few courses that everyone who wishes to claim expertise relating to computers should successfully complete. So far we have been unable to do this.

This has led to a related problem in our certification effort. We have been unable to define a set of preliminary examinations that *all* persons seeking certification by the ICCP should pass. I believe that unless we have a series of two or three preliminary exams, followed by one or more specialty exams (much like the actuarial examinations), we will be unable to gain widespread acceptance for ICCP certification.

Finally, we come to the issue of the professional status of persons in computer-related occupations. This issue is related to two of the areas discussed above: educational degree programs and certification. This issue relates to the core in much the same way these two areas relate to the core. Consider, for example, the Civil Service Commission view that a professional should have mastered a body of knowledge as evidenced by successfully completing a course of study at an accredited institution and/or passing a series of examinations administered by a professional organization. The core is that portion of this body of knowledge that would be shared by all computer-related professionals.

I hope that this letter indicates why I believe that a definition of the core should have a high priority. Although the core is related to several different existing ACM activities, its definition does not appear to be the responsibility of any one of them. I would not presume to suggest a mechanism for arriving at a definition. This is something that the Council as a whole or the Executive Committee might do.

HERBERT MAISEL
ACM Council Member,
Capital Region Representative
9432 Curran Rd.
Silver Spring, MD 20901

On Accreditation

□ We have these comments on the ACM Accreditation Committee's Computer Science curriculum guidelines (*Communications,* November 1977, pages 891-892).

On *Section 1.0* (Curriculum): All of these topics are software related. Graduates of the subsequent degree programs would be well qualified to work for vendors developing operating systems, compilers, and control programs; or to work for large-scale users as systems programmers, database administrators, or data communications programmers. The larger employment area of systems analysts and applications programmers, primarily employed by users but also a growing field with vendors, is not addressed. One or two good accounting and finance courses should be added to the curriculum, because many business systems are organized along the lines of budgeting, variance analysis, cost accounting and double-entry bookkeeping.

On *Section 2.3* (Teaching Load): Many universities presently offer five-hour courses, particularly in the student's major area. The maximum load should be at least 15 hours, with a two-course limitation on the number of different subjects taught per term. A second section of a course is not as demanding as an additional topic.

J. CLARK KEY
JACK B. SAMPSELLE
Corporate Information Services
Southwire Company
Carrollton, GA 30117

□ The accreditation guidelines for a bachelor's degree in Computer Science developed by the ACM Accreditation Committee are fine, so far as they go. However, our experience has been that we already have a serious need for people with a capability to understand the architecture of, and effectively program, microprocessors. I do not see any logical design, microprocessor architecture, microprocessor applications, use of RAMS, ROMS, PROMS and EPROMS, or mini-to-micro cross-assemblers mentioned in the Accreditation Committee's guidelines.

In addition, in my view, *Section 1.33* on Data Communications ignores basic things like intelligent terminals, message switching, circuit switching, error, delay (particularly satellite circuits), and any treatment of distributed (dispersed?) processing or the economics of data communications.

Without the items I have mentioned, your bachelor's degree should be entitled "Large Computer Programming," not "Computer Science."

H.F. Hession
Western Union
Government Systems Division
7916 Westpark Drive
McLean, VA 22101

Response

The letters coming in on the accreditation recommendations for Computer Science (the two above submitted to the Forum and others) have commented on the lack of systems analysis work and on a weakness in preparation for applications programming tasks.

This was a conscious omission by the Accreditation Committee as we worked on this recommendation. Our work with the curriculum committees of ACM and IEEE have convinced us that there is more material in the systems programming and applications programming areas than can be treated in one curriculum. Because of this we are developing accreditation recommendations for an applications programming area called Information Systems in addition to the Computer Science area.

We relied heavily on work by the Curriculum Committee for Computer Science of ACM for applicable subject areas in our work on Computer Science. We intend to work just as closely with ACM's curriculum committees working on information systems topics for our accreditation guidelines for Information Systems departments.

On topics such as teaching loads, minimum faculty, and computer resources we drew extensively from the experience of many department chairmen. We feel that changes that allow increased load on the faculty in the end produce a lower quality education for the student. We opted for some heavier loading than we thought wise but we recognized there are budgetary constraints that push for heavier loading. We stand on our recommendations. They have been thoroughly reviewed and discussed.

Our committee has always felt that the accreditation guidelines set a minimum level for acceptable programs. Departments striving for quality will use the curriculum recommendations of the ACM curriculum committees to measure their effectiveness and program strengths instead of the accreditation guidelines.

We are moving ahead and will soon have accreditation guidelines for Information Systems departments and for computer facilities at educational institutions.

GORDON E. STOKES
Chairman, ACM
Accreditation Committee

ACM Forum
Vol. 21, No. 6, June 1978, p. 511

Wrought Into the Core

□ In his ACM Forum letter of April 1978 [p. 329] Herbert Maisel calls for an appropriate corps within ACM to define a core of basic knowledge assumed to be known by all members of ACM. He pictured his proposal with a square wheel whose hub was the "core" and whose four sides were JOURNAL FOR ALL MEMBERS, EDUCATION, CERTIFICATION, and PROFESSIONAL STATUS—representing his perceptions of ACM's four principal activities.

If each of us were asked to draw a diagram showing ACM's main activities in relation to a "core," I think we would get a lot of pictures showing PUBLICATIONS, EDUCATION, CHAPTERS, and SIGS as the four main activities. Some would depict round wheels that roll forward, rather than square ones that remain stationary.

And what is in the "core"? An operational definition is the intersection of all the sets of computer knowledge of all members. ACM's present specifications invite the membership of any college graduate interested enough to invest $35, even if he has no deep knowledge of computers. Thus the operational "core" is essentially empty. Maisel's perception of a lack of a present "core" is an observation of the operational reality. An attempt by one group of ACM to develop a "core" might well be opposed by other groups of ACM. (No one wants his ox cored.) Diversity is ACM's strength. Maybe we should learn to live with it, and to capitalize on it, as the SIGs have done so successfully.

Ever since our financial crises of a few years back, we have devoted much volunteer time to meeting and planning: someone has observed that committee-meeting hours exceed technical-session hours at our annual conference. Now, I'm a believer in planning for schemes that cannot be cheaply reversed once started—for example, undertaking a new major publication. But there are many schemes which can be easily reversed —for example, if the direction and style of the *Computing Surveys* are unacceptable, we simply replace the Editor-in-Chief.

Planning is important, but it has become ACM's major activity. I think we should plan less, do more, retreat when needed from poor decisions. I would view a core-finding committee as more unneeded planning.

PETER J. DENNING
Member-at-Large of Council
Editor-in-Chief, *Computing Surveys*
Purdue University
W. Lafayette, IN 47907

Response

I am pleased to see that Peter Denning and I agree that ACM's core is essentially empty. I would prefer that we had a more substantial foundation. I do not agree that defining a core is planning—it is doing something that will be of great importance to the ACM.

I did not say that the JOURNAL FOR ALL MEMBERS, EDUCATION, CERTIFICATION, and PROFESSIONAL STATUS are the principal activities of the ACM but rather that they are "four of the more important ACM activities." These four important activities would all benefit from a definition of a core of basic knowledge.

I did not realize when I drew it that Peter planned to ride on my diagram. However, considering the direction in which he would take us, I am rather glad that I provided a square wheel for his ride.

HERBERT MAISEL
ACM Council Member
Capital Region Representative
9432 Curran Rd.
Silver Spring, MD 20901

Report
Vol. 23, No. 2, February 1980, p. 67

Curriculum '78—Is Computer Science Really that Unmathematical?

Anthony Ralston
SUNY at Buffalo

Mary Shaw
Carnegie-Mellon University

Key Words and Phrases: Curriculum '78, computer science education, discrete mathematics
CR Category: 1.5

If computer science had not developed—significantly—as a science in the ten years between Curriculum '68 [2] and Curriculum '78 [3], then perhaps all those people who wondered if computer science was really a discipline would have been correct. In 1968 computer science was searching for but had not yet found much in the way of the principles and theoretical underpinnings which characterize a (mature) science. Ten years later, there is nothing laughable about calling computer science a science. This decade has seen major advances in the theory of computation and in the utility of theoretical results in practical settings. The rapid growth of the field of computational complexity has greatly increased our ability to analyze algorithms. And perhaps most significantly, we have finally started to make real progress in developing principles and theories for the design and verification of algorithms and programs.

Are these changes evident in Curriculum '78? Sadly, no. That curriculum only lends support to the equation

Computer Science = Programming

that is mistakenly believed by so many outside the discipline. In the "Objectives of the Core Curriculum" [3] only the second objective—"be able to determine whether or not they have written a reasonably efficient and well-organized program"—recognizes that good programming requires more than just mastery of the syntax and semantics of a programming language. And even here the reference to principles and theory is, to be charitable, vague.

The principles and theories of any science give it structure and make it systematic. They should set the shape of the curriculum for that science, for

—only in that way can they provide a framework for the mastery of facts, and
—only in that way will they become the tools of the practicing scientist.

This is as true for computer science as it is for mathematics, for the physical sciences, and for any engineering curriculum. Inevitably, for any science or any engineering discipline, the fundamental principles and theories can only be understood through the medium of mathematics. In the following sections we focus on the place of mathematics in the computer science curriculum and try to show how badly Curriculum '78 fails in this respect.

But first we note one matter of crucial importance which makes an emphasis on principles and theory even more important in computer science than in other disciplines. Computer science is an evolving field. Specific skills learned today will rapidly become obsolete. The principles that underlie these skills, however, will continue to be relevant. Only by giving the student a firm grounding in these principles can he or she be protected from galloping obsolescence. Even a student who aspires only to be a programmer needs more than just programming skills. He or she needs to understand issues of design, of the capability and potential of software, hardware, and theory, and of algorithms and information organization in general.

Authors' present addresses: A. Ralston, State University of New York at Buffalo, Dept. of Computer Science, 4226 Ridge Lea Road, Amherst, NY 14226; M. Shaw, Carnegie-Mellon University, Computer Science Dept., Pittsburgh, PA 15213.

Table I. Required Mathematics Courses.

Curriculum '68		Curriculum '78	
M1	Introductory calculus	MA1	Introductory calculus
M2	Mathematical analysis I	MA2	Mathematical analysis I
M2P	Probability	MA2A	Probability
M3	Linear algebra	MA3	Linear algebra
B3	Introduction to discrete structures	MA4	Discrete structures
B4	Numerical calculus		
	plus 2 of		(Required for some students)
M4	Mathematical analysis II		
M5	Advanced multivariate calculus	MA5	Mathematical analysis II
M6	Algebraic structures	MA6	Probability and statistics
M7	Probability and statistics		

Curriculum '78 and Mathematics

A comparison between the mathematics content of Curriculum '78 and that of Curriculum '68 is instructive. It reveals that

(1) Whereas Curriculum '68 required the student to take eight (8) mathematics courses (see Table I), Curriculum '78 requires only five (5) mathematics courses.

(2) The mathematics courses in Curriculum '68 formed an integral part of its prerequisite structure (see Table II). Note, in particular, for how many courses the discrete structures course (B3) is a prerequisite. In Curriculum '78, however, there is no mathematics prerequisite for any undergraduate computer science course with the exception of three advanced and clearly quite mathematical courses (only one of which has a computer science prerequisite). True, Curriculum '78 notes that the "mathematics requirements are integral to a computer science curriculum even though specific courses are not cited as prerequisites for most computer science courses." But this was clearly an afterthought, not present in the preliminary publication [4], and added only in response to criticism of the preliminary version.[1] Moreover, if the mathematics courses are not prerequisite to the computer science courses, the latter cannot teach or use formal techniques that require mathematical literacy.

(3) The mathematics emphasized in both curricula is traditional, calculus-based continuous mathematics. In both curricula the only course which is not a common part of the undergraduate mathematics curriculum is a single course in discrete structures.

More generally, the attitudes of Curriculums '68 and '78 toward mathematics are very different. Whereas the authors of C68 aver that "an academic program in computer science must be well based on mathematics since computer science draws so heavily upon mathematical ideas and methods," the authors of C78 say only that "An understanding of and the capability to use a number of mathematical concepts and techniques are vitally important for a computer scientist." The latter, too, was an afterthought since the preliminary report stated that "It was recognized in the process of specifying this core material that no mathematical background beyond the ability to perform simple algebraic manipulation is a prerequisite to an understanding of the topics." And note that this "core material" consists of *eight* courses including one on Data Structures and Algorithm Analysis.

One would have to conclude that the authors of Curriculum '78 believe that

(1) Mathematics is less important in the computer science undergraduate curriculum today than ten years ago.
(2) Basic computer science courses have less need for mathematical prerequisites today than ten years ago.
(3) The mathematics that is appropriate for computer science undergraduates has changed not at all in general flavor over the ten-year period between the two curricula.

We think all three of these propositions are wrong, and dangerously so. In the next section we will indicate why and how we would modify Curriculum '78.

Mathematics for Computer Scientists

A key sentence in C78, also not in the preliminary version, states that "Ideally computer science and mathematics departments should cooperate in developing courses on discrete mathematics which are appropriate to the needs of computer scientists." But, as if to emphasize that this recognition of the importance of discrete mathematics was only an attempt at a quick fix in response to criticism of the preliminary proposal, C78 goes on to say that "Until such time as suitable courses become readily available, it will be necessary to rely on the most commonly offered mathematical courses for the mathematical background needed by computer science majors." And the report goes on to recommend the five courses listed in Table I, four of which are standard

[1] We think a comparison of the sections devoted to mathematics in the preliminary and final versions of Curriculum '78 clearly imply a "quick fix" which does not address the substantive issues.

Table II. Prerequisite Structure.

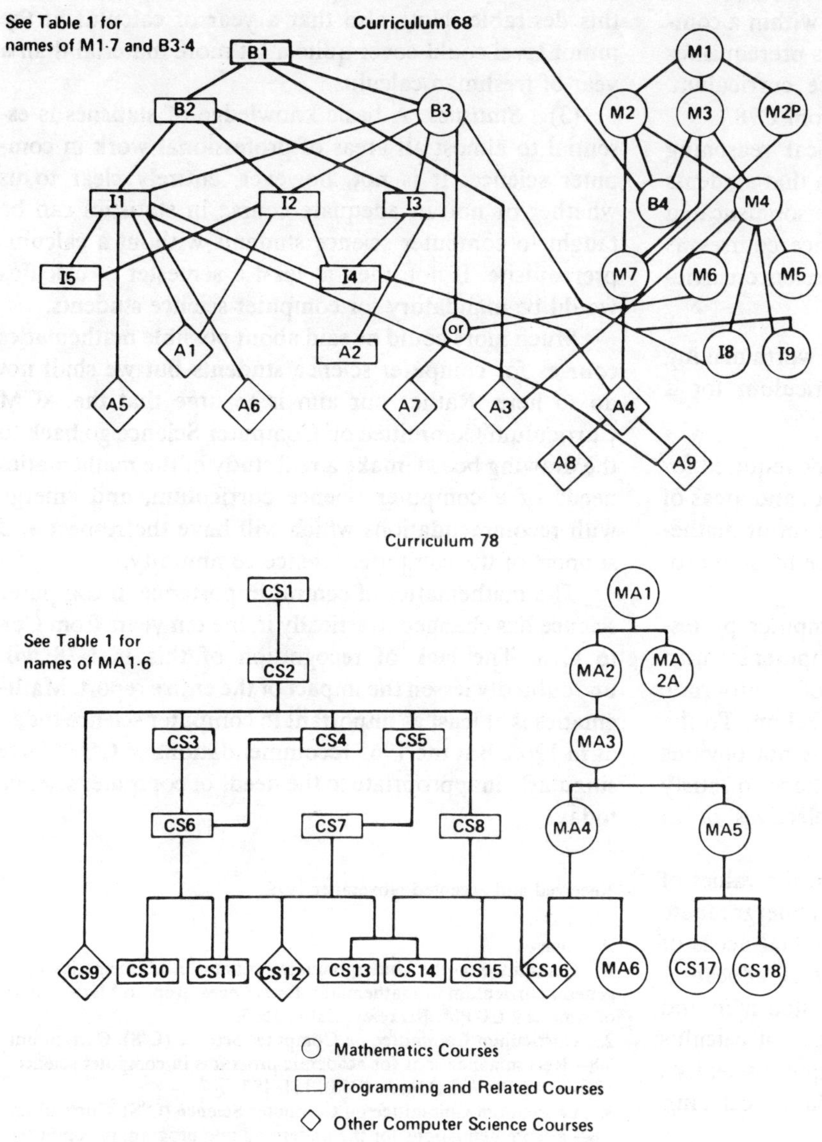

undergraduate mathematics courses from a 1965 report of the Committee on the Undergraduate Program in Mathematics (CUPM) [1] and the fifth is "a more advanced course in discrete structures than that given in C68." In other words, instead of going back to the drawing board and doing the mathematics portion of C78 properly, the authors elected to fudge the issue with pretty words and no substance.

For, of course, the quotation in the first sentence of the previous paragraph is correct and should have been the basic philosophy which informed the entire C78 report. In rather more detail this (and our) philosophy is:

(1) Mathematical reasoning does play an essential role in all areas of computer science which have developed or are developing from an art to a science. Where such reasoning plays little or no role in an area of computer science, that portion of our discipline is still in its infancy and needs the support of mathematical thinking if it is to mature. Large portions of software design, development, and testing are still in this stage.

(2) The student of computer science must be encouraged to use the tools and techniques of mathematics from the beginning of his or her computer science education. This means, for example, that even in the very first course in computer science (e.g., CS1 in C78 where, among other things, the student is to be introduced to "algorithm development") the basic ideas of the performance and correctness of algorithms and their associated mathematics need to be introduced or assumed from a parallel or prerequisite course.[2]

[2] The authors of C78 are, of course, quite correct in not making MA1, Introductory Calculus, a prerequisite for CS1; the problem is that MA1 is the wrong first mathematics course for computer science students.

(3) The mathematics curriculum for the computer science student must be designed to

—provide, either in separate courses or within a computer science course, the mathematics prerequisites appropriate to the computer science curriculum. (Obvious, no? But signally missing from C78.)

—more generally, develop mathematical reasoning ability and mathematical maturity so that students will be able to apply more and more sophisticated mathematics to their computer science courses as they progress through the computer science curriculum.

Some other, more pragmatic points are worth making before we discuss the mathematics curriculum for a computer science major in more detail:

(1) Only the quite basic courses can be required for all students. Depending upon the emphases and areas of specialization in the last year or two, one set of mathematics courses rather than another may be most appropriate.

(2) The needs of the practicing computer professional rather than those of the research computer scientist should be uppermost in consideration of appropriate mathematics for the undergraduate curriculum. To the extent that these needs are different—it is not obvious that they are—the future researcher will have to satisfy his/her needs through undergraduate electives or in graduate school.

(3) Although we believe strongly that the values of a liberal education should infuse any undergraduate program, our focus here is on the professional needs of the computer scientist not on the general education needs. Thus, it may be true that all educated men and women should be familiar with the essence of calculus but it does not *necessarily* follow that computer scientists have a significant professional need to know calculus.

What then is an appropriate sequence of mathematics courses for the computer science major?

(1) *Discrete Mathematics.* The overwhelming mathematical needs in the courses which normally comprise the first two years of a computer science major are in areas broadly covered by the rubric discrete mathematics—elementary logic, inductive proof, discrete number systems, basic combinatorics, difference equations, discrete probability, graph theory, some abstract and linear algebra, etc. We believe a two-year sequence can and must be developed (by mathematicians, if possible, but without them, if necessary) for computer science majors. This sequence should be *integrated* with the first two years of the computer science curriculum. Beyond the subject matter itself, we believe that such a sequence would be able to develop mathematical literacy and maturity at least as well as the classical two-year calculus sequence.

(2) *Calculus.* A year—but perhaps only a semester—of calculus in the junior year would be appropriate for all or almost all computer science majors. The techniques of calculus have just enough application in standard undergraduate computer science courses to make this desirable. Note also that a year of calculus at the junior level could cover quite a bit more material than a year of freshman calculus.

(3) *Statistics.* A basic knowledge of statistics is essential to almost all areas of professional work in computer science. It is not, however, entirely clear to us whether or not an adequate course in statistics can be taught to computer science students without a calculus prerequisite. If not, then at least a semester of calculus would be mandatory for computer science students.

Much more could be said about possible mathematics courses for computer science students but we shall not do so here. Rather our aim is to urge that the ACM Curriculum Committee on Computer Science go back to the drawing board, make a real study of the mathematics needs of a computer science curriculum, and emerge with recommendations which will have the respect and support of the computer science community.

The mathematics of central importance to computer science has changed drastically in the ten years from C68 to C78. The lack of recognition of this in C78 will undoubtedly lessen the impact of the entire report. Mathematics is at least as important to computer science today as in 1968. But the 1965 recommendations of CUPM are singularly inappropriate to the needs of computer science today.

Received and accepted November 1979

References

1. Committee on the Undergraduate Program in Mathematics. A general curriculum in mathematics for colleges. Rep. to Math. Assoc. of America, CUPM, Berkeley, Calif., 1965.
2. Curriculum Committee on Computer Science (C^3S). Curriculum '68—Recommendations for academic programs in computer science. *Comm. ACM 11,* 3 (March 1968), 151–197.
3. Curriculum Committee on Computer Science (C^3S). Curriculum '78—Recommendations for the undergraduate program in computer science. *Comm. ACM 22,* 3 (March 1979), 147–166.
4. Curriculum Committee on Computer Science (C^3S). Curriculum recommendations for the undergraduate program in computer science. SIGCSE Bulletin (ACM) *9,* 2 (June 1977), 1–16.

ACM Forum
Vol. 23, No. 6, June 1980, p. 356

Comments on the Mathematical Content of Curriculum '78

☐ I read with interest the Ralston-Shaw article [1] on the mathematical content of Curriculum '78 [2]. While I hesitate to overstress the mathematical principles of computer science for fear of keeping those who are not mathematically inclined away from the field, I still strongly agree with the arguments presented in this article. Historically part of the problem has been the inclusion of mathematics-based courses in the computer science curriculum (1) without sufficient emphasis on the integration of the mathematical content of these sometimes theory-based courses with the more practitioner-oriented computer science courses, and (2) without sufficient emphasis that these mathematical concepts are the principles upon which computer science is founded. The end result of this situation has been that many computer science students are not able to relate their computer science and mathematical courses (1) because the courses have not been taught in a relatable fashion and (2) because the student is not aware that the two areas are supposed to be related.

The Ralston-Shaw article focuses on the first of these two conditions and, as a long-term objective, spells out the guidelines for introducing the proper mathematical content into the curriculum. As a short-term objective, however, a solution to the second problem might be more useful. In particular, I think the following objective ought to be added to the objectives for course CS1:

(d) to foster an awareness of the mathematical principles behind computer science.

Upon completing this course the student should be able to recognize the relationship of mathematics to computer science both from a historical point of view and as regards current research and development efforts. More important, however, the student will be able to recognize the relationship of the mathematics courses in his/her curriculum to the computer science courses *regardless* of whether the course content is integrated or not. This overview of the "foundations" of computer science will also help to replace the equation

Computer Science = Programming

with a more balanced view of what computer science is all about.

A second concern I have regarding the curriculum is that it lacks a "real world" view from a career development standpoint. Too often a student completes a computer science curriculum (1) without any awareness of what he/she wants to do with the knowledge gained, or (2) without any awareness of the true nature of the available alternatives. As an illustration, consider the student who had more fun in the operating system writing course (CS6) than he/she had writing a payroll check printing program (CS2) and on that basis applies for a job at several major companies as a "systems programmer," not willing to consider a position as a "programmer/analyst." While the solution to (1) requires career guidance which is beyond the scope of this curriculum, a solution to (2) can easily be constructed.

I would like to propose the following course as an addition to the curriculum:

CS2A. Roles of a Computer Scientist (1-0-1)
Prerequisite: CS2

The objectives of this course are:
(a) to develop an understanding of the various roles that a person with a computer science education can take in society; and
(b) to develop an understanding of the basic skills and requirements needed in each of these roles.

COURSE OUTLINE

After an initial overview of the subject, an in-depth look at some of the major segments of the computer science community should be undertaken. Guest speakers should definitely be considered. A partial list of topics which should be discussed are:

A. Industry vs. Education vs. Government job segments
B. Business vs. Scientific vs. Systems programming
C. Research vs. Software/Hardware development vs. End-User programming
D. Small shops vs. Large shops
E. Outlook of demand in the various segments.

While it is not expected that such a course can be a substitute for personalized career counseling, there should be sufficient breadth and depth in the coverage of the various roles so that each student has an appreciation of the differences as well as the similarities of the requirements for each role. This course will not only give a better sense of direction to some students by giving them more definite goals, but will also give a better perspective of the integration of the total curriculum and its ultimate application to society.

As a final point, I think we can all be proud of the tremendous advances that have been made in the development of the science of computer science in the past decade and the role that ACM has played in helping to direct a corresponding development in the computer science curriculum. Curriculum '78, and Curriculum '68 before it, have had a major role in shaping the direction of computer science education. I look forward to continuing developments in this area.

ALAN RUSSELL, CDP
RD 1, Box 223C
Zionsville, PA 18092

1. Ralston, A. and Shaw, M. Curriculum '78—is computer science really that unmathematical?. *Comm. ACM 23*, 2 (Feb. 1980), 67–70.
2. Curriculum Committee on Computer Science (C^3S). Curriculum '78: Recommendations for the undergraduate program in computer science. *Comm. ACM 22*, 3 (March 1979), 147–166.

☐ The recent article by Ralston and Shaw concerning the undergraduate mathematics sequence in computer science is timely, appropriate, and absolutely correct. The February issue of *Communications* arrived as I was preparing the following in a memo to the computer science faculty here at Colorado State University:

1. Mathematics is a necessary and desirable component of computer science education. Mathematical problem solving ability is the primary skill that distinguishes a computer scientist from a programmer, and a strong foundation in mathematics is the best hedge against technical obsolescence of our graduates.

2. We are not requiring the correct math courses for our undergraduates. This conclusion is based on the following considerations:

(a) Our graduate curriculum has seven tracks: architecture, data structures and databases, graphics, languages and compilers, numerical methods, operating systems, and computing theory. Only one track (numerical methods) requires a strong calculus background. This is an indication that the undergraduate mathematics sequence is out of sync with the subject matter of computer science.

(b) I have revised the formal languages course to include a month of review of discrete structures and modern algebra. The students cannot handle the material without this review.

(c) Graduate students in my software engineering course complain that they are not equipped to read the literature in software specification techniques, proof of correctness, testing theory, etc. I believe this is also true in the graduate level compilers, data structures, database, graphics, and operating systems courses.

3. A better math sequence is:
two semesters of calculus (freshman level)
two semesters of discrete math (sophomore level)
one semester of probability and statistics (junior level)
one semester of math elective (junior or senior level)

The math elective would be geared to the students' senior level elective courses in computer science. It could be used as follows:
Numerical Methods—Linear Algebra, Advanced Calculus, or Differential Equations
Graphics—Linear Algebra or Geometry
All Others—Applied Algebra

4. Possible topics in the discrete math sequence would include:
Elementary Logic
Proof Techniques (induction in particular)
Number Systems
Combinatorics
Difference Equations
Discrete Probability
Graph Theory
Matrix Algebra
Introduction to Modern Algebra

5. I suggest that we pursue the design of a two-semester, sophomore level sequence in discrete mathematics as a joint venture with the math department.

In a subsequent letter to Ralston and Shaw, I suggested that a national committee be formed to prepare a study of undergraduate mathematics in computer science. I would like to use this forum to express my appreciation to these two authors for initiating a dialogue on the appropriate mathematics sequence in undergraduate computer science.

RICHARD E. FAIRLEY
Colorado State University
Fort Collins, CO 80523

ACM Forum
Vol. 23, No. 6, June 1980, p. 356

☐ I have read with great interest the article "Curriculum '78—Is Computer Science Really that Unmathematical?" by Ralston and Shaw, appearing in the February 1980 issue of *Communications*. It seems to me that these authors have identified a small (albeit important) issue in the very difficult task of computer science curriculum development, isolated it from its context, and arrived at conclusions which, in isolation, are very difficult to oppose. The difficulty is that, in isolation, the issue has become oversimplified.

The context of the curriculum development process can be set through the posing of a sequence of questions, many of which do not have answers agreed upon across the computing disciplines and professions.

The sequence is as follows:

1. The question of definitions.

(a) What is computer science?

(b) How does it relate to the other disciplines?

(c) How does it relate to the other computer professions?

2. The question of expectations.

(a) What does society, in general, expect of computer scientists?

(b) What does industry, in particular, that part of industry that is concerned in one way or another with computing, expect of computer scientists?

(c) What does academia expect of computer scientists?

3. The overall questions of preparation.

(a) How are practitioners to be prepared to meet the expectations of society, industry, and/or academia, as may be appropriate?

(b) What should be the division between formal training (ie. training in academic institutions) and informal training (ie. training through experience)?

4. The specific questions of academic training.

(a) What should be the division between the quantities and levels of training at training institutes, two-year undergraduate schools, four-year undergraduate schools, master's level graduate schools, and doctorate level graduate schools?

(b) What should be the division between theory and applications at each of these levels?

(c) What should be the level of specialization at the undergraduate level: liberal arts (at most one-third specialized), or professional (up to two-thirds specialized)?

(d) What are the priorities for the inclusion in the computer science program of material from other disciplines?

Part of the difficulty lies in the fact that, in the twelve years since Curriculum '68, the computing disciplines and professions themselves have become very greatly diversified. These disciplines and professions certainly include what are referred to by many as computer science, computer engineering, information science, software engineering, programming, systems design, systems analysis, data processing, etc. The questions are of identity, even of self-identity. Is there agreement as to the definitions of the foregoing fields by persons who identify themselves as practitioners of these respective fields? I think not! Before issues such as the one raised by Ralston and Shaw can be resolved, definitions of these respective subfields, and others, will have to be formulated and agreed to by a broad cross section of individuals in the computing professions. This may be a job for AFIPS. The problem is that Ralston and Shaw are using a traditional definition of computer science, one that goes back to an almost classical period in the computing profession, and certainly to a period of infancy in computer education. This was a period in which, because of immaturity in the field, agreements were more easily reached.

The 1968 definition of computer science was highly mathematical, and, as a consequence, Curriculum '68 was also highly mathematical. In the interim, there have appeared in the literature any number of complaints from the industry which we serve that our graduates were of little benefit to them. Thus, highly theoretical programs which were inspired by Curriculum '68 were of benefit only to prepare students to enter graduate school.

The bottom line, here again, is one of definitions. Industry's definition of what it wanted was different from academia's definition of what it was producing. Whether or not either is to be called a computer scientist is irrevelent. The point is that the academic institutions were producing a product of little benefit to industry. I maintain that any undergraduate curriculum which does little more than prepare students for graduate school is of little benefit to society. There is also the question of the students' expectations from their college educations. What do they see themselves wanting to be or do? It must be assumed that the majority of undergraduate students, regardless of major, at a majority of the undergraduate colleges on this continent, are not going to graduate school and therefore must be prepared for useful employment in the industrial community. I realize that this statement strikes at the heart of the concept of "liberal education," but one must realize that the students whom we serve have become extremely practical in their outlook. We must also recognize that the present high enrollments in computer science are due to the high level of employment opportunities. Accordingly, we must respond to the expectations of industry.

The specific problem, as it pertained to Curriculum '68, was that an urgent need had developed for greater applied content. There has also developed a need for greater liberal arts content, communication skills in particular. Given these new demands, and given the time limitations inherent in a four-year academic program, the only solution is a reduction in the theoretical content of the program. Indeed, it must be argued, independently, that heavy theoretical content is much more appropriate in graduate school than it is in undergraduate school. Curriculum '78 may not be perfect, but it is a step in the right direction.

Let me again return to the diversification of the last twelve years. It seems to me that this diversification is a key to future developments. The ACM, the IEEE Computer Society and other concerned agencies have, from time to time, published suggested curricula. That is all that they are, suggested curricula, or guides. Each department, in each institution, must be responsible for its own curriculum development. Curriculum development must be an ongoing activity; curricula are not static. They must be based upon several factors: (1) the department's review of societal needs, both recognized and unrecognized; (2) the department's perceived strengths and capabilities; (3) the exchange of ideas through the professional societies and the printed media; and (4) other considerations deemed appropriate by the department concerned.

Let us view the published professional differences of judgment as a positive testimonial to the maturing process taking place within our profession. The proper response to both Curriculum '78 and the Ralston-Shaw article is for each department to review its own curriculum in terms of the published material and its own local situation, and to take whatever actions seem to be appropriate to it, in a professional and collegial manner.

JULIUS A. ARCHIBALD, JR.
SUNY at Plattsburgh
Plattsburgh, NY 12901

Authors' Response:

We appreciate the support of the essential theses of our article in the letters of Fairley and Russell, and note only that there are various possible different sequences of mathematics courses which would support a computer science curriculum better than what is proposed in Curriculum '78.

As to Archibald's letter, it raises some important issues, but two things in it disturb us:

1. There is an implication—admittedly no more than this—that "mathematical" should be equated with "theoretical." We reject this. The argument in our article was addressed to all undergraduate computer science programs whether or not students in them are likely to go to graduate school. Mathematics is—or should be—a practical tool for working programmers and should be as important in their education as in that of the research computer scientist.

2. The argument that academe did not or is not producing a "product" of "benefit to industry" is a hoary one. We doubt this was ever true although it is true that some segments of industry did and do and always will complain about the education of computer science majors. And it is probably true that computer science departments are less sensitive to the current needs of prospective employers than they might be. But almost all complaints about the education of computer science majors have been short-sighted and oriented to the very short-term concerns which motivate the "expectations" of most of industry. To respond to them would be to guarantee the early obsolescence of our "products." Moreover, we don't believe that Archibald's characterization of industry's concerns is accurate. We see a significant and growing trend among industrial leaders to place a high value on the mastery of mathematical fundamentals. This often takes the form today of extensive in-house training programs.

One last point. Archibald mentions the need for the formulation of definitions of the fields and subfields encompassed by what we call computer science. In this connection we direct the attention of readers of *Communications* to the *Taxonomy of Computer Science and Engineering* which has just been published by AFIPS Press.

ANTHONY RALSTON
SUNY at Buffalo
Amherst, NY 14226
MARY SHAW
Carnegie-Mellon University
Pittsburgh, PA 15213